PRAISE FOR
Relationality

"In a time of general malaise and epidemic loneliness, David Jay offers a vision of a more connected, less isolated social experience. His willingness to look squarely at our failing social dynamics is bracing, and his notion of relationship is at once radical and sensible, with the potential to mitigate a great deal of sadness and pain."

—ANDREW SOLOMON, author of
Far From the Tree

"This is not a glib call for community, or a dire portrait of a world in which loneliness has reached epidemic proportions. David Jay offers a clear-eyed telling of what happens when we invest in relational containers—and the consequences when we don't. *Relationality* is an indictment of a society and an economy that has consistently undervalued and underinvested in real relationships and settled for its commodified imitations. And it is a playbook shared by one of our generation's most studied movement leaders about how we might do better, and how we might redirect the resources required to make it so."

—LENNON FLOWERS, cofounder and
executive director of The Dinner Party

"*Relationality* offers insight into the transformative power of relationships and calls attention to the well-being deficit many face from chronic loneliness and disconnection. I commend David for his work in breaking down these concepts to get to the heart of what we all desire and what we need now more than ever—meaningful relationships."

—JILLIAN RACOOSIN, executive director
of the Foundation for Social Connection

"A wake-up call to institutions that fail to understand the importance of relationships. Whether we succeed together or fail together depends entirely on the quality of our relationships. This book is an invaluable map to improve them."

—AZA RASKIN, cofounder of the Center
for Humane Technology

Relationality

HOW MOVING FROM TRANSACTIONAL TO TRANSFORMATIONAL RELATIONSHIPS CAN RESHAPE OUR LONELY WORLD

David Jay

North Atlantic Books
Huichin, unceded Ohlone land
Berkeley, California

Published by
North Atlantic Books
Huichin, unceded Ohlone land
Berkeley, California

Cover art and design by Carlos Esparza
Book design by Happenstance Type-O-Rama

Printed in the United States of America

Relationality: How Moving from Transactional to Transformational Relationships Can Reshape Our Lonely World is sponsored and published by North Atlantic Books, an educational nonprofit based in the unceded Ohlone land Huichin (Berkeley, CA) that collaborates with partners to develop cross-cultural perspectives; nurture holistic views of art, science, the humanities, and healing; and seed personal and global transformation by publishing work on the relationship of body, spirit, and nature.

North Atlantic Books's publications are distributed to the US trade and internationally by Penguin Random House Publisher Services. For further information, visit our website at www.northatlanticbooks.com.

Library of Congress Cataloging-in-Publication Data
Names: Jay, David (Community organizer), author.
Title: Relationality : how moving from transactional to transformational
  relationships can reshape our lonely world / David Jay.
Description: Berkeley, CA : North Atlantic Books, [2024] | Includes
  bibliographical references and index. | Summary: "An exploration of how
  investing in relational work and transformational relationships can make
  us happier and healthier"-- Provided by publisher.
Identifiers: LCCN 2023057129 (print) | LCCN 2023057130 (ebook) | ISBN
  9798889840541 (trade paperback) | ISBN 9798889840558 (ebook)
Subjects: LCSH: Social interaction. | Interpersonal relations. | Social
  change. | Community development.
Classification: LCC HM1111 .J39 2024 (print) | LCC HM1111 (ebook) | DDC
  302--dc23/eng/20231218
LC record available at https://lccn.loc.gov/2023057129
LC ebook record available at https://lccn.loc.gov/2023057130

1 2 3 4 5 6 7 8 9 KPC 29 28 27 26 25 24

For my grandparents,
David, Betty, Cynthia, and Bob,
and for my children, Tavi and Xavier

Contents

Introduction

BEFORE WE BEGIN, a quick note on grammar. Throughout this book you will occasionally hear me refer to relationship as a fluid rather than as discrete objects, to "relationship" rather than "a relationship" or "relationships." Throughout the course of this book I will invite you to conceive of relationship less as a discrete state that exists or does not exist between people ("We either have a relationship or we don't") and more as a fluid that constantly flows between and through us ("We are all in relationship to some degree"). Just as we can refer both to the "water" that we need to live and the "waters" that flow over and through the land around us, I will sometimes refer to relationship as a singular fluid and sometimes to relationships as a plural set of streams and rivers. We create the conditions for relationship by drawing on the relationships around us. To understand relationship, we must look to the relationships that have shaped us.

Over a decade ago, a university student asked me a question that would grow to become the seed of this book. I had just spoken at a queer conference that she had organized, and when the dust of the day had settled, she pulled me aside to ask for advice. In school she had discovered that the work of building community was what made her feel alive, and she'd witnessed how that work could transform not only her life and the lives of her friends but the systems of power that defined their world. Building relationship felt like the most important work there was, but she was about to graduate and was struggling to figure out how she could get paid to do that work. Everywhere she looked, relational work was either underpaid, more focused on numbers than on genuine human connection, or both. The exception seemed to be jobs building communities by and for wealthy people, but these jobs did not appeal to her values. All around her, relationships were valuable and relationships were needed, so why was it so hard to get paid to build them?

Though I could think of dozens of ways to get paid to build community, the question stuck. Why *was* it so hard? Why were so many of my friends who had joined institutions that claimed to value community frustrated that those claims were not being lived up to? Why were so many of my friends who were organizers or nonprofit professionals struggling to do work that prioritized relationships above metrics? Everywhere I looked the work of nurturing relationships simultaneously seemed extremely valuable and extremely undervalued. This book is the result of a decade-long journey to understand why that is and what we can do about it.

That journey has been both intellectual and deeply personal. It has led me to understand the growing crisis of social isolation unfolding across the globe and has been shaped by my experience as an asexual man powerfully exploring intimacy outside of sexual and romantic scripts. It has grown out of a burning scientific curiosity about what relationships are and how they weave our world together, and it has been guided by my experience building and contributing to movements for social change. It has taken me from intergenerational dance floors to the deep inner workings of Facebook, from the evolutionary properties of relational systems to the toxicity that festers when loneliness and resentment are allowed to persist. My journey away from loneliness toward a world of abundant connection is far from complete. This book is for those on a similar journey.

This is not a self-help book because I do not believe that these journeys should be taken alone. Moving from loneliness toward connection requires personal transformation, but it also requires collective action. We are not lonely because there is something wrong with us; we are lonely because the world around us does not value relationship in ways that need fixing. This is not a book about how to find or heal a romantic partnership because I am asexual and aromantic and other forms of intimacy are my area of expertise. It is also not a book about asexuality because most of what I would want to say on the topic has been said better by authors like Angela Chen and Sherronda J. Brown. It is not a book about how to make teams of professionals more cohesive and productive because in order to value the work of relationship, we must challenge notions of productivity. Relationships create value in ways that are often invisible. Understanding why so many of us are lonely and what we can do about it will require grappling with the history of that invisibility.

This is a book for people who have tasted both loneliness and moments of deep connection and who wonder why more connection doesn't exist in our world. This is a book for people whose careers are, at least in part, oriented toward the goal of creating connection. This is a book for people who have worked to create the conditions for relationship and have witnessed, time and time again, how that work is both necessary and undervalued. This is a book for people who want to get paid to build community, and for people inside institutions who want to invest in communities and movements but don't know how. This is a book for those who have found paths to connection and resilience that they are eager for the world to recognize, and a book for those still facing loneliness and looking for hope.

CHAPTER 1

Why We Need Relationship

AS A TEENAGER I was regularly told that I was incapable of real human connection. Friends and adult mentors would say things like, "Some people are just happy being alone forever," as if the most that I could aspire to in life was to become one of those people. I suspected then and know now that such people do not, in fact, exist. While some of us thrive mainly through connection with the more-than-human world of nature and ideas, relationship and human thriving are irrevocably linked. Like all of us, I needed relationship to survive, and at the time I had no idea how to go about forming them.

In 1998 I was a tall and gangly sixteen-year-old with a mop of wiry brown hair and a habit of rollerblading around my hometown of St. Louis, Missouri. Though only a sophomore I was on the path to becoming valedictorian. I played on the soccer team and speed skated, ran the tech crew for my high school's theater, and was becoming close with the clique of girls that dominated my grade socially, all of whom of had recently shaved their heads and come out as queer. Quietly and with a hint of desperation, I shared with them a secret that my middle school and high school self has been holding with trepidation.

I was not experiencing sexuality like those around me. Since elementary school, I had been told that I would begin to develop "special feelings" for those around me and that these feelings would be simultaneously confusing and the gateway to the most important relationships in my life. I had invented, more or less out of thin air, the word *asexual* to describe my condition, which I was fairly certain was a problem. In the movies I watched, the songs I listened to, and the books I read, people's lives were constantly being transformed through meaningful romantic connection that was consecrated with a kiss. I could not say that I was "in a relationship" with someone without implying that that relationship was romantic and on some level sexual. All of this meant that when I tried to envision how my very present need for human connection might be fulfilled, I was left without words to use or stories to draw on. It was one thing to fear, as almost all people fear, that I would be alone forever. It was another to live in a world that treated this loneliness as a foregone conclusion. If a core trauma has shaped my life, it is the memory of being unable to imagine a life in which I am loved.

Psychologist Clare Gardiner makes an important distinction between social isolation, the state of not having relationships, and the sensation of loneliness.[1] Loneliness is about lacking the agency to form the relationships that we want. If we move to a new city where we don't know anyone but are confident that we'll quickly make friends, we experience very little loneliness, but if we have no idea how to make friends or why anyone would want to be our friend, then our loneliness can be both overwhelming and self-fulfilling. This is why loneliness also impacts people with busy social lives: If we are surrounded by relationships but those relationships obligate us to spend time in ways that we don't want to and there's nothing we can do about it, then we can feel just as lonely as someone isolated in their home. Throughout this book I will refer to a loneliness crisis rather than a social isolation crisis to emphasize this lack of agency. The path out of loneliness can look like making friends, but it can also look like having time to connect with ourselves or with the more-than-human world. For this reason the opposite of loneliness is not connection, because sometimes more connections can make loneliness worse. We avoid loneliness by continually evolving, changing, and pruning a tapestry of relationship that fits our changing lives. I'll use the term *relational agency* to refer to this capacity to grow and change the relationship around us to meet our needs.

To my sixteen-year-old self, it was a lack of relational agency, not a lack of connection, that was overwhelming. I had friendships and was slowly learning to make them deeper, but I knew at my core that friendship, at least as it was defined in the culture around me, was not enough. Friends did not feel or express love in the way that romantic partners did. They were not expected to make the same kinds of sacrifices to stay in one another's lives. They did not form families. If a friend in my life ever decided to stop spending time with me because of a job or a romantic partner, I was expected to hide my grief and celebrate their progress. While serious commitment was something that occasionally happened between friends, it was not a thing I had a right to expect or language to ask for.

All of this meant that as an asexual person (and, as I would later come to identify, an asexual aromantic), my closest relationships could disappear at any time, often with an expectation that the friendship would pick back up again if and when we reconnected. I was destined to live a life of decreasing relevance as my friends paired off and had kids, an increasingly pitied uncle in a lonely apartment. As the oldest of three siblings and one of the oldest of thirty cousins, I knew I wanted kids, but having a family to raise them in was unimaginable. I went hunting for stories and scientific studies—anything to let me know a path to connection existed or that I was not alone in my asexuality. My hours in the library came up fruitless; my internet searches came up blank. It was during this search that I began to come out to friends and adult mentors. It was in those conversations that I was told that some people are happy being alone forever. I was looking desperately for relational agency and being told bluntly by people I trusted that it did not exist.

Molly, the ringleader of the queer kids in my grade, told me a different story. Sitting in a dimly lit café in one of St. Louis's hipper districts, they invited me to challenge the idea that a lack of sexuality made me broken. Yes, being asexual meant that I had every reason to fear a lifetime of loneliness. Yes, the world around me was shaped to deliver human connection in a way that was not accessible to me. That didn't mean I was broken; it meant that the world was. My job was to challenge that world by inviting new kinds of relationship into it.

This journey from loneliness to relational agency has defined the arc of my life. I have experienced loneliness, or the lack of relational agency, as a cloud of despair that hangs over days, weeks, or sometimes years of my life but eventually fades. When I feel a lack of agency over my relationships, even when I have many of them and even when they are loving, my life becomes defined by encroaching feelings of despair and resentment. Not just relationship, but anything good in my life feels hopelessly unimaginable.

In contrast, when I think of relational agency, I think not of seasons but of particular times and places. I recall moments of so much emerging possibility that they feel almost spiritual. A dance floor where a community of sustainability activists I love is connecting and sharing their gratitude. A weekly bike ride with friends where we discuss strategies for intervening in local politics and gossip about our personal lives. Relational agency feels like sunlight that shines on weeks and months of my life, but it feels concentrated in the particular moments where relationship happens.

I vehemently believe that these moments of relational agency are not an expression of my worth as a person. They are not destined to happen because I am conventionally attractive, economically privileged, or neurotypical. They happen because people, myself included, work to make them happen. In the same way that we grow food by creating the conditions for plants to thrive, we nurture relationship by creating specific environments that facilitate its growth. These environments look like neighborhood cafés and WhatsApp threads, like karaoke bars and conferences and hikes with old friends. When we experience relational agency, it is because we have learned to find and cocreate these environments in order to predictably create moments of connection.

Relational containers are environments that are cocreated with the goal of facilitating connection. A FaceTime call with grandparents is a relational container; so is a wedding, and so is a conflict being mediated through nonviolent communication. When we feel relational agency, it is often because the relational containers around us feel abundant and easy to access, though navigating them is an acquired skill. A capable professional networker may feel that they know exactly what events to go to, what LinkedIn searches to do, and what people to ping in order to get an in at a particular company. A seasoned community organizer may know exactly what church groups to show up at, what coffees to have, and what dinner to host in order to get a neighborhood mobilized around child safety. These people feel capable of forming the relationships they need because they understand how to show up in and contribute to the relational containers around them. Conversely, an elder alone in their apartment may experience a lack of relational agency because there are no appealing and accessible relational containers in sight. Their descent down a spiral of loneliness may start with the realization that they do not have a place to go or a person to feel a sense of connection with and have no idea how to go about finding them. Wherever relational agency exists, good relational containers exist, and wherever loneliness exists, relational containers are failing.

Like all infrastructure, relational containers are more accessible to some people than others. Sitting in that café as a sixteen-year-old ace kid (*ace* is an umbrella term for people on the asexual spectrum), I was confronted with the way that a particular genre of relational container was failing. At the time, imagining romance without sexuality was like imagining a dance party without music. "Real" relationships, the kind that evoked dramatic orchestral scores in movies and had people promise to be together forever, were born in moments that involved shared sexual attraction and desire. If I couldn't experience those moments, was I cut off from all of the security and emotional intimacy that came after them? Or was there another way in? If I could understand deeply enough what relationship was and how to evoke it, then maybe I could find a way to access it without needing to perform sexuality that felt deeply inauthentic. Understanding and building relational containers in new ways began to feel like a necessary skill of survival.

This journey to understand ace intimacy both paralleled and radically departed from my friends' early experiments in dating. I tied up my family's one phone line for hours talking to a friend named Tessa from nerd camp. She discussed her adventures trying to date as the smart kid in a small town while I tried to parse out the fundamental nature of sexuality and human connection. While it was infuriating to feel locked out of the infrastructure of human connection, I quickly learned that it was only slightly less infuriating to be welcomed into it. Dating, as a cultural construct, set of expectations, and set of functional tools for building intimacy, looked from the outside like kind of a hot mess. Meeting people and trying to judge whether they would be good partners was stressful, and almost no one I knew who was doing it was having much fun. Forming relationships based on an initial surge of strong emotion and sexuality seemed like a recipe for relationships that would crash and burn, and it often was. The relationships themselves could be great. Actually connecting with someone brought a surge of relational agency that my friends would rave about and that I would find in my own time. But the journey to find those relationships seemed to have fewer clear paths than should exist for something so important. After millennia of humans desiring and forming relationship, was this really the best system we could come up with?

From social media to philanthropy to corporate HR, our world is increasingly defined by institutions investing billions in creating the conditions for relationship and largely failing. If we as individuals are feeling increasingly lonely, it is because the relational containers around us seem to be getting worse, not better. Understanding why such a widespread failure is happening is the first step in understanding how to build institutions and infrastructure that succeed at building human connection.

The Loneliness Crisis

If humans have one defining advantage as a species, it is our ability to make relationship happen. In 1992, anthropologist Robin Dunbar performed a study to try to figure out why mammals like humans have large brains.[2] He ruled out many popular theories: It's not that we needed big brains to use tools (crows can do that) or to distinguish between many kinds of foods to know what's edible (rats can do that), or even that we needed bigger brains to exist in large groups (bison can do that). Humans' large brains seem like they should be an evolutionary dead end. They barely fit through a birth canal, making human childbirth extremely dangerous by mammalian standards. They take up 2 percent of our body weight but burn 20 percent of our calories.[3] What evolutionary advantage could be worth all of that cost?

Dunbar found that brain size correlated not with group size but with the number of complex relationships that an organism had to think about to maintain group cohesion. Thousands of fish can form a school with relatively small brains because each fish only needs to track the fish immediately around them. The same goes for flocks of starlings or herds of wildebeests. When humans get together, we need to reason about not only our relationships with everyone else in the group but everyone else in the group's relationships with one another. Among mammals that formed these sorts of complex groups, like wolf packs and monkey troops, brain size scaled with the number of complex relationships that any one animal had to think about. While group selection is still questioned in evolutionary biology, the advantages of membership in a large group are clear. Large groups can defend themselves from predators and take down prey. They can divide the labor of hunting and raising young and outcompete smaller groups for territory. If our ancestors gave us a superpower, it was the ability to reason about many complex relationships better than any other being on the planet.

It is this superpower, more than our opposable thumbs or our ability to walk upright, that has allowed our species to spread to, and for most of our history live in relative harmony with, almost every ecosystem on Earth. We have survived for so long because the environmental devastation we are experiencing today is an exception, not a human norm. We are deeply wired to connect. We build and flock to cities, construct monumental temples to gather in, and endlessly write, dance, and sing about the experience of relationship because for us to be in relationship is simultaneously to meet our need for survival, create possibility in our lives, and access the divine. Give us food and we will host a feast. Give us a drum and we will dance together. Give us a tool and we will put our enormously powerful brains together in community to figure out how to use it to create the conditions for connection.

Carry these abilities forward into modern times and we should be living in a golden age of connection. Sixty-eight percent of our species carries a supercomputer in their pockets that can instantly communicate with anyone else on the planet and access the majority of all recorded human knowledge.[4] Global supply chains and increasing telepresence mean that a small but growing number of us can summon almost any good or service that might be useful in a time ranging from days to seconds. We collaborate to form corporations and governments of unprecedented power that spend billions of dollars on mission statements like "Give people the power to build community and bring the world closer together." With our impressive brains and our historically unprecedented access to whatever we can imagine, we should be experiencing relational agency to a degree and scale unknown in human history. We should be building an ecology of relational containers that unlocks human resilience, creativity, and compassion at levels that our ancestors could barely have imagined.

We are not.

In May 2023, US Surgeon General Vivek Murthy released a dire warning about a rapidly growing global crisis of social isolation. Even before the onset of the COVID-19 pandemic, approximately half of US adults reported experiencing measurable levels of loneliness.[5] In 1990, fully 33 percent of US adults had ten or more close friends, and only 3 percent reported having none. By 2021 only 13 percent of US adults had ten or more close friends and a whopping 12 percent had no one.[6] That's about four million people—more than the populations of Wyoming, Vermont, Alaska, North Dakota, and Maine combined. If we think of lonely people as a political constituency, then there are more than enough of them to swing a presidential election. If we think of them like Dr. Murthy does, as a public health crisis, then their disease is now twice as prevalent as cancer and growing rapidly.

In 2003 the average US adult spent thirty hours per month with friends. By 2008 it had dropped to twenty-five hours, in 2019 to seventeen hours, and in the 2020 pandemic it dropped to ten.[7] Before the pandemic, those of us in the United States went from roughly seeing people we care about four times per week to seeing them only once. Outside the United States, things are not much better. A Brazilian study found that 20 percent of participants reported moderate to severe loneliness.[8] London is the world's loneliest city, with more than half of Londoners feeling lonely a significant amount of the time, creating an estimated public health cost of about $7,300 per Londoner, according to the mayor's office.[9]

To understand why all of those lonely people in London and around the world are so inconvenient to our public health budgets, we must comprehend how profoundly a lack of relational agency impacts not only our mental but also our physical health. Like sleep, exercise, and a healthy diet, relational agency is one of the panaceas of human health. Exercise makes us happier and more energetic, mentally focused, and resistant to everything from viral infection to heart disease while adding years to our lives. If it could be taken in pill form, it would become the world's most successful drug overnight. Sleep is similar, with benefits including weight loss, improved athletic performance, and a decreased risk of diabetes.[10]

Loneliness is like a lack of sleep or lack of exercise, but the harms stretch from a breakdown in our individual cells to a breakdown of our democracies. Our brains are so intensely wired for relationship—not just relationship with other humans, but with ourselves and the more-than-human world—that loneliness impacts our bodies on a profound level. When we feel a lack of relational agency, it activates the hypothalamus–pituitary–adrenal gland (HPA) axis in our bodies, releasing a chemical stress response that is felt on a cellular level.[11] Proteins are more likely to misfold and DNA is more likely to have copying errors. The immune system is suppressed.[12] There is some evidence that mitochondria, the tiny organelles that power our cells, begin to break down.[13] We get less energy from our food, less oxygen from the air, and less range and power from our muscles.[14]

These examples represent just a fraction of the many complex ways that our bodies react to loneliness, with clear and drastic impacts on our health. The lack of meaningful connection can increase our risk of premature death as much as smoking daily.[15] If we are lonely, we are 29 percent more likely to experience heart disease and 32 percent more likely to have a stroke.[16] We are more likely to suffer from diabetes,[17] 50 percent more likely to develop dementia,[18] and twice as likely to become depressed.[19] Stress from sources other than loneliness will hit us harder,[20] as will infections from viruses.[21] When our relationships fall apart, our bodies fall apart with them.

This deep link between relational and physical health is why senior public health officials like Surgeon General Murthy and Dr. Tedros Adhanom Ghebreyesus, Director-General of the World Health Organization,[22] are drawing attention to the growing global crisis of loneliness. This crisis puts a very real strain on our health care system not only because of the many ailments listed above but because people without the relational agency to seek care from their families or communities access health care services at an increased rate.[23] Seen purely for its impact on physical health, the loneliness epidemic is quickly becoming one of our most devastating and costly public health crises. But the implications do not stop there.

The mental health implications of a lack of relational agency are perhaps more intuitive. In addition to the increased risk of depression discussed earlier, loneliness creates an increased risk of alcohol abuse, sleep disorders, personality disorders, Alzheimer's disease, and suicide.[24] One of the world's most comprehensive longitudinal studies, the Harvard Study of Adult Development, found that maintaining healthy relationships was the single most important factor in happiness among participants.[25] Since 1938 the project has been regularly tracking the health and happiness of 724 men; similar studies have found that the effect holds across genders.[26] It and other longitudinal studies consistently find that fulfilling relationships are the single strongest determinant of a healthy life: more than income, achievement, or even physical health. Though many times these relationships are romantic or familial, they do not have to be, contrary to what I was led to believe in high school. Deep friendships can have just as profound an impact on our happiness as any other kind of connection.

There is a risk at this point that your eyes are beginning to glaze over at a long list of studies and citations, so let's pause to summarize. There is a thing called relational agency that encompasses our ability not only to form romantic relationships, but to form any kind of relationship with others, ourselves, or the natural world. Our brains are evolved to give us this ability, and it has defined how our species has survived and thrived. It is one of the most powerful determinants of human health and the most powerful determinant of human happiness, and for the past several decades it has been in freefall.

This freefall is impacting more than our minds and our bodies. A study by the health insurer Cigna estimated that loneliness cost US employers $154 billion between job withdrawal and increased employee turnover.[27] To put that in perspective, the US loses in loneliness every year about what it spends on consumer electronics.[28] Loneliness is slowly killing our economy, but building relationships can have the opposite effect. Engaging in social activities like volunteering makes unemployed people 25 percent more likely to find a job.[29] A landmark research collaboration between academic researchers and employees at Facebook found that relationships that cross lines of economic privilege are "among the strongest predictors of upward income mobility identified to date."[30] Relational agency determines our economic prospects as individuals and plays an especially important role in addressing economic inequality. A lonelier economy is both one that grows more slowly and one that concentrates more wealth in the hands of a few.

Reading this research, I begin to imagine the future that the loneliness crisis is leading us toward. We are sicker, sadder, and poorer. It is a future where institutions struggle and fail to take on the work that our communities used to do. Rather than receiving care from those around us, we enter acute crisis and wind up in emergency rooms. As our mental health, our sleep, and our bodies fail, our schools and employers (if we have them) struggle to institutionally simulate the human intimacy we crave. We collectively become withdrawn and less trusting.

Hannah Arendt, one of the most influential political theorists of the twentieth century, saw a deep link between this sort of loneliness and the rise of totalitarianism. After witnessing Hitler's rise to power before fleeing to the United States in 1941, Arendt sought to understand how such a terrifying and destructive form of government could emerge. To Arendt, "totalitarian movements are mass organizations of atomized, isolated, individuals."[31] Totalitarianism happened when "the masses grew out of the fragments of a highly atomized society whose competitive structure and concomitant loneliness of the individual had been held in check only through membership in a class."[32] A nation of lonely people, desperate to belong to something, will more readily embrace totalitarian rule. To isolated people, the perceived strength of a totalitarian ruler will seem appealing, the attacks on others in one's community that always come with totalitarianism will feel distant, and people with little relational agency will feel powerless to come together and push back when they themselves are attacked.

As global loneliness has spiked, democracies around the world have begun to decline. The Institute for Democracy and Electoral Administration, an international agency that tracks the health of democracies around the world, has noticed a disturbing trend that, like the loneliness epidemic, seemed to get significantly worse in the early 2010s. The IDEA's 2022 report states that "the number of democracies has stagnated," with half of the world's democracies categorized as "contracting" toward authoritarianism.[33] According to the report, "over the past six years, the number of countries moving toward authoritarianism is more than double the number moving toward democracy."[34] Meanwhile, 50 percent of nondemocracies, about one in five of the world's countries, are becoming significantly more repressive.[35]

The descent of democracy is clearly correlated with the global rise in loneliness, and it is not hard to imagine why the two might be causally linked. In addition to the powerful arguments of Hannah Arendt, there is mounting evidence that loneliness is a driving factor in violent extremism,[36] though use of this term requires a critical analysis of who is applying it and to whom it is being applied. Democracy is and always has been a messy relational project. If we feel more relational agency, then we feel like we can find a way to navigate the conflicts necessary to govern together, and democracy feels like a worthwhile project. It is when navigating those relationships feels impossible that we seek to dominate rather than collaborate with those around us. It is then that we seek the authoritarian strength to settle our disagreements through suppression.

Return now to our imagined lonely future. Not only are our cells breaking down, our bodies breaking down, our minds breaking down, our schools and our workplaces breaking down. Not only are we sleepless, anxious, addicted, and depressed. The vast wealth of our economies flows to fewer and fewer billionaires who, themselves isolated, cannot turn their unimaginable wealth into happiness. Our democracies falter and collapse, replaced by authoritarian regimes that see collective action and the human connections that lead to it as a threat. We are isolated not only from one another but from ourselves and from the more-than-human world.

In this future, can we expect to face the unprecedented global challenge of climate change? Can these authoritarian states and these broken, isolated people maintain a biosphere compatible with human survival? Without relational agency, what agency could we find to do so? Without relationship we become stagnant, we become unable to adapt to the demands of the world around us, and far too many of us will cease to exist.

Could the opposite also be true?

Instead of a lonely future, try to imagine a relational one. Not a future where everyone is connected, as we have already established that too many connections can be a bad thing. Instead, imagine a future where most of us feel that they are capable of building the relationship that they need to survive and thrive. Like relational magicians, we know how to find or cocreate relational containers capable of manifesting whatever relationships we're looking for, including professional connections, romantic partnerships, creative collaborations, and friends we can just relax with. Because we have relational agency, these relationships evolve when and how we need them to. If we need time to ourselves, we communicate about it and our friends oblige, knowing that we'll invest in time with them when we have the capacity.

Imagine that year after year for decades at a time our capacity for relationship keeps getting better. The world around us becomes more and more structured to facilitate relationship, and we become more skilled at leveraging it. What changes if the leading driver of human happiness is a thing that all of us start having more and more access to? How do our bodies feel in this world? How are our mitochondria holding up? What is it like to be in high school in this world? What is it like to be in an assisted living facility? How do our careers unfold in this world? How do our workplaces shift, with this much capacity for workers to come together in agreement? How might the structure of our economy shift as a result? What happens to any would-be authoritarian rulers who try to seek power in this world? What happens in the still unrealized project of creating a world of thriving multiracial democracies? What might our relationship with the more-than-human world begin to look like? What might our movements look like?

In this future, how might we expect to face the unprecedented global challenge of climate change? How might we adapt fast enough and nimbly enough to meet the changing world around us? When that world breaks in the ways that it inevitably will break, how might these relationships help us to grieve, survive, and thrive?

The difference between these two futures rests on whether we choose to invest in and build places where relationship happens. Creating the conditions for relationship takes deep understanding, compassion, and skill. It takes training ourselves to be present, knowing when and how to invite people in, cooking food, and creating art. It takes tapping into lineages of wisdom about how to create community that our grandparents knew but that we have begun to forget. It takes knowledge about how to facilitate generative conflict. It takes respect for the fact that people in relationship will become powerful in ways we do not anticipate. And all of this food, furniture, and skilled labor takes money. In this book I will argue that the global loneliness crisis is due in large part to the fact that most large institutions are unable to effectively fund relational work. We are starved of relationship because most of the people who build relationship are starved of resources. To get out of this crisis, we will need to understand what relationships are, how to create the spaces where they happen, and how to move resources toward the work of building them.

There are many valid ways to approach the work of creating the conditions for relationship and many relational lineages with wisdom to offer about paths from loneliness to connection. A lineage I come from and will discuss extensively in this book is movement organizing. My personal journey away from loneliness was facilitated not by sexual desire and dating apps but by places where shared struggle and shared purpose led to trusting relationships. These relationships not only met my individual need for emotional intimacy, they not only supported me and challenged me to become a better version of myself, they unlocked forms of collective power that could take on the very systems that had made me lonely in the first place. If we are to take on the systemic forces that keep us lonely, then movements have a great deal to teach us.

A Journey from Loneliness to Movement

By the year 2000, my fear of unending loneliness had begun to slip away. Supported by Molly, Tessa, and a handful of other friends, I graduated high school tentatively convinced that I was not broken. Though I had yet to speak with another asexual person, though I still had no idea how I would go about building connections that stood the test of time, I was convinced that both these things were possible. I showed up to prom with three dates, two of whom were in a couple. I came out as asexual for the first time at a summer camp

focused on social justice and spent a day in tears. I tentatively began
to talk about my closest friendships with the sense of weight that my
friends reserved for the people they were dating or sleeping with. I
had a feeling in my gut that if I was going to find a path away from
loneliness, the words used to describe intimacy would need to shift to
make room for me.

Touring college campuses with my dad, a giant-hearted if somewhat preppy Midwestern architect, I secretly scouted for a place where
I could begin to work on this shift in language and where I could hope
to find other people like me. I chose a school called Wesleyan whose
walkways were chalked with radical queer slogans and where student
organizing seemed to be the preferred campus sport. My student host
handed me the keys to his room and informed me that he had to head
off to DC to get arrested.

The following fall, once I had matriculated and settled in my dorm,
I went about the project of finding any evidence of human asexuality
outside of my lived experience. I scoured our campus library and found
only one book, which discussed women cohabitating in the 1920s. I
looked through research archives and found papers that hypothesized
the existence of asexual people, but none that discussed actually seeking to understand these people through surveys or interviews. I tentatively approached the leadership of the campus Queer Alliance (QA)
to inquire about connections that she might have.

Hailing from the rugby team, the leadership of Queer Alliance
was to my campus what football stars might be to a large state school.
A group of physically and politically intimidating women (trans and
nonbinary leadership was still a few years away), they reminded me
of Molly's crew in high school in a way that provided comfort. They
represented the hub of student organizing on campus, bridging the
campuses' many disparate groups to engage in collective action when
necessary. When students organized buses to send five hundred students to a major protest, QA led the charge. Recognizing that the
admissions office was a key lever of power on campus, they had deftly
seized control of it, infiltrating the ranks of tour guides and using sidewalk chalk and other tactics to control the expectations that incoming

students held of the kind of campus that they were joining. Even though much of their organizing was explicitly and radically pro-sex, there was something about this display of raw queer power that my scared Midwestern self found intoxicating. This is what it looked like to push back on a world that refused to make room for me until it bent.

I put in a month or two of quiet work before I made my approach. I copied and put up fliers, distributed sidewalk chalk, volunteered as a campus tour guide, and otherwise showed up for the movement before I asked it to show up for me. When I finally knocked on the door of one of the cochairs, I was met with intrigue and suspicion. What role did an asexual have in a movement combatting sexual shame? I did not seem like the enemy, since I was clear that I found sex personally unappealing rather than morally objectionable. And the journey to self-acceptance that I was on seemed to strike a chord. Like other queers I had been told that I was impossible, broken, and less than human. Like other queers I had been told that I was incapable of relationships that were socially valid and was convinced that I had been told a lie. Like other queers I was pissed about it. Though I still had no leads on finding other asexual people, tentatively and for the first time in my life, I had found a movement to hold me. The support and guidance of that movement would prove invaluable in the years head.

Over winter break I decided to fly to California to visit a high school friend on the Stanford campus. There I learned of a new search engine called Google that had just become available beyond the limits of the Stanford campus. I was skeptical. Searching the web for the term asexual had only ever turned up papers on amoebae and plant biology, and I saw no reason why this new search engine would be different.

Once I was back in Connecticut, I booted up my desktop, typed the word asexual into this new search engine and, for the first time, got a match. A zine article titled "My Life as an Asexual" described the journey of a queer person and their partner who had mutually realized that sexuality wasn't for them. I got about three paragraphs in, then spent an hour walking around campus holding back tears. After years of doubt and isolation, after endless hours of searching, I had evidence that I was not alone. I had evidence of another asexual person *in a partnership.* The side of my brain that was secretly betting on loneliness, the nagging fear that the way relationships worked in the world simply did not work for me and never would, got smaller so fast I felt vertigo. I took several minutes of deep breaths and made the journey back to my desktop.

At the bottom of the article, there was a comment section. This was before the days of YouTube comments and state-sponsored trolling. Finding an article like this took a minor miracle, and most of the people who had come to it were, like me, authentically floored to find others like them. There were dozens of testimonials. Dozens of people who had independently invented the word asexual to describe themselves and were reaching out desperately for others like them. They shared their life stories, the same intense feelings of validation and relief that were coursing through my veins at that very moment. But other than leaving comments in a single thread there was no space to hold a conversation.

I booted up a text editor and began coding a site. Nothing more than raw HTML, it included a definition of asexuality ("a person who does not experience sexual attraction"), a short FAQ, and my personal email address. I posted it to the comment thread, enlisted the help of QA to send it out to an email list of campus LGBTQ groups, and hoped for the best.

About a week later I got a response: an email from a senior at Swarthmore. After some nervous back and forth, we hopped on the phone, something we were both strongly discouraged to do with strangers we had met online, and talked for two and a half hours. We shared ways that we had felt alone for our entire lives and reveled as that feeling of loneliness slipped away: the experience of faking having a crush on someone so that we could fit in with our friends, the experience of feeling a deep shame at being unable to give the people we loved the sexuality that they wanted, and the experienced of being abandoned because relationships with us were not considered serious.

More emails started to come in, including one from a Yahoo group called Haven for the Human Amoeba, a reference to the fruitless web searches that all of us had spent years conducting. With eighteen members, it was the largest asexual community on the planet, and we set about debating the principles and values that would come to define our community. There were those who thought that the term asexual should be strictly policed to avoid confusion. They advocated that community members take a rigorous test to confirm their "true" asexuality before being admitted, and that anyone who violated this standard should be expelled. Schooled on identity by my queer elders, I advocated for a different approach. The term asexual should be a tool, not a tightly controlled brand. If someone found it useful, they should be able to pick it up, even if they used it in a way that was a little bit different from others. If they wanted to customize their tool to make it more personally useful, by amending their personal defi-nition or adding a creative adjective, then they should be encouraged to do so. If they no longer found the tool useful and wanted to put it down and pick up another, that should be celebrated, because our value as a community should be self-discovery and self-acceptance, not conformity.

I purchased the domain name asexuality.org, upgraded the site with proper online forums, and invited a handful of asexual folks from Haven for the Human Amoeba to join. Soon we had a core group that shared the values of support and self-acceptance. Appearing just as Google was coming into widespread usage, the Asexual Visibility and Education Network, or AVEN, became the top search result for anyone who typed the term asexual into what was quickly becoming the world's most widely used search bar. About once a week a new member would show up, almost always overwhelmed with the expe-rience of realizing that they were not alone. Usually they had, like me, independently invented the term *asexual* and used it for years in isolation. As Google became more widespread, those members started showing up once a day.

I knew from my own experience finding community that new arriv-als needed special attention. Like me, many would feel overwhelmed when releasing a deep feeling of loneliness that had been burdening them for years. Some would eagerly dive into the community, but others were nervous. They did not know if they would fit, did not know if our community would accept them, and needed reassurance before they would open up. From my time infiltrating the Wesleyan admissions office, I knew that the act of welcoming was both sacred and powerful. The lessons that people learn when they enter a community define the culture that will come to guide it: what parts of themselves to show to others, what behavior will let them be respected and accepted, what the community is capable of, and how they can tap into that power.

This shared experience of finding community created a bond among members that, for a time, helped to minimize the toxicity that defines many online spaces. The outpourings of emotion in welcome threads led to ongoing relationships, with people coming back first for support and then for creativity. Amid the many memes, joke threads, and vent sessions, the community began mapping the terrain of asexual experience, as the invitation to modify tools and build new ones was accepted with a flourish. The term gray a was invented to describe people on a spectrum between sexual and asexual, and demisexual to describe people who experienced sexual attraction only in close emotional relationships. Romantic people found resonance with the language of crushes and falling in love, while aromantic people (like me) did not. As our numbers expanded and diversified, it no longer felt fitting to refer to us as the asexual community, so the umbrella term *ace* was invented to describe those on the asexual spectrum. The definition of asexuality was not a box for us to fit in but a flag, visible from afar, that we could build a city around.

Every day I logged on to AVEN to personally welcome newcomers. I noticed that other members would regularly show up to provide support in welcome threads, and started communicating with them to discuss how we each approached this critical work. It was in these conversations that the community began to develop its leadership and governance. The other welcomers became moderators, then fellow administrators of the site. Our job as leaders in the ace community was to create a space where new people could explore their identities and connect with others to find support, and the people who excelled at that job were invited into power.

Nearby in the conceptual space of the early-2000s internet, another community was working through similar challenges. Involuntary celibates, or incels, at that time had a community that was similar to ours in many ways. They also had a supportive forum, started by a woman named Alana, where people who felt alone explored their incompatibility with the standards of the sexual world. While incels wanted sex and we didn't, both of us were communities dedicated to helping a diverse group of people support one another in journeys away from loneliness. But the incels were developing a problem. They'd had a harder time recruiting moderators to take on the work of welcoming new people and smoothing over conflict. As the community grew, Alana and the other moderators began to burn out, and the community began to turn toxic. Instead of focusing on support and self-acceptance, the community tilted toward self-loathing and blaming its loneliness on others. Misogyny took root, then took over, then became violent. New members learned that the way to gain attention and power was to post increasingly extremist content. In 2014 in Isla Vista, California, a man identifying as an incel killed six people in an attack motivated by these extreme posts,[37] starting a wave of mass violence that has continued since.

Today the asexual community numbers in the millions and is a respected part of the LGBTQIA+ community. Ace kids show up to high school gender and sexuality alliances and receive support. We have successfully lobbied to be delisted as a mental disorder, and thanks to some well-placed employee activism, we can find one another on OKCupid. Like all parts of the queer community, we have our flaws, but we receive grateful letters from young people who tell us that we have saved their lives. The incel community numbers in the tens of thousands and is recognized as a terrorist group by the US government.[38]

Loneliness can be a reason to transform ourselves and our world in positive ways, but it can also fester into a resentment that harms everything it touches. Building relational containers is necessary, but it is not enough: We must maintain a set of shared values that direct the transformative power of these containers. When the people maintaining those values in the incel community burned out and left, the community spiraled toward disaster. Without someone to do the work of welcoming people, holding values, and mediating conflict, relational containers will inevitably fail, often with tragic results.

Movements like AVEN are one way to scale the work of building relationship, but their impact is limited by a lack of funding. In order to understand the intersection of relational containers and money, it is helpful to understand what happens when money *is* invested in building relationship and why such investments so often fail. Just as the ace community was getting off the ground, another relational container was being built, one that would go on to become the best resourced that the world had ever seen.

Why the World's Best-Funded Relational Container Is Failing

In 2002, just as AVEN was getting off the ground, two friends from my quantum physics class invited me to preview a secret project. They booted up a browser and took me to a site called WesMatch, where participants could fill out funny surveys and be connected with compatible friends on campus. The site included profiles with uploadable pictures, a message system, and a way to track the friends you were making on campus, a mix of features that put it ahead of the then-dominant Friendster that had halfheartedly taken root.

WesMatch launched and was an on-campus success, and my friends began scaling it to other campuses. To make money they charged student governments, most of whom had discretionary budgets, to launch the platform as a benefit to students. This created a protracted sales process that slowed their growth and allowed them to be overtaken by a competing platform from Harvard called (at the time) thefacebook.

In order to discuss the need for relational containers, we need to examine why so many of the containers we have are broken. I do not place blame for the social isolation crisis solely on the shoulders of Meta or social media in general, though the strong correlation between the global rise of social isolation and the global rise in smartphone-based social media use is difficult to ignore. Meta and social media companies like it can serve as illustrative examples of a trend that both predates and spreads far beyond them.

From its foundation, Meta's explicit goal has been to build a relational container. From its founding tagline, "Thefacebook is an online directory that connects people through social networks at colleges,"[39] to Meta's mission statement today, "Giving people the power to build community and bring the world closer together,"[40] the company has focused on creating the conditions for relationships to happen. As Mark Zuckerberg began rapidly expanding thefacebook across college campuses, he set out to do what legions of people building relational containers had tried and usually failed to do: acquire funding.

All relational containers require resources to survive, and the way that they acquire those resources profoundly shapes how they operate and what they are and are not capable of. Generally, when people seek resources for the work of building relationship, they are forced to rely on anecdotes and theater to get funders to understand the power of their communities, unless they are fortunate enough to have funders who participate in that community directly. Zuckerberg had something rare and radically transformative in the world of relational funding. He had data.

Back in the days of thefacebook, a relationship was a simple line between two people. Either this line existed and the people were friends, or it didn't and they weren't. Because this insufficiently captured the complexities of campus social life, an optional label was added for people who were sleeping together or dating, called "relationship status," with options like "single," "in a relationship," and "It's complicated." Thefacebook's engineers could track when people made more friends, they could track when they viewed one another's content, they could track engagement and retention among their users, but they couldn't track when existing friends became closer to one another. The shining data that thefacebook showed to their investors felt like a proxy for relationship, but a messy one. If people were constantly logging in and looking at content posted by their friends, then surely they were becoming closer. The details of what, exactly, a relationship was and how to better go about measuring one could surely be worked out as the company grew. If metrics like engagement were a proxy for relational success, then thefacebook looked poised to be the most successful relational container the world had ever seen. To investors it looked like a powerful new engine not only for human connection but for creating predictable behaviors of scrolling and clicking that could easily be monetized. Zuckerberg acquired his first round of funding, used it to purchase the domain name facebook.com and change the company's name to Facebook, and set out to rapidly scale his new relational container across the globe.

Today tech companies like Meta still run on a more sophisticated version of the engagement metrics that Zuckerberg first reported to investors. These increasingly complex gradations of engagement flow from quarterly statements to the way that product teams and individual engineers are assessed for their work. If someone inside Meta has an idea for a product, they build it and test it on a small number of users. If that product makes the right kinds of engagement go up, it stays; if the right kinds of engagement go down or stay flat, then it is eliminated. Every button placement, every font weight, and every algorithmic content nudge is painstakingly optimized for the data that Meta believes to be correlated with meaningful relationships before it is distributed more or less uniformly on a global scale. For a time, this model of global homogeneity based on a rational meritocracy of data seemed poised to bring relational agency to the world, saving democracies and banishing social isolation in the process. But that dream did not come to pass. We live in a world that is rapidly getting lonelier and more autocratic, a world in which Meta is spectacularly failing in its mission.

The anatomy of this failure is complex and nuanced, but for the time being I want to highlight one component: the way that thefacebook, then Facebook, then Meta defined relational success to its funders. It is now broadly acknowledged that engagement metrics are not, in fact, a helpful proxy for understanding when people are becoming closer with one another. Nor is the speed at which they like, follow, or add one another to their social graphs. At the core of Meta's empire of relational containers lies a deep uncertainty about what a relationship is and how to go about building one.

While social media companies like Meta and TikTok are uniquely impacted by this problem, they are far from alone in it. The definition of a relationship that thefacebook started with was borrowed from a mathematical discipline called graph theory, which is still the dominant way that relationships are scientifically reasoned about today. While graph theory is an immensely robust and powerful mathematical tool, it offers little guidance on how to understand the growth of relationships over time. Relationships consist of nodes—representations of things that can be in relationship, like people—and edges—lines connecting them that can either exist or not exist. Graph theoretician Mason Porter refers to this as "people walking around holding sticks that other people are holding,"[41] and, like many of his colleagues, openly acknowledges how it is a gross and sometimes dangerous oversimplification of our lived relational experience. Edges can be weighted with numbers or tagged with statuses like "It's complicated," but there is not a consistent theoretical framework for describing the difference between an important relationship and an unimportant one, or measuring how relationships become more or less important over time. Meta's product teams can measure people engaging with one another's content, but they have no idea if those people are becoming closer to one another in the process.

This conceptual gap has carried over to social science, where researchers tend to categorize relationships with labels such as "strong" or "weak"[42] and by particular observable metrics such as time spent together. Once again, rigorous and highly impactful work is being done, and once again, it is highly fragmented. A good deal of research focuses on the relational health of married couples, since they pay for therapy, and on the health of relationships in the workplace, since they improve productivity and companies will pay for this expertise, but shockingly little is devoted to the topic of understanding how people form friendships or how those friendships deepen.

While it is difficult to find a citation that demonstrates a gap in a field, a helpful proxy is the disambiguation page that Wikipedia has for the word *relationship*. Wikipedia treats familial relationships, interpersonal relationships, and romantic relationships as separate and largely independent concepts,[43] with the notable exception that the research in the "interpersonal relationships" section mostly references research on romantic relationships.[44] The section on "ways that interpersonal relationships begin," a central question for anyone seeking to build relational containers or address the loneliness crisis, includes less than a hundred words and only one citation.[45]

For the profound impact that relationships have on our health, our lives, and the future of our species, shockingly little is scientifically understood about them, especially when those relationships are neither romantic nor professional. Far more is scientifically established about the impacts of loneliness than about how to support the relational agency that gets people out of it. In saying this I do not mean to minimize the excellent work of researchers who study things like adult friendship, merely to highlight how shockingly little funding and scientific interest there seems to be in this topic. Given how critical relational agency has been to our health as individuals and the history of our species, it is as if we lived in a world where the combined study of agriculture and nutrition was considered an obscure niche.

In many ways, this gap in our scientific understanding mirrors the gap in language that I struggled with as a young asexual person. Relationships seem to be worth talking about when they are on a path to heteronormative family or professional productivity, but when they are headed anywhere else that is powerful, we face a gaping void of meaningful language. This is why so many institutions wax poetic about investing in community but have almost no shared, let alone scientifically grounded, understanding of what it means to do so. This is why executives at thefacebook, then Facebook, then Meta struggled to understand what metrics indicated a path away from loneliness and eventually settled on whatever metrics brought in money. This is part of why foundations so often fail to meaningfully invest in grassroots social movements, why parents of young kids wind up isolated from their friends rather than supported by them, and why the money poured into political campaigns overwhelmingly goes toward email and text-message spam rather than toward connecting people with one another to build power. We share a deeply felt sense that relationships matter but lack the shared language to invest in building them.

Let's label this mysterious void of language **relational invisibility.** To me, relational invisibility is more than an abstract concept. It is a memory I hold, a familiar feeling in my body. It is every time I have witnessed human connection that mattered and have been told that that connection was not real or not concrete. It is the feeling of being patted on the head and told that my emotions are nice, but that things that are more grounded in reality need to take priority. Often these things are simply more easily measurable or more aligned with a scripted narrative of success. Relational invisibility is the frustration of knowing that investing in relationships will ultimately be vastly more impactful and having that knowledge ignored.

It is not ignored universally. Many of us have experiences in social movements, faith communities, or creative networks where wisdom about how to build and maintain relationship is practiced and passed on, even though these groups tend to be too underfunded (unless they cater to the wealthy) to provide us with a source of income. Relational invisibility is never more apparent than when we suddenly move from a place where relationship is everything to a place that is unable to understand its power.

If you picked up this book, you have probably experienced this frustration. It may have happened only once, or it may be a smoldering rage that you experience daily. If, like me, you are in the latter category, then I invite you to reflect on that rage and how you hold it. If we are to address the loneliness crisis, then that rage has work to do.

Relational invisibility can also be a cloak. By 2021, exactly twenty years after founding AVEN, I had established myself as one of the most effective worker organizers in the tech industry, though my work was focused on supporting employee advocacy rather than directly on unionization. Using the relational strategies that I had discovered in the early days of the asexual community and honed in numerous movements since, I was able to build trusted relationships with and between employees at major social media companies in ways that directly impacted the policies they set and the features they shipped. For example, shortly before the rebrand to Meta, a number of Facebook employees expressed concern about the rising influence of harmful conspiracy theories like QAnon and were told by higher-ups that other issues needed to take priority. Working with a few internal contacts, I was able to organize an external invite-only event on the topic that just so happened to exclusively invite Facebook employees. I created a welcoming environment, set the stage and the stakes with compelling personal stories, then stepped out of the room so that employees could connect on the issue across departments without violating their nondisclosure agreements (NDAs). The result was a block of coordinated employees who could work together and more effectively push back against the mandates of their bosses. Changes to Facebook's products came soon after.

Though I had avoided signing any of their NDAs, I tended to know more about the internal politics, if not protected trade secrets, of companies like Facebook, TikTok, Twitch, and Twitter than many of their own employees. I knew, for example, that there was substantial concern among TikTok employees about the impact that their algorithm was having on creator mental health, with mounting implications of influencer anxiety and depression sitting alongside the company's efforts to convince as many of their users as possible to become content creators. If a particularly crucial debate was raging among Twitter's executive leadership, I would quietly ensure that a well-regarded external organization would release an opinion piece to nudge it in the right direction. By understanding where relationships did not exist but were possible and how to make them happen, I was able to wield a surprising amount of power that no one in the leadership of these companies seemed to notice.

During my organizing, I went hunting for internal teams charged with addressing the gap in relational understanding that had occurred at the company's inception. If the plan had always been to get big and figure out how relationships worked along the way, then surely someone was doing that? Collaborations with external researchers had soured after the whole Cambridge Analytica business, but surely someone on the inside was tinkering away. Eventually I found them: a group of data scientists charged with something approaching the question that motivated me: what was relationship, and how could Meta know if it was happening? I hopped on Zoom to discuss statistical techniques and found a human who was frustrated and dejected. Though Facebook was gathering mountains of data on its users, there was no clear path to finding indicators of off-platform human connection within those data, nor was there any indication that this was the right kind of data to gather. What's more, the team was limited in the kinds of questions it could ask because the higher-ups at Facebook were concerned about the answer.

It was in the context of this work that I encountered a Facebook employee named Frances Haugen. It was public knowledge at that point that the north star metric for Facebook's product teams was something called Meaningful Social Interactions, or MSI.[46] This basket of metrics had been gotten to with some roundabout social science: Facebook users had been surveyed to find which ones felt a higher degree of connection, then the kinds of Facebook interactions correlated with those users had been clumped together and labeled as "meaningful." This included things like the number of emoji reactions and comments that a post received and how active users were in Facebook Groups. Everything from the ranking that posts received in the Newsfeed to which product features got greenlit was determined by MSI, which, conveniently, involved types of engagement that bolstered Facebook's market position and bottom line.

Through a shared understanding, Frances and I kept our conversations at the level of office politics about ideas that were already public knowledge. There was growing internal concern that MSI was failing and possibly causing harm. For example, the heavy emphasis on Groups had fueled the growth of antivaccine groups during the early days of the COVID-19 pandemic and the conspiracy theories that drove the attack on the US Capitol on January 6 of that year. Publicly,

Facebook denied any association, but internally there were understandable doubts.

A few months later, Frances would make a considerable personal
sacrifice to do something about it. She snapped pictures of numerous
internal documents on a disposable camera, then delivered them to the
Washington Post and applied for protection from the SEC's Office of the
Whistleblower in the largest leak from a social media company in history. Alongside other whistleblowers such as Ifeoma Ozoma, Sophie
Zhang, and Anika Collier, Frances Haugen's courageous actions gave
us a rare glimpse inside some of the largest and best-resourced relational containers in human history, and the results were damning.

Facebook's own internal research showed that Instagram was
having a negative impact on teen girls. According to an internal slide,
"32 percent of teen girls said that when they felt bad about their bodies,
Instagram made them feel worse."[47] The internal discourse on MSI was
equally troubling. Because comments and reactions were considered
signs of "meaningful social interaction," posts that generated a sense of
moral outrage were bubbling to the top, and employees could see it in
the data.[48] The leak aligned with research that indicates that when we
amplify content based on its ability to elicit emotion, the emotion of
moral outrage tends to win out.[49] Facebook had bet that content that
created an engaging emotional reaction would create relationships,
and they had been dead wrong. In the following months, Frances
Haugen testified before the US Senate, Facebook changed its name to
Meta, and its stock price dropped by over 50 percent.

It is tempting to see the loneliness that we feel as a personal failing.
If we lack the ability to build the relationships we need to survive and
thrive, we are often told that it is because we have failed to be rich
enough, thin enough, accomplished enough, or normal enough. We
have failed to cover ourselves in the right trappings of success or to
sufficiently hide our thoughts and feelings under an acceptable exte-
rior. But that is not why we are lonely. We are lonely because the vast
engines of cultural, economic, technical, and political power charged
with building environments for connection have lost sight of what a
relationship is.

Reflection Questions

- Where are you on your own journey away from loneliness?

- Where are you still struggling?

- Where are you ready to invite others into the knowledge you have gained?

- What spaces for connection do you find meaningful?

- How do you support their existence?

- How do you create them yourself?

CHAPTER 2

Three Definitions
of Relationship

RELATIONSHIP IS A FUNNY WORD. Like *health* or *life,* it is so all-encompassing as to be almost undefinable. The Oxford English Dictionary defines relationship as:

> **relationship** *(noun). The way in which two or more concepts, objects, or people are connected, or the state of being connected.*

This definition leans heavily on the word *connection,* which is unhelpfully circular:

> **connection** *(noun). A relationship in which a person, thing, or idea is linked or associated with something else.*

Both definitions hark back to the graph-theoretic definition of relationship as a line connecting two points, as "two people holding a stick." Simply saying that a relationship is a thing that either exists or doesn't between two people tells us nothing about how to make relationships appear where they don't yet exist or make relationships deeper where they do.

Definitions are tools. They should help us make sense of the world around us and how to relate to it. Yet many of the definitions of relationship that permeate our society, including Oxford's definition, Facebook's MSI, and the narrow definition of a romantic relationship headed toward marriage, are ineffective tools. They give bad advice or none at all on how to make relationships happen in our lives. They fail to contribute to or actively undermine our relational agency, and they serve as poor guides for developing effective relational infrastructure.

In this chapter, I will explore three alternative definitions of relationships, three tools that I have found immensely useful both in finding my own relational agency and in building relational infrastructure for others. They suggest the steps that we might take to make relationships happen, ways to create a shared understanding of where and how they are happening, and ways to understand the implications when they do. The definitions are:

1. A relationship is a shared understanding among two or more people about how to spend meaningful time together.

2. A relationship exists when two or more entities change one another.

3. A relationship exists when two or more entities exchange information.

These definitions are useful in different ways and in different situations. The definition about time is useful for thinking about how to build relationships, the definition about change is useful for thinking about why to build them, and the definition about information is useful for thinking about how to make measurements and predictions about them in a rigorous way. That last one involves a fair amount of abstraction and some amount of formal analysis, which I will do my best to make accessible to nonmath folks without rendering it too vague for those with a more technical bent.

If definitions are tools, then a good way to understand how to use them is to understand the particular challenges that they were designed to address. In order to explain these tools, I will need to tell their stories.

A Relationship Is a Shared Understanding Among Two or More People About How to Spend Meaningful Time Together

After graduating in 2004, I found myself struggling to navigate the realities of urban community. I had just moved to the Bay Area to explore the intersection of technology and social movements and, like anyone in a new city, was figuring out how to climb my way out of loneliness. I was meeting people I got along with, but spending time together took weeks of planning, and spending my first ten hours with someone, even when there was strong mutual interest, could easily take a year. For the first (and one of the last) times in my life, I would go a full week at a time without seeing friends beyond my housemates.

It was the earliest stages of the scenario I most feared: without a sexual partner to fill up my calendar, would it eventually empty? Would plans with friends become less frequent as they inevitably paired off until I was left to fill my time with whatever distractions I could muster? I did not yet know the terrifying research about the impact that loneliness would have on my health, only that loneliness was a fate I seemed headed for and that my survival depended on avoiding it.

While some asexual people had begun to describe themselves as "romantic" and found the rituals of dating authentic and fulfilling, I was not among them. At any given time I would have many people I was excited about for different reasons, but it felt awkward and arbitrary to assign one or more of them a special status and a script and therefore identified as "aromantic." Without sexual or romantic attraction to guide me, people weren't highlighted as shiny or special, just varying degrees of exciting to spend time with. Even if I chose someone to date, could I be able to be an appealing partner while being honest about my feelings? Tens of thousands of romantic aces have since proven that when they are grounded in authenticity, romantic relationships can work up, down, and across the ace spectrum, but romantic dating doesn't tend to work for the aromantics among us.

The problem was one of intentionality. Romantic relationships were not necessarily more important or even more emotionally powerful than friendships, but romantic scripts came packaged with tools for talking about commitment. Romantic partners could, albeit somewhat awkwardly, ask one another where their relationships were going. They could quickly escalate to seeing one another once a week or more, and know that suddenly not being able to make time for one another was a reason to check in. I had no idea how to indicate that I wanted commitment in my friendships or that I wanted to see my friends more often without sounding desperate. Friendships, in contrast to romantic relationships, were supposed to be flexible and easygoing. If someone wasn't available for a period of time, the relationship was supposed to pick up where it had left off. When friends chose to entangle their lives by living together, it was generally a matter of convenience ("Hey, it looks like both of us are looking for a place right now ..."), rather than the result of years of careful planning.

To invite intentionality into my relationships, to have something approaching the relational agency that the allosexual (not identifying on the asexual spectrum) and alloromantic (not identifying as aromantic) people around me had, I needed to expand my definition of what a relationship was. As long as I used Facebook's labeling system of "in a relationship" or "just friends," meaningful relationship was something I would be locked out of. I needed a tool that let me see beyond the label that has been slapped on a relationship to begin to appreciate the story of what it was.

As I strategized about how to fill my calendar with meaningful shared time, I began to conceive of a relationship as a **shared understanding that two or more people have of how to spend meaningful time together.** My friend Karuna and I weren't just holding two ends of a stick, we had a shared understanding that if we went to karaoke on Tuesday nights, it would make both of us happy. Our relationship started when we struck up a conversation and realized that we had a shared love of dance and music. In order for the relationship to grow, we didn't have to start dating, we just had to expand our understanding of how to spend time together by making the jump from karaoke to hiking or cooking together. The strength of our relationship could be thought of as the depth of understanding we held about how to spend time that integrated with and added to both our lives.

I like this definition of relationship because of the way that it invites inquiry into the story of a connection. How do two people like to spend time together? Is the time meaningful, or do they spend it together out of a sense of compulsion? Do they have a shared understanding of what meaningful time means, or do those understandings diverge? Does the way that they understand how to spend time regularly lead to conflict or does it enable destructive behavior? I can conceive of my relationship with myself as the understanding I have about how to spend time with myself, an understanding like any other that can grow and shift over time. If I count my relationship with myself, then every second of every day of my life is spent in some sort of relationship. How we spend our hours, our days, and our years is defined entirely by the relationships we hold.

This means that building relationship, either with ourselves, with others, or with the more-than-human world, is how we invite new possibilities into our lives. When I learned to sing karaoke with Karuna, I wasn't just building a connection with her, I was becoming familiar with an entire domain of expression that would stretch beyond our friendship. I could have learned to love karaoke on my own, religiously heading to the Shattuck Down Low on Tuesdays to sit in a corner until it was my turn to sing, but in my experience, this kind of dedication without relationship is fairly rare. Unless a relationship with myself or another being is growing along with it, it is very difficult to gain a new understanding of how to be in the world.

These understandings of how to spend time can be discovered or inherited. When I attend synagogue and read the Kaddish, I embody an understanding of how to spend time mourning in community that has roots in my ancestors over a thousand years ago. When I meet someone for the first time at a party, we must find an entirely new understanding, which is easier in some environments than others. If I meet a stranger on the New York subway, the path to shared time is narrow and murky. Social norms prohibit speaking or eye contact, and even if I were to strike up a conversation, I would have nothing but visual clues to tell me how this person likes to spend time or how we might spend it well together, nor should I expect them to have any interest in learning to spend time with me. But if I get off the subway and go to a dinner party where the host excitedly introduces me to someone who shares my interests, the path to meaningful shared time is much easier. The job of a relational container, like my friend making the introduction at his party, is to help navigate this search process.

The way that we build this understanding, and therefore the way that we build relationship, tends to follow a consistent pattern:

1. First, we **explore** new ways to spend time with someone. In a new relationship, this could look like exploring several topics of conversation to see which one resonated; in a mature one, it could look like having an explicit conversation about things that we want to try doing together.

2. We communicate about how the time spent makes us **feel.** In a new relationship, this could look like noticing someone's face light up when I mention a shared interest. In a mature one it might look like having a grounded conversation about complex feelings.

3. Once we know which ways of spending time feel good and which don't, we must **commit** to spend more time together in ways that feel good. In a new relationship, this could look like an interest in grabbing coffee; in a mature one it might look like a commitment both to spend regular time together but *not* to spend that time in certain ways. This additional time creates new opportunities for exploration, and the cycle begins again.

When relationships move through this cycle, they tend to grow. When they are blocked for some reason, they tend to stagnate. If two people have a great connection but only ever stick to the same habits, then their relationship is failing to explore new territory. These old habits may work, and they may even be reassuring if the other parts of our lives are shifting chaotically, but if the way that the two friends habitually spend time stops working for either of them, the relationship could be doomed to failure. Similarly, if two people explore lots of new possibilities but fail to feel or communicate their emotions, then the relationship will have no sense of direction. I have had amazing relationships in my life that were deeply intellectual. My friends and I would spend time so lost in our heads that we were unable to access the emotions that coursed through our bodies. As a result, the relationships began to feel unsupportive and riddled with small conflicts until we could intentionally shift our shared understanding of how to spend time together to include grounding in and communicating our feelings. Finally, relationships can fail if they lack the capacity for commitment. If two people explore amazing new ways of spending time together and express powerful emotions about them, but fail to keep and make promises about how to spend more time together, their relationship will quickly cease to exist. Commitments constitute a shared investment, a willingness to avoid spending time in other appealing ways so that it can be spent together. For this reason, breaking a commitment, especially without acknowledging or repairing the harm caused in doing so, can quickly degrade an otherwise powerful relationship.

In the same way that a map makes a city more navigable, a good relational container helps us navigate the process of learning to spend time together. When two people meet, there is an immense amount of uncertainty to navigate. The possibilities are endless: any possible topic of conversation, breaking out into spontaneous dance, screaming together at the top of their lungs. Relational containers collapse this vast possibility space into something manageable that maximizes the possibility of discovering compelling new opportunities for connection while minimizing the possibility of causing harm. It does so by helping us explore, feel, and commit. One job of the synagogue and the Kaddish is to help me feel the loss of a loved one fully so that I can understand how to spend time with them as a memory rather than as a living being. Without the community and without the prayer, I may not be able to feel deeply or consistently enough to make the transition. The container guides me to a relationship that is possible but that I could not have found my way to on my own.

If we set out to create relational containers, it is worth asking how these three steps will take place. In 2009 I befriended Avary Kent, who became frustrated after attending conferences where days were packed with back-to-back panels aggrandizing the speakers and leaving the audience isolated. This is an effective strategy for getting as many people as possible to speak, and therefore to get as many recognizable names as possible to attend, but it creates a poor relational container. If Avary had space to explore with others, it was often by asking a generic question to someone waiting with them in the lunch line and hoping to strike on a meaningful topic. The feelings Avary could express and ask about were constrained. No one was modeling openness or vulnerability, so expressing anything beyond a constrained professional approval or excitement felt uncomfortable. Because of these frustrations, Avary has devoted much of their life to the design of relational events, which emphasize trust-building among participants over broadcasting the ideas of organizers and speakers. They specialize in ensuring that the conversations that normally take place in the hallways of an event are instead centered at the core of the program.

For example, every June Avary helps to organize a group of Bay Area sustainability professionals for an event called the Greenermind Summit. Located in a campground in a gorgeous redwood grove, the event has a relatively low budget because of its strong reliance on volunteer labor. Participants prep the meals, clean up after them, set up and tear down the space, and set the agenda. People are encouraged to propose workshops and facilitated conversations on whatever their area of greatest passion is at the time, from fire spinning to the economics of open-air carbon capture. Sessions are small, highly interactive, and generously spaced around open time where people can follow up on threads that they find interesting. Open mic performances, campfire singalongs, and small children underfoot eliminate the expectation that anyone will be held to the emotional standards of professionalism. First-time attendees are identified, and a special class of volunteers is tasked with welcoming and checking in with them. At the end of the weekend, Avary prompts participants to find the people with whom they experienced the most impactful moments of the conference and express gratitude. These exchanges of gratitude often result in hugs, tears, and follow-up plans. The event has sparked book clubs, working groups, a heartbeat of get-togethers throughout the year, and countless professional collaborations.

Like all relational containers, the Greenermind Summit is designed to meet the particular relational needs of a particular community. When designing or actively participating in a relational container, it can be helpful to ask the following questions:

How does the container help participants explore? Participants are regularly put in structured small groups or one-on-one conversations with a hint about the kinds of meaningful time they might spend together. When a new person arrives, they are gently ushered into a one-on-one conversation where they can be seen, heard, and oriented to the norms of the space ("When you meet someone, don't ask what they do; ask what brings them here.") By glancing at the schedule they can see what people in the community are most passionate about both professionally and personally and focus in on the places of strongest overlap. When they show up, they will be a participant in a conversation rather than an audience member, meeting and finding overlap with the others at the conference who share their area of passion. Once this relational groundwork has been laid, and only when it has been laid, tasks like meal prep and cleanup become further opportunities for connection. A dinner cleanup shift provides a good opportunity for participants to work with their hands while gently exploring possible paths to connection with the others in the kitchen.

How does the container help participants feel? From the moment of their arrival, participants witness others openly expressing their emotions and experience a gentle curiosity about their own emotional experience. The redwood trees invite a departure from the emotional norms of their professional lives while event-specific norms around things like consent and conflict mediation are laid out explicitly. Shared, community-prepared meals elicit emotion, as does shared music, dance, and a continual invitation to articulate their greatest areas of personal passion and growth. Most group activities involve both a shared display of emotion and a focus on moving and sensing the body, where information about emotions resides.[1] Throughout the event, gratitude is expressed like a drumbeat, both to individuals and to the community as a whole, prompting participants to continually reflect on and integrate the emotions that they feel throughout the weekend. All of this means that as possibilities emerge through exploration, whether they are people to talk to, conversation topics to pursue, practices to try out, or projects to explore, participants are aware of which possibilities elicit the strongest emotional response and are continually reflecting on how to integrate that emotional information into an understanding of what to do next.

How does the container help participants commit? After every session, participants have ample open time to allocate to their emerging relationships. If they strike a resonant chord with a fellow workshop participant, they can go on a walk in the woods to let the conversation unfold rather than needing to fit a follow-up in between work calls three weeks later. Because participants are cocreating the event by making food and making the agenda, they feel increased license to pursue ideas for spontaneous shared projects. It is common for people who just met to perform together for the open mic or to cofacilitate a session. A norm of people committing not only to spend time talking but committing to take on meaningful work greatly expands the size and scope of commitments that feel possible. At the end of the event, the gratitude exercise is, in part, an explicit tool for generating follow-up commitments. Because shared commitments flow from strong shared feelings, evoking those feelings creates an environment where more commitments happen.

Asking how a relational container facilitates exploration, feeling, and commitment can tell us a great deal about what kinds of relationships will or will not happen there. This is true whether we are examining an event, a community, a physical space, or a piece of social software. In the face of the loneliness crisis, this has important ramifications. If a given group of people are lonely, as far too many are, we can observe how they prefer to explore, express emotion, and make commitments and then make informed guesses about the kinds of containers that will help them build relationships. If we see that relationships are missing across two groups—two complementary but siloed scientific fields, elderly people and high school students, or communities separated by a political divide—then we can intentionally construct spaces of exploration, feeling, and commitment to connect them. If we want to understand how these spaces are going, we can use instruments from social science to examine these three processes. How often are people encountering new possibilities that feel relevant to their lives? How powerfully are they feeling and expressing emotions about these possibilities? How many of them are committing time and other resources to exploring them further? Mixed methods approaches to answering these questions, some of which will be explored in chapter 6, can provide meaningful data on when and where relationships are forming.

This possibility for measurement is one tool with which we can begin to draw back the veil of relational invisibility. Relationships may seem like an abstraction, but we can compare two events and see which is more likely to generate evidence of follow-up conversations. We can approach someone with money who is interested in, say, investing in a youth-led reproductive justice movement and provide them with evidence of an effective relational strategy for generating student groups with a shared commitment to grassroots action, or approach a university with evidence that our conference plan will create improved evidence of cross-field collaboration, or test a relational intervention in a high school that is seeing the worst of the social isolation crisis play out. Though there are many more definitions and tools to explore, this first definition of relationship allows us to begin to imagine what it might look like for resources to flow to the relational infrastructure that our world desperately needs.

This definition and the tools that come with it also have limitations. Simply helping people spend time with one another is a start, but this definition fails to capture the complexities of why we chose to spend time together or what happens when we do. I am reminded of a night spent at a rooftop taco joint with a group of integrity workers from major tech platforms. Integrity teams, sometimes referred to as trust and safety teams, are responsible for dealing with the bad things that happen on the internet. They deal with everything from cyber-bullying to human trafficking to state-sponsored attacks on elections. Though there was laughter and full margarita pitchers, the mood was somber. Everyone at the table had seen things that their NDAs forbade them from talking about, and those things had left them with a deep feeling of unease. Most of the behavior that social media platforms encourage is to relational agency what popcorn is to nutrition. It is novel and interesting but provides no clear path to spending mean-ingful time with another human. I cautiously asked the people around me why this was the case. Could social media platforms create a pipe-line from following someone to being in conversation with others who shared that interest? Couldn't they develop ways for people in a group not only to broadcast ideas to one another but to get into small conversations where they could openly express emotions and make commitments?

Clutching their beers, they patiently answered that this did happen. It was an extremely effective way to get people into relationships with one another, and the people who did it best tended to be hate groups. Several years earlier, the relational tactics I was advocating for had been used by ISIS to lure teenagers, especially young women, from the United States, Great Britain, and Europe to join the Islamic State.[2] Propaganda would explicitly target the sense of social isolation that these young women felt, promising a utopian vision of a com-munity rooted in Muslim values. Once they expressed interest, they would be personally contacted by a recruiter who would listen to their story, offer kindness, and build trust before inviting them to a small closed community with others on a similar path. Similar tactics had been leveraged for years by white supremacist groups, who offered socially isolated young men "the seductive feeling of being part of a brotherhood, which in turn validates their manhood."[3] To extremist groups, the loneliness crisis was creating a steady stream of people so desperate for connection that they were willing to abandon their families and communities to embrace an ideology based on hate. To the integrity workers sitting with me around the table, effective relational containers were part of the problem.

Say that they *could* measure where relationships were happening. Say that they replaced MSI with a set of measures that effectively demonstrated when people were on a path to spending time together, and they optimized their vast relational infrastructure around that goal. In that world, trans kids finding support would look like success, but so would people being recruited into violent extremism. Simply defining a measure of relationship, even a great one, and making that measure go up would leave massive unanswered questions about the impact that those relationships were having on the world. To understand that impact, we need to think of relationships as more than a way to fill people's calendars, and the path to relational agency as about more than helping individuals spend time with one another and themselves. We need to grapple with the complex connection between relationship and power.

A Relationship Exists When Two or More Entities Change One Another

By the spring of 2015 my relationship with Avary had evolved into a committed aromantic partnership. Though I lived in New York, I regularly flew back to the Bay Area to Avary and their husband Zeke, with whom I was equally intentional and committed. Through a series of intention-setting conversations, the three of us had entered a long-distance aromantic partnership that had become an important part of all our lives. They were not romantic with me and not sexual with me, but that in no way diminished the power of our connection.

During one or my trips, the two of them sat me down in their small living room. "We're thinking about starting a family," they shared, "and we want you to be involved. We don't know exactly what that looks like yet, but we'd love to take time with you to figure it out." I was floored. I had known since childhood that I wanted kids and had struggled for years to envision how that might be possible. As I explored ace intimacy in my twenties, I realized that a committed relationship with a couple seemed like the most aligned and appealing way to go about having kids, but was uncertain how to make that happen beyond dropping hints. Since early in our relationship I had eyed Avary and Zeke as potential co-parents and had dropped a few of those hints, but up until that moment I'd had no idea if they'd take the bold step of actually asking. Though emotions wanted to surge through my body, much as they had after discovering that I was not alone in my asexuality, I temporarily held them back. "This could mean a lot of things," I said, holding my arms wide and waving my right hand. "On one end of a spectrum I'm visiting you regularly, but when the baby cries I give the baby back." I checked their expressions, then wiggled my left hand. "On the other end of the spectrum I'm changing diapers at three in the morning, and we're doing our best to equally carry the work and expenses of parenting." Zeke cracked a smile. "We're interested in that second one," he said. "As close to equal as we can get."

Over the next two years, the three of us had regular conversations about the kind of family we wanted to create. We discussed our families of origin and how they handled things like money, discipline, and quality time. We discussed what about those families we were excited to re-create and what about them we wanted to depart from. We briefed our parents and brought them on board, got practice watching kids together, and drafted a lengthy agreement about how we would handle any conflicts that arose. When Avary and Zeke became pregnant in December 2016, I began packing up my room in Brooklyn to move in with them. Once I arrived in their apartment, we had six months to learn how to live together, to attend birthing classes together, for me to learn to support their lives and marriage, and for them to learn to support my continually evolving constellation of relationships. We learned that, because of decades of advocacy by queer families in California, third parent adoption was an option for us, and put in motion the steps to get all three of our names on our daughter's birth certificate. Just in case, we made sure her full name included all of our last names so that it would always be easy to point at our ID and establish parentage.

In late August, our daughter was born. To say that I was learning to spend time with this new being was simultaneously true and a profound understatement. I had spent much of my life on a journey to make this kind of relationship possible, and now I stood ready for it to fully and unrecognizably transform me. I do not believe that everyone needs to be a parent to be happy, nor do I believe that being a parent is the only valid way to have children in one's life, but I was and still am someone for whom parenting holds an almost spiritual draw. When I held my daughter in my arms, I learned how sensitive she was to my embodied presence, not the words I was saying but the subtle information that the pace of my breath and the tenseness of my muscles conveyed about whether she should feel scared or comforted. This embodied presence and my capacity for care, two things that I had been socialized as a white man to disassociate from, were the only lines of communication that I had in the most important relationship of my life.

I was drawn to parenthood because parenthood is a transformation. From a young age I had observed that when I was around kids, a change came over me. Whether the two siblings and thirty cousins I grew up with or the few kids I got to spend time with in my twenties and early thirties, being around kids transformed me into a person who was more joyful, curious, and caring. I knew I wanted a kid in part because being a parent would forever change me into this more joyful, curious, and caring person. I had no idea who I would be after that change. Not knowing was part of the adventure, but I knew that I wanted to see where that change would take me.

When my child was born, I had a small startup, one that ultimately failed because of my choice to prioritize parenting. (I have no regrets.) I was in a cohort with other founders, and as I came back from parental leave, I noticed an unexpected benefit of having a kid in my life.

The other founders lived and breathed their companies. When the workday ended they took its stress and anxiety into casual conversations with their friends and into nights where they would struggle to find sleep. When I closed my laptop, whatever stress and anxiety I was holding from the day quickly evaporated. I had a much bigger, much more important relationship to have feelings about, and what it required of me was embodied presence and care. While the founders around me were running an emotionally exhausting marathon of depression and anxiety, I was running a short series of daily sprints. Avary, Zeke, and I divided the night into shifts. Zeke and Avary would nurse our daughter when she woke up during the first half of the night, and I'd take over with bottle feeding around 2 a.m. Still, when I met my cofounders for coffee, it was clear that I was better rested.

Relationships transform us, yet somehow they are also a source of resilience. My relationship with my daughter transforms me, but it also brings me back from whatever other transformations the universe has thrown at me. To understand how to build relational infrastructure, it is not simply enough to make relationships happen. We must know what to do with the transformation and resilience that they invite into the world.

Like many in the movements that I am a part of, I draw inspiration from the work of science fiction author and visionary Octavia Butler. Anyone intrigued by the ideas in this book would do well to spend time with her work and with adrienne maree brown's *Emergent Strategy* and *Pleasure Activism,* which directly apply its insights to the work of building joyful relationship in movements.[4] In Butler's *Parable of the Sower,* the protagonist, Lauren Oya Olamina, lives in a world that I could easily imagine my daughter or grandchildren growing up in, and that is eerily similar to the world that many children are growing up in today. Sheltered in a small community barely holding back the crises of a changing climate, skyrocketing inequity, and an authoritarian leader with close ties to extremist groups, Lauren's life is torn apart when her home is destroyed. Like thousands of others, she takes to the road as a refugee, with her ability to build relationships as her sole tool for survival. *Parable of the Sower* opens with a poem, one which I have found insightful in my journey to understand relationship:

> All that you touch
> You Change.
>
> All that you Change
> Changes you.
>
> The only lasting truth
> Is Change
>
> God
> Is Change[5]

To Butler, change is not a thing that happens to us or that we make happen to the world around us; it is a process of mutual resilience and transformation that shapes our lives and our world. My life looks the way that it does today because of the relationships that have shaped it—my relationship with my child and my co-parents, with Molly and the queer movements that nurtured me, with my parents and grand-parents and ancestors stretching back through time. It is shaped by the land I am on and the people, animals, plants, and fungi that have cared for that land. The physical shape of my body comes from my DNA, a biological record of the relationships that have shaped my ancestors since the time of the first living cell. As I write this sentence, I am staring at a giant oak tree, whose thick branches wind and twist over the hillside next to my home. The thickness of each branch, every twist and turn, is a record of the tree's history of relationship. Where it has found sunlight, it has grown; where it has felt the strain of wind, it has shifted and thickened; when it has had water, its rings have grown thick; and when it has experienced scarcity, they have become slivers. In this way, the shape of my life is defined in its entirety by the relationships that have changed it. So is the shape of every rock, stream, and being I have ever known. This profound role of relationship in shaping the world around us is what comes to mind when I consider the last line of Butler's poem, "God is Change."

I bring this up not to invite a religious debate, but to illustrate how a conversation about relationship can move beyond our individual need to find a path out of loneliness. At a recent conference on social isolation, I witnessed many speakers discussing treatments for loneliness as if they were shots to be administered. The disease was loneliness, and the goal was to find a cost-effective and scalable treatment for that disease, one that a relatively small group could administer to a large population with a minimum of unexpected complications. At no point was there an acknowledgment or expectation that the organization administering this treatment and transforming the lives of so many would be transformed themselves. At no time was there a discussion about how the people undergoing this treatment, newly capable through their connections with one another, might exercise their ability to assert collective power over the program that was changing their lives. They sought to be in relationship without being impacted by that relationship, to change without being changed.

To invest in relational infrastructure is to invest in transformation, both in the world around us and in ourselves. This has profound implications for the desire to create efficient, tightly controlled operations that operate at a massive scale. Every time we change someone's life by inviting more relationship into it, they change us back. This change can be welcome if we are working one-on-one or at a relatively small scale, but it can quickly become overwhelming as the number of people being invited into relationship grows. A 2022 survey found that community organizers' greatest area of concern was organizer burnout, followed closely by and deeply related to a concern about underinvestment of resources.[6] When we pay only a few people to build relationship among many people, those organizers quickly start to become changed by those in their community in many different ways simultaneously. Within a group of hundreds of people growing relationship, someone will always have an urgent need, a conflict that needs attention, or an exciting idea that needs nurturing, and organizers must constantly shift their attention to juggle these demands, expanding their working hours and rapidly leading to burnout. Changing hundreds of others while being changed back is unsustainably exhausting. As a result, organizers tend to quickly move on to other careers, failing to develop skills or pass on wisdom and institutional knowledge to those beneath them. If we are to address the loneliness crisis, if we are to learn to invest in relational infrastructure, then we need people with a skill and passion for building community to have long, rewarding, and financially attractive careers. Instead, far too many organizers are being used up and discarded.

This situation is worse when relational infrastructure becomes truly massive. Recall the group of emotionally exhausted integrity workers clutching drinks around a table. Depending on their workplace, each of those individuals was probably responsible for upward of a hundred thousand users on their respective platforms. The power imbalance between these platforms and their users, a power imbalance that these integrity workers were responsible for holding, was and is almost unfathomably large. At some companies, an issue could impact ten million people, more than the population of New York City, and still only warrant 10 percent of one employee's time. In part because of this issue, integrity workers tend to focus on the populations that they are most closely connected to, that they are most familiar with, and that are most capable of holding them accountable. Documents leaked by Frances Haugen reveal that as of 2021, Facebook devoted 87 percent of its staff time to issues in the United States.[7] That's just 13 percent devoted to every other country on Earth, with an integrity staff-to-user ratio well into the millions. At that scale, how big a change would need to occur in the world for Facebook to change back?

In 2020, another whistleblower from Facebook Integrity named Sophie Zhang came forward. While working as a data scientist, Zhang discovered that 78 percent of the likes on posts by Hungary's authoritarian leader were generated by fake accounts.[8] Before long she found a similar pattern in Albania. As she kept digging, she identified additional campaigns of large-scale coordinated inauthentic behavior operating in Azerbaijan, Mexico, Argentina, Italy, the Philippines, Afghanistan, South Korea, Bolivia, Ecuador, Iraq, Tunisia, Turkey, Taiwan, Paraguay, El Salvador, India, the Dominican Republic, Indonesia, Ukraine, Poland, and Mongolia. To her frustration, many of these reports, especially those outside Europe, would languish internally for months. At one point her superiors informed her that large-scale election manipulation in Honduras was being explicitly ignored because of a focus on the US and Europe.[9]

To be in relationship, we must both change and be changed. To be in relationship with many people at once, we must either expand our capacity to be changed or pursue a strategy of dominance and homogenization. Dominance is what happens when someone seeks to change others without being changed back. Homogenization is what happens when they use that power to make different people similar to one another so that they can be related to more efficiently. Integrity employees at Facebook are left holding the inevitable result of this dominance and homogenization, an inability to make sense of or respond to the profound harms that their attempt at building a globally dominant homogenous relational container has created. Where dominance and homogenization reign, there inevitably grows a widespread culture of relational invisibility.

I find this trio of dominance, homogenization, and invisibility all too familiar. As a cisgender white man from an elite coastal city, I have often been socialized to believe that my strength, security, and success are closely tied to my ability to change others without being changed back. In New York, San Francisco, and DC, I would regularly attend parties where people would introduce themselves by their proximity to centers of power. If someone played a role in, say, sourcing the organic produce for all of Walmart, they would casually drop it in conversation to assert their status. This proximity to power, the number of others that they could change without being changed, became the reason that they were worth talking to and the foundation of their self-respect. Without it, they held a justified fear of sliding into loneliness; with it, they felt a surge of relational agency. Embracing this dominance and homogenization required rendering the many people relationships that they had helped to dominate and homogenize invisible. Few imagined in those conversations that the millions of people who used to have a say over the produce in their local grocery stores might harbor a sense of resentment.

To N. K. Jemisin, another science fiction author whose work is a source of personal inspiration, this regime of homogenization is intricately entangled with whiteness:

> *You can support whiteness and be not white. It's a system. There are a lot of people who kind of subscribe to the idea that talking about whiteness means that you are talking about white people. And that is not the case. Whiteness in and of itself as a concept is a homogenization of Europeans.*
>
> *European immigrants came to this country with their own languages, their own culture, their own foods. And in order for the powers that be in this country to forge a coalition that could push back against the very multicultural masses, the working classes, one of the things that happened was the creation of this identity that could suck in the Irish immigrants, and the Italian immigrants, and the wealthy uptown British-descended people, and things like that, and form them into a single coalition that could work back against all of those competing forces.*
>
> *And that homogenization is harmful to white folks. It is— wouldn't you want to retain some aspect of your own home culture that your grandparents fought and struggled to come to a place where they felt that they would be free to practice?*[10]

Whiteness is a part of the history that has shaped me, but it is also a disconnection from that history. I come both from a lineage of people creating the conditions for connection and from a lineage of dominance and homogenization that has destroyed those conditions. When my friends speak of white supremacy, I often think of this lineage of dominance and homogenization, this sprawling, doomed attempt to change without being changed. Because this is a book about relationality and not racism, I will use the phrase "dominance and homogenization" throughout this text, though I consider it and the legacy of exploitation rooted in colonial history deeply intertwined.

I opened this book with a mystery at the heart of the loneliness crisis: If we are becoming more and more capable at building whatever we want, and what we want is to connect with one another, then why are we rapidly getting so much lonelier? In Facebook, we see an example of an attempt to build a relational container through a regime of dominance, homogenization, and invisibility that ultimately leads to widespread disconnection. In an economic regime rooted in colonial history, this example is by no means unique. We are lonely, at least in part, because when those with power invest resources in relational containers, they expect to change others without being changed themselves.

Though this way of thinking about scale is common among institutional investors like venture capitalists and philanthropists, it is far from the only model available. Recall the moment when I knocked on the door of the head of Queer Alliance and asked them to consider my asexuality. In that moment I was approaching not quite an institution but a movement with extraordinary cultural, political, and economic power. Like Facebook, and arguably more than Facebook, the queer movement has transformed how people across the globe relate both to themselves and to one another. It is awkward to compare a movement to a corporation, but a case could easily be made that the queer movement has more ability to mobilize human labor, more economic power, more political influence, and is responsible for vastly more intellectual and cultural innovation than any corporation on the planet. Yet as a first-year college student, I could knock on this movement's door, ask it to change, and be heard.

When operating at scale, institutions can either adopt a policy of dominance and homogenization or expand their capacity to be changed. In the early days of AVEN, members who proactively welcomed others and reflected the community's values were invited into positions of leadership. It was this ability to expand our leadership as we grew that prevented us from collapsing into burnout like other communities that quickly became toxic. While AVEN has had many issues over the two decades of its existence, this pattern of recruiting and supporting community leadership is one that shows up in successful movements throughout history. As the movement grows, potential leaders are identified and mentored on how to welcome new people, pursue the movement's strategic goals, resolve conflict, and participate in governance. As the number of leaders grows, an ecology emerges to provide various resources, mediate conflicts, weave together disparate narratives, and recognize and mobilize around opportunities to create change. While the corporate form and organizational forms like it may be extremely effective tools for building particular kinds of infrastructure, building relational infrastructure may require organizational forms that more closely resemble a movement—forms that grow their capacity to be locally changed as they scale. If this is true, and I will argue that it is, then resourcing relational infrastructure may look radically different than funding a new hospital or investing in a hot new startup. To avoid the trap of dominance and homogenization, we will need to examine more closely how organizational forms like social movements operate, an examination that will be the focus of chapter 4.

Seeing this alternative model can be difficult in part because movements are obscured by the veil of relational invisibility. Large corporations are easy to discern: they have imposing headquarters, consistent legally controlled brands, executive leadership with close to autocratic authority, and easily identifiable products and services that can be brought to market. They have balance sheets filled with things that they own and payrolls filled with employees whose lives they substantively define. We can tell where the corporation begins and where it ends by measuring what it does and does not own.

A movement, in contrast, does not own things. It may include nonprofit and even for-profit corporations with balance sheets, but these organizations are not the movement. It may include leaders who are charismatic, operational, or both, but these leaders do not issue commands to the movement as a whole with anything approaching the authority of a corporate executive. If a corporation is a bundle of ownership, a movement is a more relational entity, a network of people, institutions, and ideas changing one another in a way that somehow acts as a cohesive whole. Movements grow not by expanding what they own, but by inviting more people into aligned relationship. They succeed not through dominating a market with a homogenous product but by mobilizing the diverse relationships that constitute them to pursue even more diverse strategies to create change in the world. Where corporations can survive and thrive while building fairly subpar relational infrastructure, as anyone who has attended a mandatory corporate team-building exercise can attest, movements either excel at building relationship or quickly cease to exist.

If we are to address the urgent crisis of social isolation, then movements are one of several lineages of relational wisdom with a great deal to teach us: about how to invite people to connection, about how to deploy resources, about how to build trust and solidarity across lines of difference. We must learn to see movements as networks of relationship, as collections of people learning to spend time together, but more importantly as networks of people changing one another in ways that ripple outward to create change at a much larger scale.

The need to understand relational entities like movements is why this section's definition is "A relationship exists when two or more entities in the universe change one another" rather than "A relationship exists when two or more people change one another." Relationships do not only form between people. They form between movements, between nations, between ideas and beings in the more-than-human world. An ecosystem can be seen as a collection of organisms with particular characteristics, but it could just as easily be seen as a collection of relationships shaping those organisms through their interactions. A nation can be seen as a collection of people, laws, and lands, but it can just as validly be seen as the collection of relationships that give each of *those* things their shape. My body is made up of relationships between organs, free-floating cells, and the trillions of microbes that live in my gut. My organs are made up of relationships between cells, my cells of relationships between complex proteins, genes, and membranes. These proteins are made up of relationships between atoms, atoms of relationships between electrons and quarks, and so on down the smallest scale imaginable by science. Wherever things change one another, relationships exist.

Physicist Carlo Rovelli, a leading theorist exploring ways to knit together quantum physics and general relativity, explores how the universe operates at the Planck scale, the smallest scale that it is possible to observe under known physics.[11] At this scale, matter and energy as we understand them do not exist. Neither do space or time.

But relationship does exist. A network of tiny overlapping fields that dynamically change one another create what Rovelli calls a spinfoam, a constantly shifting web of connection from which time, space, matter and energy are all emergent properties. If we choose to see the world around us as made up of relationships, then it is relationships all the way down.

This relational lens can occasionally bring insight where a more object-oriented view cannot. A giant technology company can be seen not as a monolith but as an ecology of relationship that can be observed and invited to change. Cancer is increasingly seen not only as a mutation of individual cells but as a breakdown of relationship between cells in the body.[12] When we see the world in terms of relationship, radical new paths to transformation and resilience become possible.

This expansion of relationship into the more-than-human world brings us to our third and final definition of relationship. If movements are relational entities, networks of transformation and resilience, then what tools might let us see them clearly? What methodologies, scientific or otherwise, can we draw on to make sense of complex networks of things changing one another? It may seem counterproductive to bring in the tools of scientific measurement, tools that are so often used to further projects of dominance and homogenization, but I believe that they have a place. Science can also be a way of describing truth, of making the invisible concretely visible, and that concreteness is helpful when informing values-based decisions on what kinds of relational containers to fund. If we cannot see the relational universe and the wisdom of movements through a scientific lens, then it is far too easy for them to remain obscured behind a veil of relational invisibility. To collect the data, we will need to lift that veil. We will need to add one more definition of relationship to our toolbelt.

A Relationship Exists When Two or More Entities Exchange Information

I am named after my maternal grandfather, David Lazarus, who was a physics professor at the University of Illinois Urbana-Champaign.

Starting at the age of four, he would pull me onto his lap and explain to me the workings of the universe. Though his research in solid-state physics helped to build the foundations of the semiconductor industry, his true love was for teaching, whether at a postdoctoral level or as supplemental content to kindergarten. Before I could read, I had memorized the speed of light and knew that the only way to keep going faster if you got close to it was to slow down time. I knew that black holes were just places you had to go faster than light to get away from, which no one could do without magic.

I double-majored in physics and sociology in part to honor him. As he grew older and I came out to him as asexual, he advised me that his greatest joy in life had been parenting, and that I should do everything in my power to pursue it. He passed away in 2011, the day after his ninetieth birthday, in his sleep after a day of celebration surrounded by his friends and family. I had a chance to say good-bye to him a few hours before he died.

After his passing, I began to revisit the stories he told me as a child. I picked up a book on one of my grandfather's contemporaries, a man named Claude Shannon. While many of my grandfather's friends were working on the Manhattan Project, and he was in Boston building radar jammers to obscure the invasion of Normandy, Shannon had been just a few hours north at Bell Labs working on cryptography and telecommunications. Shannon experienced a frustration that felt eerily familiar to someone trying to turn the abstract and ephemeral world of relationship into something concrete. Prior to Shannon, the term *information* had been a poetic descriptor. A book had information, a sonnet and a painting contained information, but to try to compare that information in any formal way was an exercise in hopeless abstraction. Information was fundamentally different based on the *type* of information it was: a book, a sheet of music, a pressed cutting of a flower.[13] If Wikipedia had existed in 1948, the entry for "Information" would have been a disambiguation page.

On nights and weekends, Shannon wrote a paper titled "A Mathematical Theory of Communication" that turned this ephemeral understanding of information into something mathematical and concrete.[14] Imagine that I know a word and you are trying to guess it. For this game, we'll use the official Scrabble dictionary, which contains 187,630 unique English words.[15] The first letter is *D*. Knowing that takes us down to 10,956 possible words, eliminating almost 95 percent of the possible guesses. The second letter is *E*, and since there are just 3,800 Scrabble words that start with *DE*, our uncertainty goes again, with about 65 percent of the possible guesses eliminated. With the next letter, *S*, we're at just 405 possibilities, and when I tell you that the final letter is *K*, we're down to just one.

Every letter that I give you in this example helped you answer the question by eliminating possibilities, but some letters eliminated more possibilities than others. *D* took some 176,674 possibilities off the table, while that final *K* only eliminated 404. To Shannon, information could be quantified as a reduction of uncertainty. While both *D* and *K* are just one letter, the *D* creates a greater reduction in uncertainty and therefore contains more information. Viewing information in this way allows us to see how different types of messages can do the same job of reducing uncertainty. Instead of telling you letters in our guessing game, I could reduce uncertainty by telling you that I'm thinking of a flat surface used to write on, or I could draw you a picture of a desk, or I could sing you a song about a desk, though the latter would be a fairly inefficient way to get my point across. Shannon proved that the most efficient way to communicate information and eliminate possibilities was to communicate a number in base 2, a series of ones and zeros that we know today as bits.

Thanks to Shannon's information theory, any kind of information could be converted into bits and then converted back. Books could be made into bits, pictures could be made into bits by breaking them down into pixels, music could be made into bits by breaking it down into numerical representations of sound waves, and DNA could be converted into bits by encoding its base pairs. Questions like "Which contains more information, the human genome or *Star Wars: A New Hope?*" would have been nonsensical before Shannon, but now we have an answer: The human genome is about 750 megabytes, while *Star Wars* in 1080p format is 7.54 gigabytes.[16] This discovery had huge implications for how we build containers to process and store information. Suddenly we could build devices that stored bits and used them to store anything. We could build devices that transmitted bits and devices that processed bits and use them in an almost unthinkably broad array of applications. How we related to information and used information to change the world around us has profoundly changed as a result.

But the change did not stop there. Biologists and ecologists began to talk about information flowing inside cells and between organisms in an ecosystem.[17] It became common for physicists to describe the speed of light as a fundamental speed of information.[18] Information slowly came to mean not just a message that helped a human eliminate uncertainty, but anything that changed the probabilistic behavior of anything else. Information had become a powerful scientific tool not just for analyzing how people communicate but for understanding how things change one another.

Around 2012, remembering the sense of clarity and groundedness that I felt in those conversations with my grandfather, I began looking into ways to stitch together information theory and the growing understanding of relationship that developed out of my journey away from loneliness. I reached out to contacts at various universities, AI research teams at large tech companies, and the European Organization for Nuclear Research (CERN) to try to find existing work in this area, only to be told that what I was working on seemed to be novel and adjacent to interesting emerging areas in their fields, such as causal entropic forces, and that if I wanted to be miserable for several years I should consider getting a PhD. I suspected that I would, in fact, be miserable and that this might get in the way of my ability to form a family, so I set about building relationships with PhD students and post-docs who could advise me instead. The intellectual journey presented in this book has been advised by and accountable to those in academia rather than performed within it, and I have made a concerted effort to clarify where the ideas in that journey are purely theoretical, where they are merely backed by my own work, and where they have a more rigorous scientific foundation.

If relationships exist wherever entities in the universe change one another, then information theory provides a flexible and scientifically rigorous toolset for observing and analyzing that change. Like the word *information* once did, the word *relationship* exists today in a form that is poetic and ephemeral. Romantic relationships are different from professional relationships, which are different from the relationships that a matsutake mushroom has with the roots of a pine tree. If we want to make sense of these relationships, we need to use entirely different words and concepts. If we want to create containers to nurture them, those containers will be understandable only through rough heuristics and poetic metaphor. But the tools of information theory could change all that. They cannot be used to build one universal system for facilitating relationship in the way that the internet has become a universal system for processing information; in fact, they very quickly prove why any such project would be doomed to failure. But these scientific tools could pull back the veil of relational invisibility by creating an understanding of relational systems planted in the bedrock of fundamental physics. When a community organizer approaches a funder to talk about investing in relationships, these tools can make the statement feel as rock solid as the foundation of a new medical center.

The link between relationship and information hints at how scientific tools might be used to deepen our understanding of what relationships are and how they happen. For example, information is formally defined as a reduction in entropy. Entropy is a measure of randomness: It goes up when many outcomes are possible and down when fewer outcomes are possible. Could a local reduction in entropy, the emergence of a stable pattern from chaos, be an indicator that stable exchanges of information are forming? If so, could observing these reductions in chaos tell us where relationships are happening? Could creating the conditions for relationship allow us to hold entropy at bay? To grapple with these broadly sweeping questions and apply them to my lived relational experience, I would need to step back and gain perspective. I would need to turn the link between relationship and information into a set of practical tools that could explore the properties of relational systems, and I would need to draw on the wisdom of my grandfather.

Reflection Questions

- How do you experience relationship?

- What ways of meaningfully spending time have you discovered in your closest connections?

- What ways of spending time do you want in your life but have yet to find relationship for?

- What kinds of environments might help you connect with yourself or others to spend time in this way?

- What are ways that you welcome the process of being changed by the relationships that surround you?

- What are ways that you would like to invite your relationships into shared change?

CHAPTER 3

Understanding Relational Systems

IN 2009, AS HIS HEALTH WAS FAILING, I sat down to conduct an oral history of my grandfather. I still think about it over a decade later. In 1941, a few short months before the bombing of Pearl Harbor, my grandfather graduated with a degree in physics from the University of Chicago. He was one of only a few hundred physicists in the country, many of whom were fellow Jews, and even before the United States declared war, there was a strong desire among many in the field to do something to address the rise of fascism in Europe. Unsure what role he had to play, he and a few friends started one of the only programs in the country to train GIs on radio operation and maintenance. Radios, they surmised, would play an important part in this war, and someone had better get busy teaching the troops how to use them.

They would stay up late drafting lesson plans and practical exercises to illustrate the fundamental properties of electromagnetism and then teach them the next day to eager recruits with a high school education in mathematics. It was frenetic, skin-of-your-teeth physics, and my grandfather loved it. Their grassroots program received light support from the administration, and my grandfather and his colleagues were allowed to take over a lab where their class learned to assemble and disassemble the electronics that would help to decide the course of the war. Suddenly, down the hall, a shadowy government program began to take root. Even the program's director was a secret. Rumor had it he entered and exited the building through a side door to avoid recognition. My grandfather's friend Al Wattenberg was recruited into the project. Then the lab they had been using for classes was reassigned to it, and my grandfather was approached.

The details were hush-hush, but they wanted my grandfather's help building equipment to detect different forms of radiation. Something was going on at the University of Chicago involving neutrons and heavy metals that was being treated as a vital part of the war effort, and my grandfather had a vague idea what that thing might be. As a physicist up on the research, he was familiar with the theoretical science fiction–like properties of nuclear fission. This was why so many of his friends had joined. Who could have imagined that a handful of Jewish academics could wield a power so awesome that it could bring Hitler to submission? The assumption among his friends, he later learned, was that after the war their discovery would be modified to create electricity too cheap to meter. Who could resist the opportunity to join the best and brightest minds in their field on a project with unlimited funding to save the world?

My grandfather turned them down. Perhaps it was academic bitterness at the loss of his lab space, or perhaps he had a prescient insight about the nature of power. His friends could very well create a power awesome enough to bring Hitler to submission, but they would not be the ones to wield it. In 1945 my grandfather's friend Al Wattenberg signed a petition urging the government not to use the horrific weapon that he and his colleagues had created, but it was too late.

When I was a small child, Al would take me fishing. He never discussed his time on the Manhattan Project, and I was encouraged never to discuss it among my grandfather's contemporaries. My grandfather shared the stories with me shortly before he died, and his decision to walk away is one that I have been digesting ever since. The

Manhattan Project ushered in not just the atomic age, but the idea that one could make profound change by getting the smartest people into a room, giving them unlimited resources, and getting out of the way. The Apollo program was inspired by the teams at the University of Chicago and Los Alamos, and so was DARPA, where the internet was born. When a recruiter from Facebook approached me in the early days of the company, the pitch was similar to the one that my grandfather had received: Join the best and brightest to invent something of unspeakable power that will transform the world. As evidence, they touted Facebook's engineer-to-user ratio: the number of people whose lives I would be able to change was off the charts.

Why had my grandfather said no? He was a scientist eager to learn about the beauty of the world, but more than that, he was a teacher who longed to share that beauty with others. He authored a textbook that changed how high school physics was taught, and he jumped at opportunities to share his beautiful understanding of the world with GIs headed to the front, with dozens of graduate students, and with me as soon as my young brain could begin to comprehend it. To him physics was a tool of appreciation, a way to be in deeper relationship with the more-than-human world and to awe at our tiny place in it. Fantasies of godlike powers were not appealing even when those powers would ostensibly be used for good. Science was not a tool to dominate, a way to break complex reality down to equations that unlocked new ways to change the world. Instead, science was a tool of inquiry, an invitation to notice where rich and beautiful things were happening so that one could be present enough to connect with them.

As my personal journey to understand relationship drew more and more heavily on the tools of physics, I sought to embody my grandfather's teaching of appreciation over dominance. In 2012, when I first learned to see relationships as exchanges of information, it felt as though a vast relational world had revealed itself that I had only begun to explore. Exchanges of information, complex dances of things changing one another, made up my universe as much as, and more fundamentally than, matter and energy. If I wanted to take a few shaky steps toward appreciating them more deeply, I would need new tools for observing and making sense of them. I had a rich set of tools for observing relationship as a community organizer, but the connection between relationships and information promised something far more fundamental.

I began tinkering with simple mathematical models of information exchange. I created networks of mathematical entities that sent information to one another at random. When an entity received information, it would change how it sent information back out according to a set of rules. I could tweak these rules and also tweak the environment that the entities exchanged information in: It could be an open graph where everyone talked to everyone, or a set of tiny niches where information exchange was contained.

Once a set of rules and graph structure were in place, I would hit play and observe the entropy of the system over time. Many systems would start chaotic and stay that way, but in some, relational patterns would reliably emerge. If the starting conditions were right, random information exchange would reliably collapse into a stable, dynamically shifting pattern that I could then run further experiments on. I enlisted advisers with backgrounds in graph theory, agent-based modeling, and nonlinear dynamics to help me understand how to explore these toy relational systems. After years of struggling to understand relationality, I was watching it play out before my eyes.

My definition of the term *relationality* also became more concrete: **Relationality is the capacity of a given environment of information exchange to create relationship.** Just as the relationships in my models seemed to only emerge under the right starting conditions, real world relationships seemed very sensitive to the specific environments that they form in. Two people may sit next to one another on a bus and then meet a week later at a friend's party. They may have an immense capacity for connection, but the environment of the bus has a low relationality and does not allow that connection to manifest. Just as every physical environment in the universe has a temperature, every environment of information exchange has a relationality, from the soil beneath a forest floor to an online support group for queer dads. Like a complex field, this environment shifts based on who is interacting with it: I may not find the dirt in the forest relational in quite the same way as a morel mycelium, but there is a relationality that each of us experiences. The models I was building let me see this relationality playing out in minute detail. In the real world the information flowing back and forth and changing things was invisible and impossible to measure; here I could see it with perfect clarity.

Could these mathematical constructs teach me anything about relationality in the real world? Compared to any real-world human relationship, or even the relationships between molecules inside a cell, these models were incredibly simple. It felt like I was trying to use a baking soda-and-vinegar volcano to understand a living organism. I couldn't do anything like modeling real-world relationships, but I could explore very basic principles. Was there anything consistent about the starting conditions that reliably led to relationship? Once relationship had developed in a given system, how would it respond to being poked and prodded? If I created two very similar systems, how would their relationships stay similar, and how would they diverge? In these questions I let my experience as an organizer be a guide. When the models seemed to echo the dynamics that I observed in movements, I would stop and look closer. They often did, and it was often a sign that something interesting was happening.

Properties began to emerge from these models that seemed to be consistent across networks of information exchange in the human and more-than-human world. Because all relationship in the universe is made up of information exchange, and all information conforms to mathematical rules, there is reason to believe that all relational networks have a few basic things in common. The following is a list of hypotheses about what these fundamental properties might be, though I will be the first to admit that turning these hypotheses into a defensible theory is beyond my current abilities. I present them here because they will prove a helpful foundation for the rest of this book. If they are true, they provide a helpful insight into how we might go about creating the conditions for connection.

Properties of Relationship

1. Relationship drives resilience.

2. Relationship drives transformation.

3. All entities have a limited capacity for relationship.

4. Relationship forms through a process of evolution.

5. We can create the conditions for relationship by creating the conditions for evolution.

6. We can predict the conditions that lead to relationship, but not where that relationship will lead.

1. Relationship Drives Resilience

One of the first things I observed in these relational models was a sense of resilience. Once they had found a relational pattern, I could hit them with chaotic information and they would bounce back. Some networks would bounce back more readily than others; some would break and have to reform their relational threads from scratch. But there seemed to be a direct correlation between relationality and resilience.

Things in relationship stay together, and things not in relationship fall apart. Because relationship is an exchange of information, and information creates a reduction in entropy, entities that are in relationship are likely to resist the effects of entropy in their environment. A rock is more resistant to change than a pile of sand because the atoms in a rock are in stronger relationship with one another. Cut my arm, and the relationships that make up my body will deliver platelets, immune cells, and nutrients to the cut so that it can heal. As relationships become stronger and more dynamic, they make the entities that they constitute more resistant to disruption.

This happens through a process similar to what I experienced as a new parent with a startup. During the workday I would be hit by entropy; packets of information would fly in from random directions and change me in random ways, threatening to shake me apart. But my relationship with my kid was steady. She sent me a consistent kind of information. She changed me in a consistent set of ways. When the entropy of the world tried to shake me into randomness, the information I received from her snapped me back.

For this resilience to impact me, the relationships I'm in must change me in ways that are integrated with one another. If I love my partner, but how he changes me varies widely from day to day, then I won't feel resilience. If I love my partner and love my job, but they each ask me to be very different people, then I may experience entropy from the constant need to shift back and forth. But if my partner, my job, and my community all transform me in ways that are mutually compatible, if the relationships integrate with one another in ways that are complementary, then deepening any one relationship will make me more capable and resilient in all the others.

We see this resilience play out in research about disasters. In the summer of 1995 an intense heatwave hit the city of Chicago and over seven hundred people lost their lives.[1] Afterward, public health researchers combed through data about the heatwave to better understand how deaths could be prevented, and they found that the single biggest factor in survival was social connection. People in relationship got checked on, and elders in relationship had neighbors delivering them water and evacuating them to cooling centers in a way that socially isolated seniors did not. When we are in relationship, we tend to be changed in ways that promote our shared survival. A similar trend played out during the outbreak of COVID-19, where low death rates were correlated most strongly not with GDP per capita or with preparedness for a global pandemic but by measures of interpersonal trust.[2]

The fact that a particular instantiation of relationship is resilient does not necessarily mean it creates resilience around it. An addict's relationship with alcohol may be resilient in the sense that it persists over time and resists attempts at disruption, but it may actively undermine the resilience of relationships with family and friends that sit beside it. A hate group may be internally resilient but similarly undermine resilience elsewhere, while a group offering gender-affirming care may, after some rockiness, have a strong positive impact on the resilience of relationships with family and friends. In this way, resilience is not only a property but a fascinating lens through which to view the relational world.

Is it any wonder that our bodies, our minds, and our democracies fall apart when starved of relationship? It's not just that a lack of relationships makes us scared and releases stress hormones. When we are not in relationship, the world disrupts our lives in random ways, and we have nothing to bring us back to center. This property of resilience also creates a compelling reason to invest in relational infrastructure: Investment in relationship comes back as resilience to outside disruption. A community facing climate change might invest in relational infrastructure as a form of disaster preparedness; a political campaign that invests in relational infrastructure will be more likely to hold together through the chaos of the election cycle. This property also gives us a tool for observing where relationships are happening. We generally cannot see information flying back and forth. Without massive invasions of privacy we cannot see where and how people are changing one another. But we can observe that some places seem more resilient than others and infer where relationships exist.

2. Relationship Drives Transformation

The models hinted at a deep connection between relationship and the process of transformation. By definition, when a relational entity received information from its environment, it would change. When the information was random, these changes would also be random, and the entity would wildly oscillate between different states and chaotically send its own information out to the world. But when the information it received became stable, it would transform into something that behaved in relatively stable and consistent ways. When the relationships around it would inevitably change, it would change with them. What was true of individual mathematical entities seemed to be true of relational networks as well. A sufficiently stable network of entities seemed to behave as a stable entity of its own, forming and responding to relationships on a larger scale until the conditions for its relationality ceased and it fell apart.

Paradoxically, relationships are both how things stay the same and how they change. If a houseplant gets sun on its right side, and I turn its pot so that it gets sun on its left side, it will change the direction in which it grows. If a hummingbird gets its food from a flower and the flower changes, the hummingbird will evolve to change with it. No relational entity, whether it is a person, a mycelial network, or an idea, has relationships that are entirely static. Information is constantly shifting how it moves through the world, sometimes gradually and sometimes abruptly, and when it changes, the entities in relationship must change with it. If we want something to change, it can be powerful to ask what relationships might change it. If we observe something changing, we can infer that the relationships around it must be changing as well.

I experience this interplay between resilience and transformation in my relationship as a parent. My daughter changes me, but how she changes me as a five-year-old is radically different from how she changed me at five months. As each of us has grown and changed, and as the other relationships around us have grown and changed, our relationship has been a stable but continually shifting thread.

Without these resilient threads it can be difficult for a consistent process of transformation or growth to happen. Around 2011 there was a wave of excitement about the ways that massive open online courses, or MOOCs, could transform education.[3] By broadcasting classes online, the best educators in the world could be accessible not only to students at elite universities but to anyone with the motivation to learn. But the results did not live up to the hype. Completion rates for courses reliably fell below 13 percent.[4] Learners, even highly motivated ones, were struggling to complete course materials at anything approaching the rate of even unmotivated students on college campuses. Further investigation found that students taking courses with friends had a significantly higher completion rate.[5] In order to commit to learning, it seemed that students very often needed a relationship to turn their intentions into action.

To succeed, a transformative process must be resilient. Students who were initially excited about an online course would easily see their interests succumb to entropy: They would be pulled away as new interests and unexpected struggles would demand their attention. But people who shared the learning process with friends would find their learning journey imbued with a sense of resilience. When something pulled them away from the course, their friendship was there to pull them back.

In this way, resilience and transformation are inexorably linked. To be transformed we must receive similar information from a similar source over an extended period of time, and the relationship transforming us must be resilient. To be resilient, a relationship must grow and adapt to changing circumstances. It must have the ability to transform.

This transformative property creates another compelling reason to invest in relationships. If we want something in the world to change—perhaps a low rate of voter turnout in a key electoral district—then a powerful strategy can be to invest in relationships that drive that change. A relationship does not mean a one-way burst of communication; it means a stream of information that persists over time in which all parties involved are changed. Creating environments that allow these streams of information to form and evolve over time is necessary in order for meaningful transformation to take place.

Transformation without resilience can exist, but it is often disruptive. I will be transformed if I am punched in the face, but probably not in a way that integrates with and supports the other relationships that help me survive and thrive. How the punch in the face transformed me will have less to do with the punch itself and more to do with how the relationships around me help me to heal and grow in response to injury. It is rare for brief, powerful interventions to result in change, and even rarer for them to result in change that is helpful. When they do, it is almost always because other relationships that persist over time deserve credit.

In a relational environment, transformation is almost never attributable to a single discrete cause. Transformation hints at a more complex story about the way that beings in an environment are changing one another over time. Examining where transformation takes place generally does not point to a neat and singular cause, but it can be a powerful way to observe where relationships exist and how they are shifting.

3. All Entities Have a Limited Capacity for Relationship

As the models I was building grew larger, an interesting dynamic emerged. Entities that found relationships would slowly shift from chaos to stability for a while, but if more and more relationships were added, they would descend into chaos again. One or two relationships changing them in one or two compatible ways was manageable and could result in a robust relational network, but dozens of relationships changing them in dozens of unique ways would cause them to collapse into chaos. I could tweak the system to expand and contract this capacity for relationship, but a limited capacity always seemed to exist.

If we keep adding relationships to a system, they stop being a stabilizing force and become a source of entropy. Because all information that a relational entity receives changes it in some way, hitting it with too many changes at once will eventually overwhelm the relational resilience that keeps it together. Living in the Bay Area, I occasionally run into people who aspire to be in loving relationship with every living being in the universe. While the desire behind this sentiment is valid, being simultaneously changed in so many ways at once would quickly lead to overwhelm and burnout, perhaps literally. There are so many living beings in the universe that receiving unique information from all of them would physically heat up a human body until it combusted. Try to connect to the entire universe and you will explode.

While it is true that we are part of a network of relationship that spans the entire universe, we also each have a unique position in that network. We are changed more directly and deeply by some things than by others. The information that shapes us must come from a narrow sliver of the universe around us, not from all of it at once.

Failing to acknowledge this positionality and the kinds of information it both provides us and denies us prevents us from hearing what the world has to teach us. We are all part of a great web of connection, but our unique positions in that web matter a great deal.

To have relationships that are resilient and transformative, we must honor our limited capacity for relationship. That capacity can expand, but the capacity of any relational entity to be in different kinds of relationship is always finite. Because of this, all relational systems thrive in a place of balance. Too little information flying around and there isn't enough opportunity for new relationships to emerge. Too much information flying around and the relationships that exist get drowned out by noise, and the entities forming them begin to shake apart. Like Goldilocks, relationships thrive in environments that are not too hot and not too cold.

This limited capacity for relationship is part of why so many community organizers burn out and integrity teams at social media companies struggle to respond to even large-scale crises. When one relational entity wants to relate to many others, it needs to do so in ways that are consistent (homogenization) in order to avoid being shaken apart. Often this requires it to exert a high degree of control over those relationships (dominance). This removes the capacity of relationships to dynamically transform, resulting in relational systems that are relatively stagnant and brittle.

An alternative strategy for allowing many relationships to exist in a system is to expand its relational capacity. An environment with many tiny niches, like a coral reef, allows each niche to maintain a comfortable level of information exchange even if the overall system grows to include a massive amount of information exchange and level of diversity. Imagine the difference between two hundred people in a circle trying to have a conversation and those same two hundred people being allowed to cluster in groups of three or four around a space filled with nooks and crannies that they can freely navigate between. These fractal patterns appear in a wide range of effective relational containers, and we will return to them when discussing the structure of social movements in chapter 4.

This constraint has implications for how we go about investing in and gathering resources for relational work. We cannot be in relationship with everyone ourselves, and we must acknowledge and work from the relational position we occupy. Often we must trust others to hold relationship that we do not have the capacity to hold. How we place this trust, and how we allocate our limited capacity for deep relationship, will determine the path of transformation and resilience that shapes our lives and our work. Chapter 6 will focus on this practice of trust-building to deploy resources in a nested relational environment.

This limitation on relational capacity can also help us observe relationship in the world. Where many relationships exist, there will often be evidence of a nested fractal structure for them to exist in. It is common for the word *community* to be thrown around by everyone from social media influencers to corporate HR departments. One way to quickly gauge if such a community actually exists is to look for small niches where people can freely connect.

4. Relationship Forms Through a Process of Evolution

As I observed the entities in my models struggling to form relationships, something about that struggle seemed eerily familiar. The entities would form relationship by iterating through many possibilities, find a few that fit, and then collapse their probabilistic wave forms around whatever option was most stable. It would be a stretch to say that they were having feelings and making commitments, but they were going through some process that seemed to rhyme with the exploration-feelings-commitments cycle. As I chatted with my advisers and dove into the literature, I found that what I was observing had all of the hallmarks of evolution.

All relationships seem to grow from a place of randomness to a place of stability through a kind of search process. The cycle of exploration, feelings, and commitments is what this process looks like when we navigate topics of conversation or decide how to spend time with our friends, but a more general version happens whether relationships are forming between people, atoms, or ideas. When a relationship begins, it is always in a state of randomness. Many different kinds of information are flying around in many different directions. To get from this state of randomness to something stable and resilient, all relationships need to iterate through a cycle:

1. **Exploration:** The relationship needs to generate many possible states across a probability curve. In a conversation, this could look like randomly guessing at topics that might be interesting. To an octopus, this may look like randomly trying strategies to open up a jar with a tasty snack inside. To an atom, this may look like randomly bumping around into the atoms around it.

2. **Differentiation:** The relationship needs to differentiate some of those states. In conversation, this could look like finding a topic that creates emotional resonance. To an octopus, it may look like finding a strategy that gets the jar to budge. To an atom, it may look like entering the range of an atom with a particularly strong electric field.

3. **Selection:** The relationship needs to update its probability curve to narrow in on the differentiated states. In a conversation, that looks like releasing the other possible topics and focusing in on the resonant one. To an octopus, it may look like abandoning the other strategies that it's been trying and focusing on a promising one. To an atom, it may look like shifting its range or probable motion to stay attached to another atom in a crystal lattice.

Within the models there was no way to go from randomness to stability, no way to reduce entropy, without some version of this evolutionary process. Where evolution thrived, relationships thrived. Where evolution stagnated, relationships became static and brittle. If I intervened in a model to eliminate its capacity for exploration or its ability to select, then its relationality would reliably flatline, and wherever relationality was present, some version of this evolutionary process was visible.

This seemed, at least intuitively, to be true in the world outside my models as well. In my organizing work I had observed how taking people through nested cycles of exploring new and compelling possibilities, helping them differentiate those possibilities (often with embodied emotion), and then inviting them to select a few possibilities and let the rest fade away was often a powerful way to make new relationships happen. There is a clear link between relationship and evolution in ecological and microbiological contexts, and even relationships between atoms seem to form through a process of rapidly exploring many possible states and collapsing into those with minimum free energy. When renowned physicist Richard Feynman examined quantum fields, he came to a similar conclusion, seeing them not as bubbles in space-time but as crackles of connection that probabilistically iterated through many states and collapsed into stability under certain environmental conditions.[6]

If true, this link between evolution and relationality has some exciting implications. If our goal is to create the conditions for relationship, then an understanding of evolution can help us to appreciate where and why those conditions exist. Where we observe the conditions for evolution, we can make meaningful predictions about relationality, and vice versa. Those predictions can be tested. Scientifically speaking, we're starting to get somewhere.

Just as I had been able to study things changing one another by borrowing the scientific tool set of information theory, I began hunting for existing scientific methodologies for studying how evolutionary processes play out in differing environments. Ecologists and computational biologists have an especially interesting one. Using an analysis of something called evolutionary rate, these scientists can look at two different ecosystems and have a pretty good hunch about which one will evolve faster. For a while now, scientists have been developing tools to look at environmental conditions and make predictions about how quickly evolution will happen. Could those same heuristics be used to make predictions about the conditions for relationship?

Heuristics for High Evolutionary Rate

1. **Edge zones:** Evolution tends to happen more quickly where differing ecologies intersect.[7]

2. **Fractal geometry:** Evolution tends to happen quickly in environments full of niches with other smaller niches branching off of them.[8]

3. **Cyclical fluctuations:** Evolution tends to happen more quickly in environments with patterns of activity that rise and fall at a steady rate.[9]

4. **Punctuated equilibrium:** Evolution tends to accelerate when the status quo is occasionally disrupted and then given time to recover.[10]

A compelling case can be made that these heuristics apply to the work of creating environments for human connection as much as they apply to predicting the evolutionary rate of ecosystems. A dinner party that thoughtfully brings two groups together will be more interesting than one that is homogenous. A room filled with tiny nooks for conversation will generally be a better place for many people to get in conversion than a large open gymnasium. If the metaphor holds, then it has exciting implications for the work of creating paths out of loneliness.

5. We Can Create the Conditions for Relationship by Creating the Conditions for Evolution

This book opens with a discussion about relational containers. The fact that we are facing a global crisis of social isolation means that the relational containers we have are failing. The fact that so many of us feel so lonely, so lacking in relational agency, is tied to the fact that we do not know how to find and cocreate the places where the relationships we need will manifest. Creating relational containers is work that the world needs, and the link between relationality and evolutionary rate provides us with a theoretical foundation for going about that work. We can create and strengthen relationships by shaping the environments in which they evolve.

My good friend Brandon is a wedding DJ, and he excels at reading a crowd and predicting what music in what combinations will get people across generations onto a dance floor. This process of iterative observation, prediction, and intervention is how relational containers are cocreated. My friend is not the sole creator; he is making an informed prediction about how to create the conditions for relationship. So is the cool grandma who decides to get up and get things started again after a lull, and so is the three-year-old who runs out to join her. Each decision creates a more relational environment that invites others to come and make it even more relational. To quote biologist Janine Benyus, life creates the conditions for life.

This iterative and shared process is why I often refer to relational containers as being cocreated rather than designed. Sometimes one individual has outsized power in that process of cocreation: the host of a dinner party, the facilitator of a meeting, or the planner of a conference. These individuals can do a great deal to set the stage for relationship, but their work only matters if others cocreate on top of it. My parents, Dan and Mary Ann, who met in architecture school, have devoted much of their careers to understanding communities both human and more-than-human and designing spaces that would allow those communities to thrive. I learned from them that the power to place walls and doors is a critical but small piece of what it takes to make an environment come to life with relationship. They needed to spend a great deal of time getting to know the community that they were building with and the land that they were building on in order to intervene in a way that would add to rather than disrupt the relationships that were already happening. We create the conditions for relationship with sustained, grounded presence more than we create it with moments of powerful action.

Creating the conditions for relationship is patient, deliberate, and often joyful work, like tending to a fire. There is a lot of work creating conditions and breathing things to life at the beginning, and then a good deal of sitting back, enjoying the warmth, and feeding things as needed. It is important, both when building a fire and tending one, to think about how it might cause harm and to maintain boundaries that prevent that harm from taking place, but in a well-managed fire this need not detract from the sense of ease and joy. It is not about the one person who lights the fire; it is about the many people who sit by the fire.

When I am present in this way in a relational environment, most of what I do is patient observation. There is usually a long complicated history to the place I am in and the people who are present, and learning about that history will help me make sense of the relationships there. I see where sparks of relationship emerge and where they fizzle, where people have created boundaries to prevent harm and where they have lit up with excitement. I ask for stories about why people have chosen the paths that they have chosen, because these stories often reveal a great deal about the relationships that shape them and the relationships that they are seeking. From these observations I can, like my friend Brandon looking out at a dance floor, begin to construct a mental model of the relationships that exist in my environment and how those relationships might be helped along. Stated formally, I am constructing a model of information flowing through my environment based on observation of proxy variables and then making a prediction about what interventions will accelerate evolution to achieve desired relational outcomes, but I experience this analysis as a grounded intuition that the quiet person in the corner probably has something meaningful to contribute and should be gently invited in.

As we will discuss in more detail in chapter 4, this cycle of patient observation, prediction, and intervention is an unfathomably complex superpower of the human brain that human cultures have been refining and improving for millennia. It is one that our most sophisticated machine-learning models cannot mimic, and probably will not be able to for quite some time, because it requires a kind of modeling and analysis wholly unlike the statistical models on which these algorithms and most other systems of sophisticated statistical prediction are built. Our capacity to subtly nudge our environment in ways that make it more relational is arguably the defining characteristic of humanity (though we are far from the only species to possess it). It cannot be automated or homogeneously mass-produced, but it can be cultivated by practicing relational work, by tapping into the lineages of relational wisdom that stretch back to before recorded history, by building our capacity for embodied presence.

Because the work of creating relational containers is about presence, it does not always correlate with traditional forms of power. The most relationally powerful person at a company is often not the CEO. The work of shaping a relational container can be done by anyone who shows up and understands how to work from the relational position they are in. It is not limited to dinner party hosts and others in positions of leadership. When I influenced social media companies as an outsider, it was by wielding this sort of relational power, by seeing where evolution that people wanted was blocked and helping to create spaces where that evolution could happen. Even without formal authority, it is surprising how much this kind of power can accomplish.

This power, which I referred to in chapter 1 as relational agency, happens when I have a clear understanding of my relational world and how to navigate it. I understand the relationships that exist, where they are thriving, where they are blocked, and the thousands of ways that I might move them forward. I have felt this relational agency in my personal life when inviting new forms of connection into my community, and I have felt it as the movements that I am part of grow in size and power. An important part of embracing this power is understanding how it works differently from other forms of power. Relational power is not about wish fulfillment. I cannot declare a thing that I want and then construct a relational container that will make it appear in my hand. To claim relational agency, I must accept the unpredictable and release my need for control.

6. We Can Predict the Conditions That Will Lead to Relationship but Not Where Those Relationships Will Lead

In 1951, a decade after his encounter with the Manhattan Project, my grandfather was once again pulled into the orbit of an ambitious government program to create a weapon of unimaginable power. His expertise in solid-state physics was requested for a lavishly funded Army program to build the world's largest electronic computer. As far as he could surmise, the Army wanted to put something on top of a rocket and shoot it more or less accurately at the other side of the planet, and they needed a hefty computer to calculate the trajectory. After Hiroshima, Nagasaki, and the start of the Cold War, my grandfather and his colleagues were understandably concerned about what that thing on top of a rocket might be, so the Army sweetened the deal. Build a computer for Uncle Sam and they'd get additional funding to build a second computer to play with however they wanted. My grandfather once again opted out, but enough physicists agreed that ORDVAC (for ordinance) and ILLIAC (for the University of Illinois) were born.

ILLIAC was a room-size monstrosity of vacuum tubes that were constantly burning out and needing replacement, but it had a speed and flexibility unlike anything that had come before.[11] As one of the first computers in the world to separate memory from the CPU, ILLIAC and ORDVAC helped to lay the foundation for all of modern computing. Quickly, researchers from around the world began flying in, joining my grandparents for dinner, clutching briefcases with problems that had been unsolvable for decades or centuries: mathematicians with geometric quandaries that would require years of manual effort to calculate, biochemists curious to see if the new toy could help uncover the secrets of proteins. Most ambitious of all were the meteorologists. What was weather prediction, after all, but a long and exhaustive series of calculations? With this new tool, they would be able to predict the weather accurately years in advance. By seeding a cloud here or turning on a giant fan there, they might even be able to control it. My grandfather could not help but wonder if the Army's decision to fund ILLIAC had involved a few discrete letters from these weather scientists. With the Cold War quickly escalating, the ability to control the weather could be even more powerful than nuclear armaments in ensuring America's global dominance. Fleets could be battered with storms, food supplies cut off with drought. Countries deciding which side of the Iron Curtain to ally with could get a gentle or not-so-gentle gust of wind to push them in the right direction.

This dream led to a decade of frustrated research into weather prediction before, in 1961, a young researcher named Edward Lorenz would hit an insurmountable problem.[12] He inputted a set of conditions into a weather model, got a result, then inputted the same numbers a second time and get an entirely different one. After frustratedly rebooting his computer and checking for bugs, Lorenz realized that something deeper was going on. When he entered the numbers a second time, small deviations had crept in. He had entered a wrong number in the fourth decimal place or rounded a variable to a few millionths to save time. These small variations in input should lead to small variations in output, but they didn't—they were compounding. A 0.00001 percent deviation was quickly becoming a 0.1 percent deviation, then a 10 percent deviation, then a 99.9999 percent deviation. Small changes in initial conditions sent the model in a radically different direction.

Grappling with the implications of this exponentially increasing error would lead Lorenz to help found the field of nonlinear dynamics, or chaos theory. Scrambling to title a talk on this phenomenon, Lorenz came up with the metaphor of a butterfly flapping its wings in Brazil and setting off a tornado in Texas.[13] Lorenz's findings meant that in order to accurately predict the weather, the US Army would need to measure not just every butterfly wing, but every atom in the atmosphere and anything else that might move them. Without such accurate measurement, the errors in weather prediction would compound and make precise predictions hopelessly inaccurate after about ten days. No increase in the number of weather stations or computational power could get around the problem. The universe, it seemed, had strong opinions about what could be predicted and controlled, and weather was not on the list.

When I began mathematically modeling systems of information exchange, I was curious what would happen if I repeated Lorenz's experiment. I created two relational models with identical starting conditions and modified one of them by a tiny fraction of one percent. When I ran the models, they looked similar at first, but quickly diverged in a familiar pattern of compounding error. Not too surprisingly, relational systems are chaotic. They sat firmly in the category of phenomena that the universe does not want us to be able to predict over long time horizons with a high degree of accuracy. We can build relational containers that make powerful things happen; we just can't know precisely what those things will be at the outset.

As in most nonlinear systems, this unpredictability contains patterns. In my models, relational systems seemed drawn to particular zones, what Lorenz refers to as strange attractors, even if precisely where in those zones they would land was impossible to predict. A rich set of dynamics of information exchange appeared that I have barely begun to explore, but one trend was clear: The more relational a system was, the more quickly its rivers of information evolved into new and stable forms, then the more quickly its small errors would compound into big ones. Conversely, if I modeled a system that *didn't* contain exponentially increasing error, it would be so rigidly controlled that no new relationships would form. There was an unavoidable trade-off between relationality and predictability.

As with the weather, the universe seems to have a strong opinion about whether we can predict and control relational systems: we can predict the conditions that lead to relationships, but not where those relationships will lead. Conversely, we can control the outcomes of relational systems, but doing so unavoidably constricts their ability to evolve and eventually kills them. I call this trade-off between relationship and predictability the curse of transactionality. If you need to know exactly what you're getting, you won't be getting relationship.

To navigate and make sense of the world, we must make predictions about it, and to accomplish this, our minds employ two different modes of prediction. The first, which I'll call transactional prediction, we use to understand complicated but arelational phenomena. From a child catching a ball who learns to predict its parabola to an engineer fine-tuning the probabilistic calculations in a quantum computer, this mode of prediction is reliable and precise but brittle. Things will go exactly the way we want them to as long as we can prevent any unexpected relationships from emerging and messing with our neatly arranged variables. For this reason, transactional prediction is closely tied to the concept of ownership, an awkward kind of relationship that is about preventing others from relating to something even if you rarely relate to it yourself. Owning something doesn't mean that we need to be in relationship with it, just that we can prevent others from relating to it so that it remains nice and predictable. Transactional prediction is not bad; it is a critical tool for navigating our world, but like any tool, it is ineffective if used in every circumstance. Because transactional prediction is relatively straightforward, we can write it down in paragraphs and equations and quickly communicate the rationale of our prediction to others.

The second mode, which I'll call relational prediction, we use to understand complex relational phenomena like ecosystems, artistic expression, and other people. From a child learning to share to a diplomat leading peace negotiations, we perform this mode of prediction by modeling relationships in our environment and predicting which interventions might allow them to evolve in beneficial ways. Things will not go precisely the way that we want them to, but we learn that this is often a good thing. The world is unpredictable, and our relationships need to be resilient to that unpredictability. Often they transform us in ways that we did not ask for but are grateful for in hindsight. Rather than trying to precisely control our relationships, we learn to nudge them and create spaces for them to thrive and surprise us. By tweaking the way an environment differentiates here, and sensing and leaning into a strange attractor there, our minds, in a feat that would seem impossible if it were not everyday, reliably navigate the chaos to wind up in a place of stable information exchange. We generally cannot write down the complex series of cognitive tasks that got us there, nor would they be directly applicable to any other relational situation if we could. Instead, we use stories to help others glimpse the relational world as we see it.

Relational and transactional prediction have very different relationships with time. While transactional prediction tends to steadily collapse from certainty to uncertainty all at once, relational prediction can provide a cocktail of certainty and uncertainty that stretches forward in time. I can know that a relationship will change me for the better without knowing how it will change me. I can know that I will look back on a decision with gratitude a decade from now without knowing precisely why. Because investments in relationship are investments in dynamic resilience, their effects can reach much further into the future than transactional ones. If we want to invest in things that will benefit our children's children and their children's children, relational prediction is often our most powerful tool.

When it comes to the allocation of resources, there is often an extreme focus on transactional rather than relational prediction and on building transactional rather than relational power. Very arguably, a grassroots movement of GI radio operators and the physicists training them was a strategic thing for the Pentagon to be investing in, but it was invisible next to the draw of the world's most powerful bomb. When transactional prediction is our only tool for understanding the future, the only futures worth investing in are ones where we hold as much power as possible. How can we ensure that those we love will be safe and happy if we don't personally hold the power to keep them that way? What better way to create a world we want to live in than accumulating as much power as possible to shape that world? Without the ability to think in relationships, the only alternative to death is dominance.

As we will discuss in more detail in chapter 6, this focus on predictability and transactionality sits at the heart of how most modern institutions allocate resources. If I go to the corner store and buy a packet of peanut M&Ms, I know exactly what my $1.79 is buying me. The branding on the package, the pressure required to tear the paper, and the thickness of the chocolate and candy shell have all been engineered for maximum consistency. The peanuts at the center, a vestige of the unpredictability of the more-than-human world, have no doubt been tamed by hundreds of millions of dollars of investment in research and engineering. The M&Ms come from a factory that has itself been precisely engineered to produce these outcomes, where workers perform repetitive tasks and constant maintenance to stop the pieces of metal and plastic shaped into factory components from relating in new and interesting ways. These workers are also prevented from forming new and interesting relationships with one another lest they unionize, a possibility that the Mars Corporation has no doubt invested significant resources in avoiding. The money used to build the factory was invested because of this predictability. The number of M&Ms produced and the gross revenue per M&M were calculated, accounting for the costs of maintenance, union busting, and the wrangling of uncooperative peanuts, to yield a return on investment, or ROI. If the ROI is competitive with other things that investors could be betting on, then money is deployed; if it is not competitive, then money is not. One thing that reliably kills an investment's ROI is risk. Anything that causes the factory not to behave as predicted, like a union or a widespread grassroots movement to educate kids about healthy eating, is a risk that makes the investment less appealing. This risk is mitigated through constant measurement of the factory and surveillance of its employees, which are bundled into a set of key performance indicators, or KPIs, which the factory's management uses to let the higher-ups and their investors know that everything is going according to plan. Even though peanut M&Ms are advertised as a candy to share with friends, and even though the factory manager may hold a company cookout and use words like "community" and "family" to describe their colleagues, when it comes time to allocate resources, every decision is optimized for predictability and, by extension, for the suppression of relationship.

This critique of industrialized society is hardly original, but the curse of transactionality allows us to connect it to the loneliness crisis at a foundational level. Our disconnection from relational lineage, the fact that community organizers are under-resourced and burning out, the failure of Facebook to live up to its promise of creating social connection, and the rising teen suicide rate may all have to do with the mistaken idea that the only things worth deploying resources to are precisely predictable. The exceptions to this rule almost always occur outside mainstream institutions. Parents invest in children because we directly feel the benefit of relationship with them. Organizations like Burning Man can be well resourced because they bring largely wealthy people into relationship, and those wealthy people can deploy resources without having to rationalize the ROI to their boards. But when it comes to institutions making institutionalized decisions about the deployment of capital, there are shockingly few examples of relationality being prioritized over predictability. Concrete proposals with clear outcomes and neat metrics of success get funded, and it is mathematically impossible for relational strategies to meet that standard or predictability.

Like most hegemonies, this focus on transactional outcomes is both widespread and faces widespread resistance. In every institution I have encountered that deploys resources based on a narrow focus on predictable metrics, there are people fighting back. Sometimes it is their own experience of relationship that drives them; sometimes it is an instinct passed on through relational lineage, but like integrity employees at social media companies, they walk a tenuous line between enabling systems of predictability and control and resisting them.

Inside government agencies, small businesses, schools, and philanthropic foundations, these relational insurgents run into a consistent problem. Their plan to create the conditions for relationship sounds like exactly the kind of thing that the institution would love to support. There's just a little paperwork to fill out. What are the expected outcomes of this initiative? What metrics can be used to gauge its success? All of this dynamic connection sounds great, but we need to consider the risk involved. Best to bring in someone from legal.

Chapter 6 will explore many more examples of how the link between investment and precise predictability undermines the conditions for relationship, but for now let us consider the genuine predicament that these institutions are in. Can they responsibly deploy resources *without* prediction? If they have no idea what the resources they are deploying will create, then they aren't inviting a more relational world, they're inviting entropy and chaos. They can listen to their gut, to that initial feeling that a plan centering relationship is worth the money, but what happens when people's gut instincts disagree? How many times can a program officer at a foundation justify a gut instinct to their board before the board begins to demand some system of accountability? Trusting individual gut instincts leads to cults of personality and creates the conditions for rampant corruption, so institutions rightly demand that resource allocation decisions be transparent and accountable. ROI must be calculated, and the people up the chain must be able to check the math. To deploy resources inside an institution, we not only need to make a prediction, we need to be able to help our colleagues and bosses quickly come to the same conclusion.

This need to write down and defend the predictions that we make has far-reaching implications. In most other domains, we exchange transactional and relational information with equal ease. We sit down with a friend to discuss the new man in his life and knowingly wink at relational predictions, backing our points up with stories when necessary. But in the workplace, especially when money is being deployed, this so-called lack of rigor is forbidden. We need cold hard numbers to justify an expense, and the result is institutions that, the vast majority of the time, try to tackle challenges with transactional prediction even when relational prediction is vastly more appropriate. The problem is not that relationships are unpredictable; we predict them constantly when navigating daily life. It's that almost all of our institutions that deploy capital have lost the capacity to predict them.

Chapter 8 explores what the world might look like if this capacity was restored. What might the world look like if all of those institutional insurgents who understand the power of relationship had a shared language of relational prediction with their superiors? How might money be deployed differently if people seeking to deploy resources to make change in the world had access to relational as well as transactional strategies, if they sought resilience and transformation as much by passing on power as by accumulating it? What might people skilled at relational reasoning and rooted in evolving relational lineages accomplish on behalf of their communities with these sorts of resources? Though it may not be solely sufficient to address the challenges that our world is facing, a titanic shift is possible simply by giving our institutions the capacity to think in relationships.

To deepen our understanding of relational prediction and what institutions that center it look like, we must look to our history. Humans have been building relationships for a long, long time, and modern transaction-focused institutions are fairly ahistorical in their inability to see it. To create the conditions for relationship in the world, we will need to reach outside those institutions to embrace lineages of relational wisdom that have far more to teach us than toy mathematical models ever could.

Reflection Questions

- How do you reason about relationship?

- How might relationship provide greater resilience in your world?

- How might relationship enable transformation where transformation is needed?

- How do the relationships that matter to you evolve over time?

- Where might that process of evolution be blocked?

- Where do you notice yourself or others working to predict relational outcomes that are intrinsically unpredictable?

- How might you accept what is knowable and unknowable about these outcomes?

CHAPTER 4

Lineages of Relational Wisdom

IN BETWEEN LEARNING physics from my grandfather, I would spend time in the kitchen or the garden helping my grandmother, Betty Lazarus, who knew how to fill a room with a sense of raw matriarchal power. Born Betty Rosenblatt to a well-off Jewish family in Chicago in 1923, she was the subject of scientific research as a child for her extraordinary reading speed. When David was building radar jammers at Harvard during the war, Betty worked at a book shop in Harvard Square, where she would purchase a book every day and finish it before stepping off the Boston T to cook dinner. After the war, my grandfather was recruited to the University of Illinois, where his buddies who had gone off to Los Alamos seemed to be congregating, and Betty got busy mapping and tending to the relational fabric of the physics department. She drew meticulous seating arrangements for dinner parties with notes about conversation topics and relevant community events scrawled in the margins like my grandfather might have annotated the properties of a crystalline structure. In a community of the people who first split the atom, she was a loud-spoken antinuclear activist, a fact that in no way diminished her popularity or influence.

Relational reasoning is the extraordinary ability that human and some other-than-human minds have of making predictions about relationships, and my grandmother possessed it in spades. She helped to weave together a close-knit neighborhood where my mother and her siblings could run between neighbors' houses to play. She deftly navigated an academic community trying to navigate through complex egos, McCarthyism, and the presence of actual Soviet spies there to steal nuclear secrets. When the head of the department invited Japanese graduate students back to study solid-state physics, my grandmother conspired to make sure that they would feel welcome in an environment where the effects of racist anti-Japanese propaganda were still rampant. Some of these students would eventually go back to help found the semiconductor industry in Japan, laying the groundwork for the consumer electronics industry we know today. Through all of this, she was a passionate advocate, reading voraciously, writing op-eds, and tirelessly organizing for social change. Before she passed, she became enamored with a young Illinois state senator named Barack Obama and organized passionately on his behalf.

This kind of relational work is often labeled "soft" and hand-waved away as intuitive and unrigorous, and while it is true that intuition and emotional intelligence play an important role, my grandmother was also engaging in a deep form of prediction that was, in many ways, more sophisticated than my grandfather's work on atoms falling into crystals. Although both my grandparents navigated complex relational worlds, the sexism of the 1950s meant that relational reasoning was the main outlet for my grandmother's considerable intellectual muscle. If my grandfather David shaped my love of science, my grandmother helped to shape my love of organizing. In her home I saw what it looked like to bring community together, to weave communities of care that stretched beyond the confines of a single nuclear family. I learned from her and her children how to see that the world needed changing and then step up to enact that change. My mother and her two surviving siblings are all prominent environmentalists who have shaped successful careers around a deeply felt sense of purpose, a testament to Betty's unwavering sense of purpose. If I want to understand myself and what I am capable of in the world, it helps to understand how Betty has shaped me, the parts of her that came to me through relationship and live on.

Betty and David are not the only lineage I hold. There is Bob, who spent his life working a job in a New York bank that he despised so that he could have the money to take my father and his seven siblings to remote places in the wilderness. He taught my father and by extension me the transformative power of the more-than-human world. There is his wife, Cynthia, who is still alive today quoting lengthy poems from memory and telling stories about fleeing the Nazis as a child in Bavaria alongside the Von Trapps, an honored matriarch with tremendous intellect and creativity. She taught me joyful creativity and grit in the face of adversity and a love of the written word. This lineage is not limited to my genetic ancestors; it encompasses anyone who has deeply shaped me. Queer elders are part of my lineage, and so are the friends who helped me discover what deep connection felt like, and so are organizers like Grace Lee Boggs who helped shape my understanding of movements that has guided much of my life. People who I have merely studied or been inspired by are part of my lineage, but in a much less profound way than if my life had been deeply shaped by theirs. I cannot simply acquire a new lineage by picking up a book or taking a workshop or by parachuting in for a design intensive. Lineage, like all forms of deep relationship, requires being shaped through sustained presence.

Solving Real-World Relational Challenges

This lineage provides me with a set of tools for solving relational challenges. If the oversized neocortex discussed in chapter 1 is hardware, this relational lineage is software. This understanding, passed on through stories, modeling, and sustained experience, is to the analytical definition of relationship discussed in the last chapter what a high school understanding of photosynthesis is to a towering redwood tree. This small scientific understanding can help us marvel at the wonder of what sits before us and to barely fathom how much knowledge there is about combining water, sunlight, air, and soil in the thing that stands before us. It is not a replacement.

When we engage in relational prediction in the real world, we do so by leveraging our remarkable brains and the wisdom passed down to us by ancestors who have been experimenting and refining methods to build relationship for a long, long time. In principle these methods can be viewed as environmental interventions designed to alter evolutionary rate, but they do not need to be analyzed in this way in order to be valid or effective. In this book I have tried to present my understanding of relationship not as some greater truth, but as an expression of my lineage that I hope others may find helpful. I see and understand relationship in the way that my lineage has taught me to see and understand it, even if the understanding I hold is a unique evolution of that lineage.

My capacity for relational prediction, my relational agency, is deeply tied to the way that I leverage this relational lineage to solve challenges in my daily life. All humans, including (and sometimes especially) those with neurodiverse cognitive experiences, have a tremendous capacity for this relational prediction, but like a muscle it strengthens or atrophies based on how we use it. Someone who primarily identifies with their ability to write elegant software and who meets most of their needs through transactions in a marketplace may have an atrophied capacity for relational prediction compared to a disabled person whose day-to-day ability to survive and thrive is deeply entrenched in their ability to maintain trusting relationships in a community of care. Both possess minds that are barely fathomable wonders of relational reasoning, but people who engage in this reasoning regularly and with intention tend to have an edge.

This edge is often but not always inversely tied to power and privilege. Someone like me who is a white nondisabled cis man with access to economic resources can more easily take on complex relational challenges because I choose to and not because I have to. The professional settings I navigate do not require the constant and exhausting work of code-switching. I do not have to develop the skill of constantly monitoring for and sidestepping sexual harassment or transphobia. When

I want food or shelter, I can reliably purchase these things rather than needing to occasionally rely on the community around me as a safety net. I may develop equally powerful relational skills in other ways, but I am more likely to have the option of moving through the world with minimal relational foresight and obligating those around me to clean up the mess.

If relational agency is acquired through practice, it is also contextual. My grandmother's experience growing up and navigating relationships in a largely secularized Jewish community was applicable to the task of facilitating relationships with people from postwar Japan, but that applicability had a limit, and it was critical for her to understand that limit and switch to passing on power and building trust when she hit it. If we build relationships by shaping environments where they can evolve, then the details of that ecology matter. Like living things, relationships will thrive in ecosystems that feel familiar. Someone who has mastered the social scene of their Connecticut country club may be wholly incompetent at constructing relational containers for queer youth, and the queer youth lead at an LGBTQ center may have no idea how to navigate the relational dynamics at a nearby Black church.

This is one reason why investments in relational containers cannot be centralized. To make relationships happen in a wide variety of contexts, resources must be pushed out to people who are skilled at working relationally in those contexts. There is no universally scalable strategy for building relationships, no software platform or AI system that can encode relational reasoning into a globally homogenous piece of software. If we want a path out of the loneliness crisis, a lot of local organizers who have been doing underappreciated work for decades are going to have to start getting paid.

The details of how to do that, and how to distribute resources to a diverse but values-aligned network of people skilled at relational reasoning in communities they deeply understand, will be the subject of chapter 7. When navigating these communities and looking for skilled organizers with whom to build trust, relational lineage can be a helpful guide. Understanding where strong connections to lineage exist and where those connections have atrophied or have been severed can help to build a picture of where relational agency exists and where it is needed.

Connection and Disconnection from Lineage: Building Communities of Care

Shortly before writing this chapter I had the honor of meeting Mia Birdsong, author of the incredible *How We Show Up,* which chronicles how the people she respects most invest in relationships with their friends, families, and communities. In the chapter on family, she illustrates how Black families have a rich history of raising children in communities of care.

> *Despite the persistent and erroneous idea that the best family forma-tion is two married people raising children on their own, for hundreds of years Black people have maintained an approach to family that taps into the support, knowledge, and capacity of "the village." So many Black folks are raised not just by their parents but by grandparents, aunties, and friends—finding home in a rotation of houses depending on the season (summers with grandparents), their age (Uncle James is particularly good with teenagers), or other resources (Aunt Viv lives in a good school district). I know so many Black folks who didn't find out until they were grown that Uncle James or Aunt Viv are not the biological siblings of their parents.*
>
> *For decades, Black families have been described as "broken." This is in part because of the misogyny that insists that children do best when raised in a home with two, "opposite-sex" married parents, not just with their mother. There is plenty of data to dispute this claim and the biased research behind it.[1] But part of what is both harmful and boring about that narrow lens is that [it] misses what is beautiful, resilient, supportive, and brilliant about the breadth and fluidity of so many Black families.[2]*

This capacity to consciously construct chosen family is also part of a lineage of queer family to which I personally owe a deep debt of gratitude. The law that allowed me to adopt my daughter as a third parent and the frameworks that guided the conversations that resulted in my family would not have existed without a queer lineage that reaches back to the chosen families of queer ballroom culture that faced down the AIDS crisis. These chosen families trace their roots to people like William Dorsey Swann, a formerly enslaved man who started hosting private balls that were the first recorded instances of the word *drag*.[3]

As a queer parent reading Birdsong, I sense a rootedness in a lineage of relational wisdom that entangles with but diverges from my own. My connection with queer lineage stretched from my high school discussions with my friend Molly through to mentorship from sex-positive activists like Carol Queen. When I was embarking on my journey to become a parent, a queer elder named S. Bear Bergman knew when to pull me aside at a conference to check in and nudge me onto a more helpful path. It comes through my co-mom's mother, a pastor who provided spiritual solace on the front lines of the AIDS epidemic and raised a daughter who understood the power of queer family. I have had to struggle to find my path away from loneliness, but my struggle builds on the struggles of those who came before me. Remembering the deep wisdom that they have to share has been a potent antidote to my own experiences of loneliness.

For this reason, connection to lineage is both an important part of cultivating my own relational practice and a thing to look for when trusting the relational practice of others. If I am seeking relational wisdom on how to raise money to support a community, I may recognize that wisdom exists in communities of faith. Their practice of gathering people in spiritual communion and passing a plate has resulted in some of the most resilient and longest-lived institutions in human history, and while many of those institutions have a flawed history of exploitation, they have just as powerful a history of resisting it. If I want to draw on that history, I could show up at a church with a notepad, jot down a few pithy observations, and call myself an expert, or I could build trust with someone who comes from that lineage. My friend Andrew, a queer-friendly evangelical who leads a national multifaith network, serves as such a guide. Rather than trying to absorb the wisdom of a relational lineage in the abstract, I invite those deeply shaped by that lineage to shape me.

Recognizing these lineages of relational wisdom can be a tool for connection across political divides. When discussing queer family with a conservative friend, I learned that my approach of creating loving communities of care around whatever arrangement of legal parents existed failed to acknowledge a relational lineage that was central to him: that of fatherhood. In his life and his lineage, fully present and loving fathers mattered, and the risk that this wisdom would be forgotten and that young men would no longer be taught to be fathers felt like a clear and present threat. Out of this fear sprouted a hesitation about trans dads, a subtle pause about lesbian couples raising children, and an uncertainty about celebrating single moms by choice. Hearing this provocation changed me. It challenged me to more deeply honor my own father, whose unwavering loving presence taught me the power of stillness in nature. I told the story of how to celebrate my graduation from sixth grade, my father took me to the north face of the Grand Canyon. At three o'clock in the afternoon, he pointed to a rock and told me to sit and watch the sunset. I shared how, for three hours, we sat in silence and watched as shadows crept up the canyon. Then I shared the stories of the trans fathers I knew, of solo moms who worked hard to ensure that their children grew up around a loving community of all genders. I too had been shaped by fatherhood and had seen how the lineage of that shaping was evolving. We do not honor lineage by clinging to the past; we honor it by creating the conditions for it to survive and evolve.

Sometimes addressing a relational challenge is a matter of understanding which lineages to draw on and amplify. I hold and honor powerful lineages of both traditional and queer families. My parents and both sets of my grandparents had marriages that stood the test of time, loving partnerships free of abuse or deep betrayals of trust. After meeting in architecture school at Washington University, my parents took jobs out of school at firms that they would stay in for their entire careers. Both rose to the senior ranks of their companies while advocating for accessibility and sustainable design. Both were active in successful efforts to revitalize St. Louis, a city decimated by redlining and white flight. They masterfully put in the work to maintain a healthy marriage and raise three children, always prioritizing their presence with us above all else.

Yet when I look out on the world, celebration of this model of nuclear family is not lacking. Stories, software, self-help books, and relational containers abound to help with the project of raising children in a monogamous partnership, while very little exists to help with the project of building communities of care around partnerships that start out or wind up looking different. Since announcing my journey to become a third parent six years ago, I have received a steady stream of messages from people tentatively exploring similar journeys. About once a week I will go on a hike or take a phone call with someone interested in doing some form of parenting with someone who is not a romantic partner. Sometimes these are straight couples afraid of becoming isolated from their friends, or child-free people who still desire regular, committed, but less than full-time relationships with kids in their lives. Sometimes they are people considering becoming known genetic donors who will play a less than full-time role in a child's life; sometimes they are solo moms planning baby showers that are more focused on weaving committed communities of care than exchanging gifts.

These people often sit close to but are disconnected from a lineage of relational wisdom about building chosen family. Though they are by no means the only models for doing so, the deeply intertwined lineages of Black and queer chosen families both have a long history of being silenced and criminalized. Rather than applauding Black mothers for helping to build neighborhood-level communities of care, the state focused on shaming them for failing to marry the Black men that it was locking up. Rather than applauding queer families as sites of resilience and compassionate care during the AIDS crisis, the state used shame about their deviance to deny critical public health services. With this history of shame and institutional hostility to chosen family, is it any wonder that so many of today's young parents feel isolated and overwhelmed?

In "The Nuclear Family Was a Mistake," David Brooks outlines why functional nuclear families like the one I was raised in are a historical fluke that occurred mostly among white Americans from 1950 to 1965.[4] According to Brooks, "The period when the nuclear family flourished was not normal. It was a freakish historical moment when all of society conspired to obscure its essential fragility."[5] Everything from the postwar economy to broadly accepted misogyny coincided to make a monogamous couple raising kids in relative isolation seem like a good idea. For the rest of humanity during that time and the rest of human history, broader networks of care have been essential to the work of raising healthy kids and supporting healthy adults.

That means that there are many, many lineages of relational wisdom about how to build these networks of care and repair them when they falter. The fact that so many people reach out to my family as if parenting with more than two adults is a thing that we invented is evidence of a deep rupture in relational lineage. Not a severing, but a fraying that makes knowledge about the intentional construction of chosen family difficult for most people to access.

Where such a fraying exists, there is immense potential for relational impact. The combination of many people isolated in a shared struggle and an unrealized disconnection from relational lineage has all the makings of a rapid and transformative shift in relational agency. In the long difficult fight against loneliness, these are the quick wins. Where loneliness and frayed connection to lineage coexist, it can be powerful to invest in the work of repair.

Healing Disrupted Lineages of Wisdom and Acknowledging Lineages of Harm

Beginning in the 1980s, La Donna Harris, founder of America for Indian Opportunity (AIO), began hosting meetings among Indigenous peoples of North America to discuss the values shared across their widely disparate cultures.[6] I imagine that the challenge was daunting. *Indigeneity,* the word chosen by Harris and her contemporaries to describe their work, is almost unfathomably broad. The word is asked to encompass the relational wisdom of all people not displaced intentionally or forcefully in a project of colonialism, the sociological equivalent of finding the common themes in all noninsect life.

After years of deep conversation, themes began to emerge. Perhaps there was a shared sense of relational lineages that had been frayed but were needed, even if articulating them at the generic level of indigeneity robbed them of the rich context and nuance needed for real understanding. To people like me who are disconnected from these lineages, they are a guide to these deeper stories, a messy communal invitation to learn to trust lineages of wisdom that I do not understand but that my world can deeply benefit from. As someone who has witnessed the impact of a rupture in the lineage of family creation, I can sense that this network of Indigenous leaders is calling attention to a rupture vastly larger in size and scope. Rather than trying to summarize a lineage that is not mine, I will provide an excerpt of the description written by Harris:

> *A result of the initial meetings in the 1980s and early 1990s was the identification and articulation of four core values which cross generation, geography, and tribe. We have come to call these four core values the Four R's: Relationship, Responsibility, Reciprocity, and Redistribution. Each of these values manifests itself in a core obligation in Indigenous societies.*
>
> Relationship is the kinship obligation, *the profound sense that we human beings are related, not only to each other, but to all things, animals, plants, rocks—in fact, to the very stuff the stars are made of. This relationship is a kinship relationship. Everyone/everything is related to us as if they were our blood relatives. We, thus, live in a family that includes all creation, and everyone/everything in this extended family is valued and has a valued contribution to make. So, our societal task is to make sure that everyone feels included and feels that they can make their contribution to our common good. This is one reason why we value making decisions by consensus because it allows everyone to make a contribution.*
>
> Responsibility is the community obligation. *This obligation rests on the understanding that we have a responsibility to care for*

all of our relatives. Our relatives include everything in our ecological niche, animals, and plants, as well as humans, even the stones, since everything that exists is alive. Many North American Indians refer to the subsistence triad of plants—corn, beans, and squash—as the Three Sisters. Indigenous leadership arises from the assumption of responsibilities arising out of our relationships and the roles in society these relationships engender, not from an ability to exercise force over others. Responsible Indigenous leadership is based on an ethos of care, not of coercion. The most important responsibility of a leader is to create the social space in which productive relationships can be established and take place.

Reciprocity is the cyclical obligation. *It underscores the fact that in nature things are circular: for example, the cycle of the seasons and the cycle of life, as well as the dynamics between any two entities in relationship with each other. Once we have encountered another, we are in relationship with them. The relationship I have with the woman with whom I founded OIO, Iola Hayden, began when her great grandfather captured my great grandfather in the 19th century down in Mexico soon after my great-grandfather's family had emigrated from Spain. They became social "brothers." Therefore, our families have been "in relationship" since then, engaging in an ongoing set of uneven reciprocal exchange obligations. At any given moment the exchanges going on in a relationship may be uneven. The Indigenous idea of reciprocity is based on very long relational dynamics in which we are all seen as "kin" to each other.*

Redistribution is the sharing obligation. *Its primary purpose is to balance and rebalance relationships. Comanche society, for example, was an almost totally flat society, socially, politically, and economically. It had many, many ways of redistributing material and social goods. In principle one should not own anything one is not willing to give away. Possessions do not own you. The point is not to acquire things. The point is to give them away. Generosity is the most highly valued human quality. The basic principle is to keep everything moving, to keep everything in circulation.*

> *To mark one's accomplishments, one sponsors a "give away."*
> *Instead of receiving gifts, the person who has accomplished something*
> *gives gifts to all those who have helped them along the way to their*
> *accomplishment. This is what my elder daughter, Katherine Tijerina,*
> *did in our home community of Walters, Oklahoma, when she grad-*
> *uated from Stanford Law School.*[7]

As someone who has spent my life struggling with relational invisibility, it is powerful to see the concept of relationship front and center
in this definition. The responsibility to create spaces of care resonates
deeply with my movement lineage, as does the notion that relationships must be balanced by reciprocity. As someone struggling to
imagine how we might direct funding toward the work of building
relationship, this feels filled with richness and possibility, even though
that richness is not mine to claim. The example of a giveaway—an
inversion of the idea I was raised with, that accomplishments should
lead to personal wealth—is especially powerful. If the central question
of this book is about effectively distributing resources to address the
loneliness crisis, then the values described by Harris and her compa-
triots hint at a way that this resourcing of relationships can be deeply
ingrained into community values and daily practice. This value of
reciprocity is further illustrated by Robin Wall Kimmerer in *Braiding
Sweetgrass*:

> *From the viewpoint of a private property economy, the "gift" is*
> *deemed to be "free" because we obtain it free of charge, at no cost. But*
> *in the gift economy, gifts are not free. The essence of the gift is that*
> *it creates a set of relationships. The currency of a gift economy is, at*
> *its root, reciprocity. In Western thinking, private land is understood*
> *to be a "bundle of rights," whereas in a gift economy, property has a*
> *"bundle of responsibilities" attached.*[8]

Witnessing the richness of this lineage brings up a stir of complex
emotion. I recall as a young child sitting around tables with my father's
extended family and hearing stories about how Native land was stolen
by my ancestors. I remember taking a train from New York with

my grandmother, who pointed out the towns that were named after people in my family tree. Although I was horrified, these stories were often presented as clever and noble deeds that illustrated my family's contribution to our nation's legacy. My lineage holds wisdom about how to build relationship, but that same lineage also holds responsibility for harm.

If Indigenous perspectives are something that I want to see more of in the world, then I must contend with the reasons why those perspectives are so absent. The relational lineage I am inspired by has been disrupted by centuries of genocide, broken treaties, and land theft in which my ancestors were active participants. It has been disrupted by over a century of Indian Boarding Schools, which from 1860 to 1978 sought to fully disconnect Native people from Native culture.

> *Students were stripped of all things associated with Native life. Their long hair, a source of pride for many Native peoples, was cut short, usually into identical bowl haircuts. They exchanged traditional clothing for uniforms, and embarked on a life influenced by strict military-style regimentation. Students were physically punished for speaking their Native languages. Contact with family and community members was discouraged or forbidden altogether. Survivors have described a culture of pervasive physical and sexual abuse at the schools. Food and medical attention were often scarce; many students died. Their parents sometimes learned of their death only after they had been buried in school cemeteries, some of which were unmarked.[9]*

This violent severing of lineage has created a gap in relational agency that spreads far beyond the Native communities where it is most apparent. If I, as a white person, read La Donna Harris and feel inspired, I am witnessing that gap. This is not an invitation to pick up a disrupted lineage and appropriate it; this is an invitation to participate from the position I hold in the work of healing that lineage.

Connecting with relational lineage is a powerful tool in the fight against loneliness, but it fails if we do not contend with the history of how those lineages were disrupted. If I seek to engage with Indigenous wisdom and bring with me unexamined lessons passed down from my ancestors who stole Indigenous land, the results could be disastrous. I have been shaped by movement lineages that resisted widespread anti–Black racism in my hometown of St. Louis, but I have also been shaped by lineages that perpetuated that racism. Reflecting on this history of harm comes with its own important relational lessons. While lineage about queer chosen family is one that has shaped me and that I can embody and teach to others, claiming Indigenous lineage would invoke not the wisdom I am inspired by but a lineage of disrupting that wisdom. If reflecting on lineages of wisdom gives me tools, reflecting on how those lineages have caused harm provides equally important warnings. I must be cautious about the way that I claim and take up space, especially if I show up with imbalanced power. I must be cautious about appropriating ideas and making them my own rather than pointing clearly to the people and lineages they come from. If I want to see relationship, responsibility, reciprocity, and redistribution in the world, then this caution can help to guide me toward an appropriate place in that process of healing. It will mean recognizing the complex relational wisdom that Native folks today hold rather than seeking an abstract ideal that was only ever imagined. I do not come from this lineage, so my role is to pass on attention, resources, and power to people who do.

I am still figuring out how to do this. It is a vulnerable and messy process that I regularly mess up. But it is necessary. Just as the landscape of relational lineage is filled with underappreciate wisdom, it is filled with underacknowledged harm. I am learning to see this harm not as a reason for guilt, shame, or moral righteousness but as another path to the process of healing that is necessary if we are to build a more relational world.

If we are to chart a path out of the loneliness crisis, it will be by learning from, evolving, and healing lineages of relational wisdom. The answers that we seek are, more often than not, answers that our grandparents and their grandparents knew, even if they must be evolved to fit a new context. We must contend with the ways that these lineages have been disrupted and the reasons that they have been disrupted and direct resources to communities where people can engage in the work of repair. The tools we seek to build relationship do not need to be built anew; they are bountiful and buried just below the surface, even when the map to find them has been torn to pieces.

To further illustrate the power of learning from lineage, I will turn to a lineage that has profoundly shaped my life: that of movement organizing. If our task is not only to connect on a personal level but to heal deep societal wounds and invite a more relational world into being, then movements have a track record of social change that is worth examining. Movements can help us to understand the deep link between relationship, resilience, and transformation in practice. They can help us understand what it means to build distributed relational power.

Reflection Questions

- What relational lineages do you hold?

- How did you learn to create the conditions for relationship?

- Which of these learnings do you want to embody and pass on?

- Which of these learnings do you want to find alternatives to or evolve?

- How are you shaped by lineages responsible for disruption and harm?

- What from these lineages do you hope to unlearn or heal?

- Where do disrupted lineages exist that you wish to repair?

- What might this work of repair look like?

- How might you be supported in it or support the work of others?

CHAPTER 5

How Movements Nurture Relationship

I HAVE HAD FEW opportunities in my life to experience the magic of an intergenerational dance floor. They usually happen at weddings, where grandparents and toddlers grin at one another while swaying to the same beat, but one such dance floor is the highlight of a prominent queer conference. Everyone over the age of twenty-five needs to be entertained while the younger activists and organizers have a mixer, so the AARP gets a DJ for people over the age of fifty and their allies. On that dance floor, the too-few elders who survived the AIDS crisis and transphobic violence are there alongside the generation who both fought for marriage equality and were ignored in that fight alongside the generation of activists fighting for gender-affirming care. It is the mid-2010s and the room is filled with an unapologetic intergenerational joy. It is filled with people who have defied the odds and survived, with people who have pushed through shame and pulled others out of it to find relationships filled with purpose and pleasure, with impossible worlds that have been imagined and manifested only to have a new generation of radical imagining grow up within them. It is filled with people who are finding their way and reveling, heads back and mouths screaming, as their loneliness slips away. Earlier that day I cried at a drag workshop where young people were pushed, many for the first time, to embody a gender that felt right in their bodies, to wild applause. I was not the only one in tears.

I attend conferences regularly, hosted by tech giants and philanthropic foundations on topics ranging from impact investing to the technology of peace-building to nonlinear dynamics. These academic and industry conferences are well-funded but often dry, while the conferences hosted and populated by movements often hold the magic of a rich and capable relational lineage. Many lineages could be the subject of this chapter, but movements—specifically movements for queer liberation, climate justice, and tech reform—are relational lineages that have shaped me and that I can therefore speak to. They are also lineages with rich insight about how to not only build relationship but coordinate and resource people working to build relationship at a large scale.

Living in Bay Area tech culture I often encounter people who see history as a story of technologies and the powerful corporate titans that wield them. They imagine US history as being shaped by railroads in the 1850s, urban electrification in the 1910s, the rise of the shipping container in the 1950s; it's a steady march of technological progress and economic growth. And while this history shapes our daily lives, movement history shapes them as much or more. From the movement to abolish slavery in the 1850s to the suffragettes of the 1910s to the anticolonial movements of the 1950s, groups of people organized around a shared struggle have reliably reshaped our world as much or more than people organized in governments or corporations.

Throughout my education I was schooled in civics. My teachers drew diagrams that illustrated how the three branches of the US government work, how elections work, and how a bill becomes a law. I was told that I would need to get a job to survive and was schooled on the basics of the corporate form: on balance sheets, executive teams, and other institutional standards that have spread from for-profit corporations into the nonprofit and government sectors. But I was not really told how movements work. If I expressed a desire to make change in the world, I was encouraged to look for a job at a social venture or to vaguely "get involved," but my formal education had little to say about what movements were, how I could intentionally help in the work of building them, or how my life might be improved if I did. I learned these things from movement elders, but to most of my teachers, my employers, my funders, and my news sources, movements were like a kind of weather. Movements were an environmental condition that would blow in and blow away uncontrollably, a thing to prepare for and predict but not participate in. To them, movements were hashtags like #blacklivesmatter or #metoo that could be harnessed by seeing which way the wind was blowing. When they came pouring down, one could choose either to dance in the streets or to shelter indoors, but movements were not organizational forms to be built in the way that corporations and governments are built.

This view of movements as weather is reflected in much of the academic literature, which often focuses on the external conditions that lead to movements rather than the things that individuals can do to help build them. Early studies of social movements treated them as a sort of mass mental illness, a delusion that caused mobs to form in the streets and make unreasonable demands of their betters.[1] This gave way to more modern frameworks such as resource mobilization theory, which sees movements as emerging from the meteorological combination of collective grievances and resources such as money and shared knowledge.[2] The framing perspective on movements shifts the focus from resources to the framing of ideas in the public discourse, centering the precise language that movement leaders use rather than the operational realities that make movements possible.[3] New social movements theory emphasizes the importance of identity construction through small informal networks but lacks a clear understanding of what the relationships making up these networks are or how they evolve. This chapter will seek to build on these frameworks, especially new social movements theory, by viewing movements as organizations created by and for the work of building relationships.

As legendary Detroit organizer Grace Lee Boggs once said, "Movements are born of critical connections rather than critical mass."[4] Just as for-profit corporations are an organizational form that uses money to organize human labor to make more money, movements are an organizational form that uses relationships to organize human labor to make more relationships. Movements are far from the only organizational form that builds relationship in this way: faith communities, artist networks, and organized fan bases can all provide equally compelling examples, but movements are unique for their ability to creatively coordinate around a shared goal of systemic change. If we face a systemic crisis of loneliness, then there are many intersecting reasons why movements may be part of the solution.

At numerous points throughout my life, movements have provided a path out of loneliness. When I was in my early twenties, anxiously wondering how to fill my calendar after moving to the Bay Area, I happened across a poster for the League of Pissed Off Voters, a group I'd joined in St. Louis that drafted and distributed voter guides that encouraged young people to make it to the polls. I showed up nervously to my first meeting and received a warm greeting from Heather, an organizer who I am still close with almost twenty years later. Before and after the meeting started, Heather made a point of asking me about my story and introducing me to others in the group. I started coming back regularly both because I cared about progressive youth voices in San Francisco politics and because the meetings were a convenient way to spend time with my friends. The meetings would regularly be followed by raucous laughter at a nearby taqueria, and it was in those spaces after our meetings that my friendships began to blossom. If I went to a professional networking session, I would present my dry professional identity and exchange business cards. If I went to a club, I could find connection, but it was difficult to take that connection off the dance floor without sex on the table. For similar reasons, dating apps were beyond useless. But in movement spaces, all of the ingredients were there: regular time together, shared passion, and a constantly shifting political landscape that invited us to creatively explore together.

Over a few short months, my relationships began to blossom. My weeks filled up with rallies, movie nights at anarchist co-ops, underground house parties, and long hikes with movement friends. Every Monday, three friends and I would meet up at San Francisco's Ferry Building and make the sixteen-mile trek out to Ocean Beach and then back home to the Mission. Aliza, Poonam, and Steve came on bikes; as a former speed skater, I kept to my rollerblades. The rules were strict: Heading toward the Pacific, we talked politics, the responsibility we had as transplants to oppose city policies that furthered gentrification, and the latest on how our power company was maneuvering to block clean energy legislation at city hall. Heading back home through Golden Gate Park, we gossiped about our love lives.

While the others stuck to the people who had caught their fancy, I talked about movements. Different groups in the Bay Area seemed to have different strategies for getting new arrivals into relationship with one another, with the more successful groups often growing and claiming power. I was sampling the relational dynamics of the Bay Area activist scene, systematically showing up for groups that resonated with my values and often finding a deep relationship or two in the process. Implicit (and before long, explicit) in these conversations was the fact that Aliza, Poonam, and Steve were the wildest successes of this operation, relationships brimming with laughter, mutual care, and creativity. Before long we were crashing our power company's press conferences in gorilla costumes, handing out well-researched fact sheets, and taking the resulting press coverage to our elected representatives. It wasn't long before the energy legislation we discussed on our bike rides began to pass.

Victories in social movements occasionally come from thousands of people taking to the streets, but it is far more common for them to come from coordinated groups of friends engaging in strategic local action. If corporations are generally made up of a hierarchical structure of teams, movements are generally made up of a coral reef–like network of intersecting affinity groups. To survive, thrive, and create change, movements must evolve strategies for forming and coordinating these small groups of friends. I like to break this process down into four layers of involvement that make movements possible:

1. **Broadcast.** The movement broadcasts a compelling message into public discourse and gives people who resonate with that message a time and place to show up.

2. **Gathering.** The movement creates a relational container where people who resonate with its message can learn more, tell their stories, make friends, and engage in mass mobilization. Sometimes the relationships formed through gathering gel into affinity groups; sometimes people are recruited from these spaces and routed to affinity groups where they can make friends and contribute.

3. **Action.** Small groups of friends who have built trust outside formal gathering spaces imagine and execute actions that align with the movement's values and shared strategic goals. This could look like creating a legal resource team for a protest, or organizing an open mic night for poets in the movement to share their work.

4. **Cohesion.** People who have built trust and respect through work in affinity groups listen to what various groups are doing, weave together a cohesive narrative that speaks to them, route resources like money and attention where they are needed, and mediate inevitable conflicts.

These four functions roughly map to the journey that one takes into a movement, from hearing a resonant message to collaboratively guiding the movement as a trusted elder. Every movement goes about these things differently, and no movement accomplishes these things without some degree of friction. A movement that fails to gather, for example, may command a large following but find it difficult to build affinity groups engaged in creative action. A movement that fails at the coordination layer may see its affinity groups splinter and focus their creative energy on fighting over attention and resources. This relational view of movements allows us to view them from the inside out, focusing not on the external conditions that create opportunities for a movement but on the ways that individuals form and navigate relationships within a movement to seize on those opportunities and create change.

The Broadcast Layer

Sometimes you work for years to build awareness only to have it hit you like a tidal wave. In the fall of 2004, AVEN had about fifteen hundred members, almost all of whom had found us by independently inventing the word *asexual* and typing it into Google. I was leading the community along with a handful of other volunteer admins while holding down my first job out of college, running a voter registration program at universities in the St. Louis area in the buildup to the 2004 presidential election. In the second week of October, just three weeks before the polls, I received an email from a reporter from a British magazine I had spoken with earlier that summer. Her magazine would be publishing a feature article on our community in just under forty-eight hours, and from the summary she included, the article looked to be compelling and well researched. At that point, most people in the world assumed that sexual attraction was an intrinsic part of the human experience, like eating or breathing. Stories from our community backed by some recent scientific research were about to shatter that assumption.

I reached out to the other leaders of AVEN, quickly recruited volunteers throughout Britain who could speak to the press, and put together a basic media training. We had a public email address that received one or two letters a week, and I recruited a dozen volunteers to forward those letters to in case we got a deluge. I messaged everyone who was in the habit of welcoming new people to our community and told them to get ready. On the day of the article's release, I woke up at 6 a.m. central time, noon UK time, to find over forty emails from major British news publications along with almost a dozen voice mails.

I scrambled to respond to the London *Times* and took radio interviews with various BBC outlets from my kitchen phone. In between interviews, I checked in with my media team, passing journalists on to trained aces in their area and routing over a hundred emails coming in from asexual people across Britain who had just learned that they were not alone. I knew from experience that every one of those emails came from someone who was in a moment of fragile uncertainty, and getting them each a response from a warm human was paramount. Our forums received a deluge of new members, and the community rallied to make sure that they felt welcomed and seen. After arranging a flight to London at 7 a.m. the next morning to appear on live British television, I reached out to my boss to let him know that I would need time off. He informed me that no one was allowed time off three weeks before the election, so I quit. Four days later, when I was back in the Midwest and the interviews had simmered down to a few a day, all of which could conveniently be taken in the early morning central time, I showed up at work to continue running the voter registration and mobilization team without pay.

Over the next few years, our press coverage continued in waves, jumping the Atlantic to the United States. We were featured on the front page of the *New York Times,* on *20/20,* CNN, and *The View* along with countless smaller publications and radio stations. I remained the spokesperson that journalists wanted to talk to. As a conventionally attractive and articulate man in my early twenties, I looked like someone who should be in their sexual prime, and the contrast was appealing to the press. It also posed a problem. I was a representative that could garner attention and introduce the concept of asexuality, but I was mostly making room for aces like me. I was easy to accept because I was expected to have agency over my sexuality in a way that many in our community were not. I did not have a history of sexual trauma, or a visible disability, or significant neurodiversity, or a gender or an age or a faith or a race that would cause people to write off my asexuality as something else: as a failure to possess the kind of mind and body that was allowed to experience sexual agency in the first place. I was what the community called a "gold star" asexual, someone whose identity was easy to accept because it was supported by other forms of privilege. Most people in the community did not have that gold star, and while amplifying my story was making some of our shared experience visible, it wasn't creating a world where most aces could find acceptance.

I continued to take the media opportunities that insisted on my involvement but passed opportunities on to or lifted up others in the community whenever possible. We didn't need one face and one story; we needed many faces and many stories. Toward the end of 2005, when *The View* called and invited me on, it was clear that they were expecting someone timid about sexuality who the hosts could poke fun at. Because it was going to be an adversarial interview where my gold-star status would come in handy, I took it. The hosts attacked me relentlessly, trying to make me squeamish about sex and asking why a bunch of asexual people would ever want to leave our homes to meet one another and organize. I knew that the story they wanted to tell about our movement, a funny story about strange and unreasonable people making a big deal out of nothing, was far less compelling than the truth. I told them how, as an asexual person, I felt a deep desire for connection with others. I told them about the ways that desire had been denied and rendered invisible and how profoundly showing up in a place with other asexual people had changed that. I made sure to mention our website. When the show aired, thousands of asexual people who had felt alone for their entire lives showed up at our doorstep. We were ready to meet them.

To grow, relational movements tell public stories that invite people to sites of connection. These stories are different from the public brands maintained by most modern corporations. As defined by David Aaker in *Building Strong Brands,* a brand is a promise about the kind of experience that customers will receive every time they interact with a company.[5] A brand is consistent and tightly controlled. It allows customers to make a transactional prediction about exactly what will happen if they exchange money for a good or service. Movement stories, in contrast, are designed to help people make relational predictions. They do not tell us exactly what to expect; they tell us that a kind of transformation is possible and invite us to show up in community to discover it for ourselves. If someone feels hopeless about the global climate crisis, a movement may tell them a story about someone whose hopelessness has been transformed, someone who moved from feeling isolated and afraid to feeling part of a community with the power to transform the world around them. Movements must tell many types of stories rather than one tightly controlled brand narrative to give a sense of the range of transformations that are possible.

While movements often argue that change is needed, laying out a logical case is generally not enough to drive meaningful action. People may nod their heads in agreement with facts and figures that outline a critical social problem; they may even open their wallets to help people who are suffering, but urgent awareness of a problem will not make many people actually show up to a movement and participate. Inviting participation in movements requires a particular structure of story, one that helps people imagine how they might personally be transformed. Marshall Ganz, a professor at the Kennedy School of Public Policy who once organized with Cesar Chavez and Dolores Huerta of the National Farm Workers Association, describes the stories that movements tell as having three parts:[6]

1. **Challenge:** a form of adversity that someone faces, usually tied to a feeling of isolation and powerlessness. A college student feeling hopeless in the face of the climate crisis or a Black mom feeling unable to protect her son from racist police.

2. **Choice:** a choice made in the face of that challenge, very often a choice that involves showing up to form a relationship. A survivor of sexual assault finding support and speaking out, or a Walmart factory worker grabbing drinks with their fellow workers to discuss their shared struggle.

3. **Outcome:** a transformation that happens both internally and in the world because of that relationship. A climate activist who felt alone and hopeless now feels empowered and is working with others to pass local legislation. A trans man who

was struggling with loneliness and anxiety now has an amazing chosen family and is working to support the next generation of trans youth.

If brand stories exist to answer the question, "What do I buy to be happy?", movement stories exist to answer the question, "Where do I show up and how do I show up to find resilience and transformation through relationship?" They map the paths that others have taken to journey from isolation and hopelessness to relationship and power so that we might chart our own path. In the last few chapters, we have discussed the remarkable ability of the human mind to make predictions about relationships. Stories, like the stories told by movements, are the kind of data best suited to help our minds make those predictions.

Sometimes these stories are about relationships forming in isolation: a friend seeking support, or someone courageously speaking up when silence is the norm. But for movements to grow, they must invite people to build relationships collectively. In order for the movement to grow, stories in the broadcast layer must point to an accessible relational container where people can experience the transformation and resilience that the movement offers. This could be a meeting, a rally, a march, or an encampment. It could be a website like AVEN with social functionality, so long as people are doing the work of making sure that newcomers can be heard and integrated. It is not an invitation to like and subscribe, or a link to a donation page, because these are not invitations to both change and be changed. To grow, movements must use their public stories to invite people to gather.

The Gathering Layer

Recently I was invited to give a talk at Boston University along with my friend Angela Chen. Angela is the author of the excellent book *Ace,* which, along with Sherronda J. Brown's *Refusing Compulsory Sexuality,* I strongly recommend to anyone interested in the ace topics that this book touches on only briefly. The two of us had a friendly conversation in front of a room of about eighty, many of whom sported the black, gray, white, and purple of the ace flag. We spoke for forty minutes, took questions from the audience for another twenty minutes, then thanked the room to polite applause. Angela went to a table to sign books, and everyone else stood up to leave.

I raised my voice. "If I could have your attention for one moment. Many of you came here because you are curious about ace experience, and if that curiosity has been satiated, feel free to head out. But many of you are here because you are ace and you've never been in a room with this many other ace people in your life. I see from the schools on your shirts that not everyone is here from BU. I know that some of you are local leaders of ace groups, and I imagine that some of you saw a poster for this talk and have never spoken to another ace person in your life. So if you want to stay, you can stay. Anyone who wants to is welcome to grab a chair and form circles of about five in front of the stage. I have a workshop that will help us get to know one another."

About forty percent of the room took me up on my offer. I seeded a few questions, and stories began flowing about the struggles that people were having with friends, the beautiful and unscripted relationships that they were exploring, and the fan fiction they were writing to unpack ace experience. I jumped between the groups facilitating, making sure that quiet people were offered space to speak, and identifying established and organically emerging leaders who could help to drive the conversation. After ninety minutes I invited anyone who wanted to make an invitation to the group to briefly do so, and half a dozen hands shot up with invitations to local events, writers circles, and campus clubs. The head of the LGBTQ center informed us that we were about to get kicked out of the room, but she and I had planned for this eventuality. Snacks and drinks were waiting in the campus LGBTQ center if we wanted to keep the conversation going, so still furiously talking, we marched across campus and began nourishing our bodies and making extensive use of the center's whiteboard to explore emerging ideas. This second gathering was less formal. People followed up with those who had expressed invitations or paired off to discuss threads of conversation that the larger groups had been unable to dive into. Young people asked me for advice on navigating their relationships, their intersecting identities, and their faiths. One person, who had kept with the group but stayed mostly silent, took me aside to share that finding the community had saved their life several years earlier. For them, being in the room and not speaking was enough. Eventually only the leadership of the local ace communities remained, and we went out to grab dinner and discuss organizing strategy.

A lecture that began at 10 a.m. and lasted for one hour sparked a gathering that didn't end until 9 p.m. In those ten hours of conversation, new relationships were formed, new initiatives were launched, and new leaders were identified and routed to groups where they could connect and collaborate around their areas of passion. I had asked for snacks and drinks to be placed in the campus LGBTQ center because I had seen this kind of gathering play out dozens of times before, spawning campus groups and intercampus coalitions in schools throughout the United States and Canada.

Movements succeed by gathering people in relational containers. After extending invitations through stories in the broadcast layer, movements need to create and maintain an abundant ecosystem of places where people can connect. These containers need to be accessible so that uncertain people can show up without too much effort, and they need to be highly relational so that the movements can build connections that build power. Unlike corporations, which can maintain fairly poor relational practices and still make enough money to pay people to show up, movements face strong evolutionary pressure to build spaces that keep people coming back. Movements that gather relationally attract members and thrive, and movements that fail to do so wither, so in my experience the gatherings that movements create are often radically more relational than the dry networking events and team-building exercises that pass for relationality in the corporate world. Examining how movements gather can teach us a great deal about how to create relational containers that work.

When someone shows up to a movement, whether they are showing up to Tahrir Square or a lecture about asexuality, they show up with a feeling of loneliness and powerlessness that they are ready to transform. This transformation cannot happen through listening alone; their personal story must be spoken, heard, and integrated with the story of the group. When working with the National Farm Workers Association, Marshall Ganz observed how leaders like Cesar Chavez organized farm workers that most unions had given up on.[7] Most organizers had come in, given passionate speeches about the benefits of unionization, and then passed out sign-up sheets to little avail. The National Farm Workers Association took a different approach. They told powerful stories of their own struggles and then asked others in the room to share. They wove those stories together to create a sense of shared identity and then explained why that identity was poised to make substantive change in the world. Ganz describes these three interweaving stories as:

The Story of Self

Organizers highlight the choice that everyone in the room has made to show up to the meeting. They tell a compelling personal story about why they have chosen to show up, one that illustrates how showing up to the movement has been transformational to both their internal and their external world. Then they invite others in the room to share. To manage time effectively, the room is generally broken up into groups of four to six, enough for everyone to be heard without spending an uncomfortable amount of time listening to others. If the movement is organizing around something meaningful, then most people will find that they have powerful stories to share. Personal struggles will come to the surface that could not be understood anywhere else, and in articulating these struggles, people will begin to feel them transform.

This culture of personal story is part of why, in my early twenties, I found movements such powerful places to form relationships. These stories provide a powerful map of the room and the opportunities for connection within it. They reveal who in the room I share a struggle with—often a struggle that both of us have been holding for years in isolation. They reveal who is still in a struggle that I have worked to overcome, highlighting powerful opportunities for mentorship.

Gone is the uncertainty about who in the room I should be talking to. Gone is the awkwardness of small talk as we try to fumble our way to an interesting topic of conversation. Good organizing efficiently highlights where everyone in the room can find conversations that get straight to the transformative path out of loneliness that they are seeking.

The exercise also trains people in movements to introduce themselves differently. Instead of opening with their employer, the city or neighborhood they hail from, and their favorite sports team, it is common in movement cultures I am part of to introduce oneself with a condensed version of challenge, choice, and outcome. If conversations are a search process to find topics that invite shared transformation through relationship, then these stories are an algorithm that reliably bears fruit.

The Story of Us

After organizers have had an opportunity to hear the stories of people in the room, they reflect back themes to the larger group. In the ace community, the fear of social isolation is often a theme that comes up, alongside frustration at a society that tells us that we are broken without sexuality. There is also often an insurgent joy at proving that society wrong, at showing that we can love and be loved fully outside of sexual scripts. When I name themes like this I will sometimes encourage people to raise their hands or snap if the theme resonates. I will call on people to briefly share to the entire group how this experience resonates with them.

After Stories of Self have been shared, they must be woven together to form a sense of collective identity, a shared struggle being addressed with shared values that lead to a shared sense of hope. Identities, like the word *asexual,* are tools that we use to understand ourselves and express our experiences to others. Everyone's identity is different, a unique reflection of their story, but it shares themes with others that make connection much easier. If I ask someone for the story of their aceness and share my own, we'll probably discover some ways of spending time together that are meaningful, since both of our stories are filled with related challenges we're facing and skills we've developed to overcome them. When properly rooted, an identity is a pointer to a Story of Self, a flag that says, "This person has a story that you're likely to resonate with, even if now is not the moment to share it."

Stories of Us and the identities they form also create a critical set of shared values. In most corporate institutions I have been part of, values are a list of words like *respect* and *efficiency* that are applied in the abstract or more often ignored. In the movements I have joined, values are intersecting personal stories that evoke a felt sense in the body. I can tell you that as an ace person I value relationship, but I have not communicated the value until I've shared a story about my journey away from loneliness that has created a sense of embodied resonance. Once you've felt it, this value is a powerful relational tool. It lets you predict which topics of conversation I'll find resonant and which I'll find dissonant. It gives you a great deal of information about how to offer me support and about what kind of support I might be seeking. It tells you a great deal about how to earn my respect and time on my calendar.

If we think of relationships as a process of exploration, differentiation, and selection, then shared values are a way for the differentiation functions of everyone in a movement to line up. Without any central coordinating authority, everyone in the movement has a shared sense of what they and others in the movement will find meaningful. If two people at the edge of a movement have a wild idea to create something that is aligned with the movement's values, they can accurately predict that this work will be recognized, respected, and rewarded. A strong Story of Us, rooted in a felt set of shared values, is the difference between a movement that splinters into hundreds of factions and one that evolves thousands of unique strategies to pursue an aligned but unpredictable outcome.

The other beautiful thing about our Stories of Us is that they evolve. When I knocked on the door of the head of my campus Queer Alliance, I was firmly outside an understanding of shared queer identity. People who talked about their queerness shared stories of sexual liberation and radically rejecting sexual shame, things that could hardly apply to someone identifying as asexual. But when I shared my story of struggling with compulsory sexuality, even though I did not yet have that exact phrase, it resonated with a shared value that was part of queerness. Did respecting the right not to be sexual, especially if that decision was part of a journey away from sexual shame, align with a value of sexual liberation? Did that feel right in the body? For several years, answers varied across queer communities, but eventually a consensus was reached that it did. Ace folks had a place in a collective queer identity because we resonated with queer values. Our ace stories had found their way into a broader story of us.

The Story of Now

Once a Story of Us has been established, organizers switch to telling a story about the moment we're living in. As organizer Grace Lee Boggs would often say, "What time is it on the clock of the world?" This Story of Now hinges on a choice. The people in the room can do nothing—they can go about their lives and see to the other worthwhile priorities in their lives, or they can choose to act. If they do nothing, the movement will fail, and a story of fear will unfold. The values revealed by the Story of Us that tie them together will be ignored and undermined, and a future will play out in which other, dissonant values hold the power to shape the world. But if they choose to act, then there is a possibility, sometimes slim and sometimes a near certainty, of a story of hope. In this story, the values that unite the people in the room spill out to shape the reality around them. A different future, one that reflects their shared values, becomes possible, and within that future, those who took action can expect connection, resilience, and transformation. In this future, their lives will abundantly embody the values that today they struggle to make real.

You are probably reading this book because you, like me, value relationship. I have not had the opportunity to hear the story of why you value it, but one day I hope to. You may also be reading this book because you, like me, are aware that we are facing a global crisis of social isolation. If things proceed as they are, if we fail to act, then that crisis of disconnection will get worse until it kills us. It will kill our bodies, kill our democracies, kill our capacity to meet the crisis of climate change, and then kill us in wars between petty autocrats over dwindling resources. But that fate is not inevitable. We can reconnect with the lineages of relational wisdom that are, as you read these words, being forgotten. We can study the science of relationship formation both scientifically and humbly to better interpret the wisdom that these lineages have to offer. We can teach the institutions that we are part of to invest resources in the necessary work of building relational containers, using both scientific insight and relational lineage as a guide. Once money is flowing, we can pursue new careers and entire new sectors of our economy dedicated to reliably creating the conditions for connection where connection is needed. In that future, a future of abundant access to relationship and widespread relational agency, our other values may thrive as well. Our health, our families, our communities, our schools, our democracies, and our relationship with the ecosystems that hold us may all be radically transformed for the better if we gain a richer capacity for connection. But we must come together and we must act.

If a room full of people only has a Story of Us, if all they've done is uncover a set of shared values, they can have good conversations but don't yet have a compelling reason to spend time together. All of their lives are probably filled with other priorities, and after the meeting they can easily go back to those priorities with a slightly improved sense of self-awareness. Without a Story of Now, the only people motivated to come back to a meeting are those facing acute personal struggle. The movement becomes a sort of self-help group and social club without a compelling sense of direction. With a Story of Now, the stakes of both action and inaction are clear. People, even people not facing an acute personal struggle, have a compelling reason to keep showing up and to collaborate around creative projects on the side. Everyone in the room suddenly has a reason to make time in their calendars for everyone else.

After a good Story of Now, people will usually glance around the room with excitement. They'll applaud the organizer, but their eyes will dart to everyone else. One of the most significant barriers to connection comes down to a kind of game theory. If I'm willing to put aside all of the other things that I could be spending my time doing to spend it with a particular person, will that person meet me with their own investment? If I put a commitment on the table, will the other person or people I'm with match that commitment and follow through? A well-executed Story of Now does the work of removing that uncertainty. It provides a clear path to transformation and a certainty that others will join you on that path. With that certainty comes a rush of relational agency. You came to the meeting because on some level some part of you is lonely, and now you know what it feels like for that lonely part of you to feel seen, woven into a community, and invited into relational agency. A clear path from that loneliness to connection and power stands before you. All you have to do is step into it. You will not be stepping alone.

Once these stories have been shared, the formal relational part of the meeting is over and the logistical portion can begin. Participants may break up into working groups to start planning an action, hear instructions about how to join an action that has already been planned, or roleplay conversations that they will have about the movement with others. I'll leave discussion of these facilitation tactics to other excellent resources to avoid this section ballooning too much in size. I recommend Momentum (www.momentumcommunity.org) and Movement Strategy Center (https://movementstrategy.org) as starting places. Instead I will fast-forward to the end of the meeting. At this point everyone is buzzing with a sense of relational possibility. They are excited, motivated, and have a concrete action plan for how they will contribute to the work. The organizer may manifest this energy in a song, a chant, or a primal scream followed by thunderous applause. Then the meeting is over and it's time to go home.

Don't.

Afterspaces

When the meeting ends, there may be a table with drinks and snacks waiting in the corner, or the organizer may shout out that anyone who wants to is welcome to join them at a restaurant down the street. From a relational standpoint, everything that has happened up until now, from storytelling to planning the actions that you will take to screaming at the top of your lungs together, has been setting the stage for the main event. As a participant you've learned who in the room has stories you might resonate with or is involved in actions that you might want to join. You've gained a huge amount of context about who in this community you might want to be in relationship with and how you might go about being in relationship with them, but you haven't actually had a space to make those relationships happen. Every moment of your time has been focused by the organizer and the structure of the meeting. The marvelous engine of relational prediction inside your skull hasn't been given the freedom to do what it does best. The afterspace is where it gets that freedom.

In my experience good afterspaces involve four components:

1. **There is a freedom to leave.** The room boils down to the most committed—in my experience often between 15 and 40 percent.

2. **There is freedom of movement.** People can talk to whoever they want to about whatever they want to. If the meeting has done a good job, then all an organizer needs to do is get out of their way, though sometimes it can be necessary to break up a large group conversation into clusters of two to four. Physical movement also helps people's bodies feel comfortable after sitting in a lengthy meeting.

3. **There is a distant end time.** The conversation keeps going as long as people are willing to stay or until the restaurant or bar closes, ideally not for several hours. It's fine if the organizer leaves before everyone else, though they should have a way to check in on what happened after they left and make sure that someone is there who is capable of addressing values-misaligned behavior and managing conflict.

4. **There is food.** After an energetic meeting, people are hungry, and if their conversations are good, they'll get hungrier. Sharing food also cements connections forming among the group.

Relationships take time to establish themselves: usually four to five hours at a minimum. If two people exchange contact information at the end of a meeting and are extremely motivated, the first of those hours may show up as a video call in the middle of their workdays two weeks after the buzz of the meeting has ended. Follow-ups can lead to relationships, but they face many barriers to success. In a good afterspace, those four to five hours happen right away, at the moment when people's minds and bodies are most primed to connect. The likelihood of relationship goes up, and with it the power of the movement to face hardship and enact transformation.

This tactic must also be used with caution. Parents of young children, no matter how motivated, may not have the flexibility to spend time after an event. A transition to an afterspace that is not wheelchair-accessible or is too loud for participants on the autistic spectrum may bar those people from participation. An afterspace at a bar may not be accessible to an alcoholic on a journey of recovery. These challenges are surmountable with creativity. An afternoon gathering in a park next to a playground may be great for parents, for example. No matter how accessible the afterspace I'm creating is to the people I want to organize, some motivated people will inevitably have other plans and leave. That's fine. The people I'm interested in are the people who stay, so long as people with important perspectives aren't being structurally excluded. The people who stay are most likely to form relationships and therefore have the greatest capacity to engage in acts of care and creative transformation. As an organizer I am constantly recruiting and mentoring the next generation of the movement's leadership, and afterspaces are the relational containers where that recruitment happens.

The Action Layer

The *Diagnostic and Statistics Manual,* or *DSM,* has a profound impact on the lives of queer folks around the world. Published by the American Psychiatric Association (APA), it is the definitive guide, both in the United States and for much of the rest of the planet, on what

constitutes a mental disorder. Until 1973 the document listed homosexuality as a disorder,[8] and it was only removed after extensive activism from the queer community. Its shift in 2013 from "gender identity
disorder" to "gender affirming care" helped lay the groundwork for
the necessary and life-saving gender-affirming care to which far too
many are still being denied access. In 2008, changing the DSM was
unimaginable to young queer upstarts like the ace community, especially when big pharma companies were actively working to oppose
us. To illustrate how movements take action, I want to share the story
of how we took on the DSM and won.

The office of the National Center for Transgender Equality is one
of the only places I have ever been recognized in an elevator. While
stopping by for a visit in 2008, an energetic intern clocked me as
"that asexual organizer" and ran to grab the executive director, Mara
Keisling. Mara was a DC powerhouse who had noticed the burgeon-
ing ace community and would, once or twice a year, swoop in for a
fifteen-minute conversation to nudge us in a helpful direction. I didn't
expect her to make time for me, but she grabbed us a meeting room
in the nearby National Gay and Lesbian Task Force. After spending
thirty seconds on a signature cheesy joke, she cut to the chase. "The
next edition of the DSM is getting written, and we're going after
gender identity disorder. You all should help us, and you should go
after hypoactive sexual desire disorder." I was floored. "Yeah, HSDD
is in there, but y'all have national infrastructure and institutional allies.
We're an online forum with a zine. There's no way we can take on
something this big." Mara looked at me and then checked her watch.
"You're ready," she said. "Go for it."

Hypoactive sexual desire disorder was the DSM's classification for
people who didn't like sex enough. Diagnosis with HSDD required
two conditions: not liking sex enough ("enough" was left to the dis-
cretion of the clinician) and "patient or partner distress." In other
words, if you didn't like sex and were worried about it, you had a
mental disorder. As a community awash in people who had been told
that they would spend their lives alone, we were all too familiar with
this distress, but the way to address it was to accept ourselves and

embrace an expanded definition of intimacy, not to force ourselves to want a thing we didn't want. Much worse was the inclusion of "partner distress." If a patient didn't experience sexual attraction and was fine with it, but it made their romantic partner uncomfortable, then the less sexual person had a disorder that required fixing. This highly questionable logic was included because the majority of patients diagnosed with HSDD were heterosexual women who were seeking treatment because their husbands told them that they weren't sexual enough. As I would soon learn, large pharmaceutical companies were developing a "female Viagra," a repurposed antidepressant that these women could use to severely alter their brain chemistry in order to marginally address this "problem." Treatments such as mindfulness meditation and improved communication with partners had already been proven to be vastly more effective at improving sexual experience and removing distress around low sexual desire than their pill, but these treatments could not be packaged and sold. Big pharma was also lobbying the APA, and the last thing they wanted was a bunch of aces parachuting in to mess up their diagnosis.

I maintained regular relationships with other activists in the ace community, including a bunch of promising organizers who were new to the community and eager to get involved. Out of this group I handpicked a *DSM* Task Force that included established ace researchers, respected leaders in the community with backgrounds in psychology and statistics, and an eager, capable newer member named Jessica who could project-manage and maintain momentum. The people we needed to get to, the Paraphilia Committee of the APA, were barred from speaking to community activists directly. One ally of ours who was on the committee, an incredible Canadian researcher named Dr. Lori Brotto, wrote back to share that she had to cease communication with us while the committee was active. So we hopped on a video call and came up with a plan.

As students of history, we knew that research mattered. Poorly designed and executed research on trans people had set the development of effective gender-affirming care back decades, and early on, the ace community had decided that we didn't want the same thing to happen to us. An eager community member named Andrew had started a team of research liaisons. When a social scientist who wanted to interview or survey members of our community came knocking, they were welcomed, vetted for ethics, and educated on how the ace community understood ourselves. We did not want to direct the research about our community; we wanted to learn from science as much as anyone, but we wanted to make sure that researchers interpreting data about us at least understood how we in the community interpreted that same data. As a result, we had close relationships with the authors of almost every research paper in existence on asexuality and knew that those papers universally supported the argument that we did not have a disorder.

The six of us began rallying these researchers and compiling their papers, reaching out to refine our case and ask for support. The members of the Paraphilia Committee couldn't talk to us, but we could compile a cohesive argument and send it to them. They could also talk to their colleagues in the research community, and it was there that we focused. We wanted the scientific argument against HSDD to be a surround sound from anyone in the research community who had bothered to look. While we were at it, we encouraged those researchers to read up on and speak about the need to recategorize gender identity disorder.

On the other side, big pharma was putting on the pressure at academic conferences. We would later learn about stacked panels and campaigns to undermine the legitimacy of researchers who had studied asexuality. But at the end of the day, the pharma lobbyists were outmatched. They had highly paid teams with high-level connections and years of experience, but when it came to this topic we had stronger supporting research and a broader network of trust. A volunteer team of six people that probably invested less than 250 hours in the project was enough to move the needle because we had the relationships that mattered, we knew how to use them, and we had the legacy of a powerful queer movement to build on.

HSDD was removed from the fifth edition of the *DSM,* although pharma companies were still able to push their drug through despite loud concerns about its effectiveness, only to meet abject failure in the marketplace.

In *Prisms of the People,* doctors Hahrie Han, Elizabeth McKenna, and Michelle Oyakawa explore why movements win. A systematic review of social movements identifies that much of what captures the public imagination, like mass protest and trending hashtags, is poorly correlated with victory. So are the things that most large movement-affiliated nonprofits ask for: signatures on email petitions, the size of newsletter lists, and the number of small-dollar donations (though such donations will play an important role later in this book). Movements win when they have the right relationships at the right time and a diverse network of leaders who can turn those relationships into action. In the case of the *DSM* task force, it took a few relationships: my connection to Mara Keisling to push us into action, Andrew's connections to researchers, and Jessica's efforts to keep us connected and focused while we juggled other priorities in the ace community and in our lives. We could not have predicted that trust with researchers over years could have resulted in this outcome, but we did it because it was aligned with our values, and one of us was passionate about doing it. To understand why movements have such a long history of driving social change, we must view them through this lens of relational rather than transactional strategy. Movements are not armies with generals who see opportunities and then deploy assets to exploit them. Movements are landscapes where values-aligned relationships are planted, nourished, and then mobilized in unexpected ways as reality shifts to meet them.

Hahn, McKenna, and Oyakawa describe this flowering of relational possibility as a "strategic choice set."[9] When movements build networks of relationships, especially if those relationships bridge lines of class, race, faith, and organizational affiliation, the number of strategic things that they can mobilize those relationships to do grows exponentially. What starts as a few people without real power or influence building a space for connection can steadily grow to a network of trust that is positioned to respond to a wide range of political conditions. Unlike a nonprofit or for-profit corporation, which would need to keep people on the payroll to maintain a particular strategic capacity, movements can maintain an extremely broad portfolio of people who show up, find the movement meaningful, and are ready to be mobilized at a moment's notice. Growing, maintaining, and eventually mobilizing these networks of trust takes work. It takes people who cook meals, mediate conflicts, welcome new members, and update websites. This work, both the slow work of growing relational capacity and the fast work of mobilizing it into action, is often done by small groups of friends called affinity groups.

Affinity Groups

In June of 2011 a group of one hundred Walmart workers from across the United States gathered to share their stories.[10] Most were low-wage workers who faced constantly changing shifts and uncertain health care. They drafted a "Declaration of Respect" that wove their stories together in a set of clear demands for how Walmart could change as an employer and then went back to their communities, eager to continue the work of storytelling and listening that had connected them. The Organization United for Respect at Walmart, or OUR Walmart, had begun.

Out of the original hundred organizers emerged those who began inviting fellow workers into small circles to share their stories and support one another. Marianne Manilov, a personal friend and mentor who consulted with OUR Walmart on organizing strategy, said that "we wanted to see how people were already supporting each other. We looked for informal places where people had a depth of trust and connection."[11] One member started a Facebook Group called "Treasures" that focused on positive affirmations and support, and the group became an entry point for people who were invited into deeper networks of care. Since many workers were facing acute struggles tied to poverty and a lack of health care, community care was often the first priority of these small groups. When one member was inappropriately discharged from a hospital, other members showed up to advocate for her and stay with her, ensuring that she received care that eventually saved her life.

This focus on being there for one another was encouraged among OUR Walmart's leaders. Those who focused primarily on providing care were respected alongside those who engaged more directly in action, though often the two were linked. Andrea Dehlendorf, co-director of OUR Walmart, states that "OUR Walmart focuses on people leading in whatever ways they lead, not just people taking specific actions like signing a petition or going to a march. A distributive network like this builds on existing relationships and pushes power to the edges rather than trying to centralize it."[12]

From these local networks of care, opportunities for meaningful action began to emerge. In 2013, Walmart Associate Girshriela Green became pregnant and was afraid that if she informed her manager, she would lose her job or put her baby's health at risk. After connecting with other Walmart workers who had been fired because of pregnancy or forced to do heavy lifting despite doctors' notes, Girshriela cofounded an OUR Walmart affinity group called "Respect the Bump." What started as a small support group quickly grew into a series of meetings and events, then a campaign calling for Walmart to change their policies. Respect the Bump members were profiled in the *Washington Post* and invited to the Obama White House, applying enough pressure that Walmart shifted their policies to allow people with high-risk pregnancies to receive accommodations, a policy that Respect the Bump continued to fight to expand.

As OUR Walmart's small networks of care continued to expand and overlap, they were able to exert substantial pressure on the world's largest employer, winning $1 billion in wage increases for 500,000 workers. This required embracing strategic opportunities like the Respect the Bump campaign, which emerged out of small affinity groups. Because Walmart workers had a place to show up, be heard, and receive care, they were committed to showing up and building power.

In the broadcast layer, people are numbers: email list sizes, click-through rates, and event sign-ups in a massive funnel that leads toward gathering. In the gathering layer, they are stories: a fluid of insight, struggle, and opportunity that the movement can learn and draw resources from. In the action layer, they are strategic capacity. Once individuals have been pulled into affinity groups, they are accountable to the relationships that keep them there and the values on which those relationships are built, not to any central authority. If any one of those affinity groups comes across a strategic opportunity that furthers the transformative goals of the movement and resonates with its values, they can, barring internal fracturing and inaccessibility, quickly pull in people from other affinity groups to mobilize resources and take action. Like the academic researchers mobilized to change the *DSM,* the relationships that exist across a movement are ready, at least in principle, for any affinity group in the movement to mobilize into action. Doing so will deepen those relationships and make the movement stronger so long as, like a muscle, these relationships do not exceed their capacity and have time to rest.

When affinity groups hold a coherent set of values, and the inevitable conflicts between them are managed generativity, they can feel euphoric. In *Twitter and Teargas,* Zeynep Tufekci writes that during the 2013 civil unrest in Turkey, many stayed in Istanbul's Gezi Park not only because they wished to protest the government, but because life being teargassed in the 24-7 relational container of tents and affinity groups was vastly preferable to the more comfortable routine of their jobs and apartments.

> *Gezi Park was frequently teargassed, and I witnessed significant injuries to some protesters, including life-threatening head traumas. Many people lost their sight to tear gas canisters that were shot directly at them rather than angled into the sky, as police are supposed to do in order to avoid such injuries. Overall, seven protesters died in the protests around the country from various causes … [but] many described the protests as the best days of their lives—not as a means to dismiss the deaths, but as a description of the meaning they found in collective rebellion. Similarly, the "Gezi spirit" is talked about with nostalgia and longing.*
>
> *Obviously, protesters are not pining for death or threats, but rather for the interruption of ordinary life they experience under conditions*

of mutual altruism. Many protesters I talk with especially hold dear the moments when a total stranger helped them through tear gas, pressurized water, live bullets, camel attacks, or whatever came their way. For many, the protest is the pinnacle of an existential moment of solidarity when strangers become family, united in rebellion. For many, that feeling of solidarity is a core part of why they protest; rebellion is a place for extraordinary communities, however brief or lengthy they may be. And the participatory impulse is not an after-thought, but another dimension of those extraordinary communities, however long they last.[13]

If relationships are central to how humans (and all living organisms) survive, thrive, and create, then the affinity group structures of a move-ment, especially when those affinity groups are aligned and resourced, provides a rare opportunity for people to experience the transforma-tive and healing power that those relationships can bring. People do not only participate in movements because they believe in the cause; they participate because believing in that cause with others unlocks relationships that feel amazing. While those in the broadcast layer are content to simply hear stories about those relationships from afar, and those in the gathering layer experience them in periodic events, those who earn trust in the action layer experience these relationships to their fullest potential.

As with all relational lineages, the wisdom that movements hold can provide inspiration about how relationships can be built any-where, from petri dishes to preschools. Critically, the action layer of movements provides a hint at how the work required to create rela-tional environments can be self-reproducing and therefore scalable. An intervention to address loneliness that invests heavily in relation-ships with just eight people hardly seems scalable, but if those eight people each seed new affinity groups, it quickly can be. And while the exploration of affinity groups described here is rooted in a movement lineage, similar structures are common elsewhere. Faith communities recruit committee members out of fellowship gatherings that take place after services. Fan communities flourish in the late-night afterparties of a convention, forming bonds of trust that will fuel creative marvels throughout the year, and which companies like Disney will be more than happy to harvest. Seeing these structures and encouraging their growth can unlock immensely powerful strategies to not only invest in relationship, but to change the world while doing it.

The very significant caveat to the power of action-layer affinity groups comes in keeping them at least loosely aligned. As different groups of friends with different life experiences evolve new and powerful strategies, their values and priorities will inevitably diverge. While many resources are self-generating, some are not: signal boosting on physical stages and social media, the time and attention of well-regarded organizers, or the usually very limited discretionary budget to which movement leaders have access. As movements grow in size and complexity, disagreements over values and related struggles over resources can spiral out of control, creating fractures that weaken a movement or tear it apart entirely. While affinity groups that are aligned and manifesting their power feel euphoric, affinity groups caught in a toxic spiral of fragmentation and infighting can be deeply traumatizing. These internal conflicts are not necessarily bad; generative conflict can be an important part of how movements evolve their thinking. But conflicts that lose sight of a movement's core values can become immensely destructive. This need for cohesion and conflict management leads to the final layer of social movements discussed in this chapter, one generally reserved for affinity group members who have earned widespread trust and respect.

The Cohesion Layer

I was able to spend only one afternoon at New York City's Zuccotti Park during Occupy Wall Street in the fall of 2011, although I spent more time in the Occupy camp in Justin Herman Plaza in San Francisco. When I visited, the park was packed with people, many holding or making signs, many organized into affinity groups that provided mutual aid services such as food, medical care, or education. One group in particular caught my attention. They sat behind a table, wore blue vests, and were trained experts in nonviolent communication (NVC). They offered NVC training services to anyone who was interested and were available to mediate conflicts if people wanted help.

An hour or so after I swung by the NVC table and asked questions, I heard yelling. A fight had broken out, and the crowd around them had swarmed to intervene. Like most of the people around me, I looked over to see two men being physically separated by about six people while the call went out for mediators. Calmly but firmly asking for a path, the two NVC experts in blue vests parted the crowd and arrived at the scene, splitting up to each engage with one of the parties in conflict. The crowd calmed and began to go about its business, while a few volunteers stayed on hand to make sure that the mediators were adequately supported.

In the heart of a movement, I had just witnessed something that few outside my friends in the prison abolition movement had ever named as possible: an organized response to violence that did not involve more violence, incarceration, excommunication, or even a centralized authority. The nonviolent communication rapid response team was not the cops of Occupy; they did not enforce laws determined by a central body. Instead they resolved conflict in a way that aligned with the broader values of the movement. Participants in Occupy ranged from anarchists to libertarians to unhoused folks of no strong political affiliation who had come to share food and wisdom. Conflicts, ideological and otherwise, were commonplace, but there was strong reason to share a mutual dislike of violent policing.

To maintain its cohesion, the camp developed a way to resolve conflicts that not only reflected its shared values but leveraged those shared values to manage disagreements in ways that would otherwise have been impossible. No one person or executive council decided that mediators were the way that conflicts would be resolved. A shared sense of values alignment from the members of the camp meant that the mediation affinity group received support that other affinity groups did not, which made them an established part of the camp's infrastructure. This meant that the camp was more resourced in its ability to resolve conflict without relying on a central authority, trusting in its shared values and the strength of its relationships to keep the movement aligned and effective.

Movements can employ a wide range of leadership strategies, from powerful union bosses to the highly decentralized anarchists who opposed the World Trade Organization during the 2007 Battle in Seattle. In recent decades, many successful movements have tended toward a nonhierarchical approach. One researcher described the environmentalist movement of the 1970s as "having multiple, often temporary, and sometimes competing leaders or centers of influence,"[14] while movement scholar Darcy Leach argues that "the real problem is not how to avoid the tyranny of structurelessness, but how to sustain structures of tyrannylessness."[15] There is a pull, particularly in the progressive social movements to which I owe lineage, to imagine and practice means of maintaining strategic direction and group cohesion that replace centralized authority with a sophisticated understanding of the power of relationship.

In *The Purpose of Power,* activist Alicia Garza, one of the founders of the Black Lives Matter movement, describes the intentional choice not to center the movement on any central publicly recognizable figures like Martin Luther King Jr., Malcolm X, or Huey P. Newton.[16] Such leaders became single points of failure, vulnerable to either co-opting by the state, corruption from within, or in the case of all three leaders listed above, assassination. Instead, Garza argues for a "leader–full" structure:

> *Black Lives Matter designates itself a leader-full organization. That means that there isn't one leader but many. This isn't just rhetoric. Each chapter has chapter leads, and those leads develop leadership inside their chapters. They make decisions about the work of their own chapters, but they also help to make decisions about the activities and the positions of the larger network. And they reject the notion that one leader, or even three, can speak for all or make decisions for all. Trust me—I know this from firsthand experience. Leaders within Black Lives Matter will tell you that I am not the leader, and they will remind me of this fact as well if they believe I am unilaterally*

speaking for the network. I have become much more deliberate about being transparent about what opinions are mine and what statements are official—debated on and decided by the network itself.

Decentralization also has another purpose, however. It allows for an organization—or a group of people trying to accomplish something together, if you will—to get ideas, leadership, strategy, and input from more people. From that perspective, decentralization is simply smarter: It opens your organization to the contributions of everyone.[17]

This level of decentralization is unthinkable in most of our institutions. While some corporations include relatively flat structures, they still maintain a CEO who holds final say over company strategy and who resolves otherwise unresolvable conflicts. Sociologist Max Weber, who coined the term *bureaucracy,* argued that rigid hierarchies with strict rules are the only efficient way for large numbers of people to coordinate their work,[18] and most modern institutions seem to agree. Yet, without such rules or formal leadership, the Black Lives Matter movement created the largest protest movement in US history,[19] dramatically altering the national dialogue on systemic racism and policing in a way that more bureaucratically professional institutions had been trying and failing to do for decades. With no central leadership to make and enforce rules, what kept the movement aligned enough to be so effective? With so many leaders providing so much strategic input, what stood in the way of that infighting tearing the movement apart?

Movements do not have a hierarchy of command, like an army with generals, but they do have a loose hierarchy of reputation. Some people in the action layer, because they have successfully enacted the movement's values, gain trust and recognition from those around them. They may not command budgets or staff, but their names are known and their voices are heard. If they are effective leaders, they also listen. They hear the stories of new people joining the movement and have regular check-ins with affinity group leaders who look to them for advice and support. They do not speak for the movement, but their voices are louder than those who are showing up for the first time because they have put in the work to build trust.

It is the job of these more trusted leaders to absorb what is happening both within and outside the movement and reflect it back as a cohesive story, aligned with the movement's values, that weaves everyone else's work together. For movements to stay united, they must maintain a cohesive Story of Us and Story of Now, and it is the role of these trusted individuals to cohere it. Often these people in the middle are friends, but they can and should have disagreements. Based on what they hear and how they synthesize, they share different stories out to the movement, different evolutions of the movement's values and strategic next steps. Some of these stories resonate strongly with the embodied values of the movement's participants. They inspire affinity groups into action and mobilize resources through trusted relationships to create change. Others resonate less strongly or strike a dissonant chord. These stories fail to build trust and may even harm the reputation of the central figure who articulated them. Central leaders who fail to align with the movement's values, or who simply opt to pass on the torch, will fade from centrality and create room for new leaders to emerge.

Resources in a movement are spread out among the hearts, minds, and affinity groups of its members rather than accumulated in a centralized headquarters or bank account. As a result, leaders only hold power to the extent that they continually mobilize those resources by speaking to the movement's values. These values, stored in the minds and bodies of the movement's membership and expressed through its relationships, are the guiding force that sets the movement's direction, not the whims of those in positions of relative leadership. If any one charismatic leader emerges, a Dr. King or a Malcolm X, then there is a risk that this accountability to values might be broken. The movement may devolve into a cult of personality, or if that leader is removed, it may create a vacuum that other leaders are unable to fill. When shared values and a strong network of relationships are in place across the movement, it is preferable to have many leaders articulating different strategies so that those in the movement can decide which resonates most strongly and vote with their feet. It is preferable for these positions of central influence to be held temporarily so that room is made for new perspectives and so that the taxing work of being central in a movement can give way to the more spacious work of conflict mediation and mentorship.

For a time, I played a role in the cohesion layer of the ace community, but these days I am mostly retired. I spent several years as the community's poster child, speaking to the press and strategizing about our public story. When opportunities like the *DSM* Task Force were put before me, I was well positioned to mobilize the resources necessary to bring them to fruition. But I did my best not to cling to this position. The ace community has never been my paid job. We intentionally chose not to raise a large budget and hire professional staff. Our highly impactful, globe-spanning network runs on a budget of about $3,000 a year in server fees, which are collected through crowdfunding. As a result, stepping back from leadership in the community did not mean giving up my livelihood or sense of self-worth. After the *DSM* campaign of 2008, I gradually shifted my focus to other projects, other movements, and my uncertain journey toward family. The movement too was ready for new leadership. Today the most recognizable face in the ace community is Yasmin Benoit, a Black asexual activist from Britain whose work has created a new wave of awareness and forced the community to grapple with internalized racism. A distributed network of leaders maintains our servers, organizes gatherings, and maintains a presence across the internet while I occasionally serve as a mentor or dabble in an affinity group working on an interesting project. Because our movement pursued leaderful strategies, stepping back from central leadership after a period of time was both straightforward and necessary.

The powerful history of nonviolence in movements resisting authoritarian power is a testament to this improved capacity to manage conflict. Nonviolence is not a vow that movements and their participants take to remain morally pure; it is a set of sophisticated strategies for managing and de-escalating conflict that can prove tremendously resilient and effective. When facing authoritarian regimes, nonviolent movements are ten times as likely as violent ones to result in democratic change.[20] Nonviolence does not mean the absence of conflict, nor does it mean the absence of the perception of violence. For example, Black protestors may be labeled as violent for engaging in behavior that would be labeled as nonviolent if performed by white protesters. Nonviolence is a set of strategies for actively engaging in conflict while minimizing the risk that that conflict will escalate to violence. Often this conflict is necessary to prevent ongoing violence by the state, so avoiding conflict is not a meaningful way to avoid violence. The fact that this capacity for nonviolence within movements has such a long and powerful history of success hints at the ways in which movements may hold wisdom not only about how to create the conditions for shared creativity, but about how to create a widespread understanding of how to avoid being creative in ways that cause harm. Movements with the capacity for nonviolence are generally decentralized, but a set of shared values, principles, and peer education helps individuals within a movement assess where risks of violence exist and understand how to engage in conflict while minimizing that risk.

When a movement is skilled at generative conflict, powerful new forms of governance become possible. The values that live in peoples bodies can be articulated and the tensions between them worked out without relying on a central authority or demanding homogeneity among a movement's members. The movement can hold a diversity of participants and of strategies while working toward a shared set of values. It can evolve far faster than centrally controlled organizations, and this high evolutionary rate can be a source of immense power. This is one reason why, throughout history, movements that are massively outresourced by authoritarian organizations have won.

Like so many of the world's other relational lineages, movements are extraordinary. They can unlock unparalleled creativity, take on society's most powerful institutions and win, and take on entrenched systemic challenges in a way that no other organizational form can match. What's more, they do all of these things while cultivating relationships that invite millions out of loneliness, healing their bodies, minds, and spirits and creating ripples in culture and community that echo far beyond their immediate goals. And while they do these things with shockingly few financial resources, I will argue that they succeed despite a lack of money and not because of it. People in movements need to make rent. They need to buy food for their kids and their community's kids. They need resources to pass on in mutual aid and free time to devote to organizing. And when organizers either go without income or try to balance organizing with an unrelated job or jobs, they get burned out. The movements we see today, powerful as they are, are a small fraction of what would be possible if the people keeping those movements alive were financially supported for the powerful impact that they create.

Given their effectiveness, we would expect a substantial portion of the roughly $500 billion in annual US philanthropic giving to flow toward movements organizing. We could expect the $5 billion deployed in US presidential campaigns to go largely toward the relational organizing that has proven a reliable path toward victory, and a substantial portion of the money invested in corporate social responsibility to flow toward the work of movements. If it was, it is possible that we would not be facing the crisis of social isolation that is becoming a steadily greater threat to our individual health and collective survival. The fact that we do live in that world points to the fact that, in the vast majority of cases, financial institutions either fail to invest in relational work entirely or do so with stipulations that undermine its effectiveness. If the path out of the social isolation crisis involves resourcing lineages of relational wisdom and the people who put them into action, we must contend with why such investments so often fail.

Reflection Questions

- Which communities and movements do you choose to show up for?

- How do these communities and movements contribute to your personal journey?

- What values hold these communities and movements together?

- What experiences in your life have led you to hold these values?

- What do these communities have to teach you about how to:

  - tell stories?

  - bring people together?

  - take action?

  - mediate conflict around shared values?

- Where are there gaps in this ability to broadcast stories, gather, take action, or build cohesion that you might help to fill?

- Who might you invite in to help share this work?

CHAPTER 6

Why We Fail to Invest in Relationship

IN EARLY 2015 I attended a panel discussion at the Ford Foundation on best practices for funding social movements. The setting was intimidating: the top floor of a towering Manhattan building with a gaping central atrium. The foundation's recently appointed president, Darren Walker, gave a speech designed to counteract the aura of the architecture. This was not a time for the field of philanthropy to speak with expertise and authority, but a time to listen and learn.

Six months earlier, Michael Brown had been murdered on the streets of Ferguson, Missouri, just a few minutes north of the home where I grew up. The resulting waves of protest in Ferguson were moving forward an agenda around racial injustice and mass incarceration that many program officers in the room had been struggling to strategize around and fund for decades. Systems change is slow, difficult work, and even experts with hundreds of millions of dollars to dispense had struggled to move the needle. Now thousands of activists were forming affinity groups in church basements in Missouri, and few could deny that the needle was jumping.

Although others across the philanthropic sector had reservations about this upstart movement knocking the pieces around their carefully arranged chessboards, there was little debate among the panelists that the waves of action happening in Ferguson were worth funding. In many cases, the growing movement was directly aligned with their institutions' strategic goals and with their personal passions, and there was general agreement that church basements in Missouri were currently where some of the most critical work around racial justice was happening. There was just one problem.

Moving money took work. A typical large foundation might seek to give away funding in at least the $200,000 range to organizations with a multiyear track record in a grant cycle that could easily take eighteen months. Those eighteen months would be filled with substantial amounts of highly skilled labor on both the grantor and grantee sides, as program officers and development directors reviewed and refined the details of a proposal and got buy-in from their respective teams, not counting the sometimes years of brand-building and trust-building required before a grant was first submitted and the years of detailed reporting that would come after. Grants had to be fairly large because the work of giving and receiving them did not scale. A smaller grant might easily be dwarfed by the cost on both sides of writing, reviewing, and refining the application. But activists in Ferguson didn't need $200,000 eighteen months after they had built established organizations; they needed $2,000 in the next forty-eight hours.

Several smaller community organizations were quick to point out that this sort of rapid-response funding was not only possible but was already happening. They had invested time in building trusting relationships with activists on the ground and those who knew and supported them, and they had convened boards of these trusted activists to help direct funding. When the protests in Ferguson had begun, these trusted networks had been activated, and money, along with other forms of support, had begun to flow through them to the places it was needed, even if the resources available to flow in this way were relatively meager. To staff at larger institutions, this focus on relationship and trust seemed great in theory but difficult to navigate in practice. These program officers were besieged from all sides by people interested in building trust with them to access their money. Deciding which of these people to make time for, let alone which of them to fund, required a rigorous and labor-intensive process of strategic justification to their governing boards. Simply making friends with people who seem to be doing values-aligned work and deploying money to them, or more scandalously yet giving them some agency over the grantmaking process, seemed dangerously unaccountable. Still, few could deny that organizations moving at the speed of bureaucracy were failing to get the job done while institutions moving at the speed of trust were.

For the small community foundations and the movements with which they shared lineage, relationship was core to the way that resources were moved. By tracking who in the movement was building relationship, resolving conflict, and weaving together stories in ways that aligned with their values, they could make strategic decisions about who to build trust with and then lean on that trust to quickly deploy resources, receive information, or be held accountable when accountability was warranted. This trust-building took time, but it paid off when information and resources suddenly needed to move quickly. For larger, generally better resourced foundations, this kind of relational thinking seemed dangerously unprofessional. To them, professional grantmaking hinged on the ability to make a prediction about impact and justify it to others. An ideal grantee worked like a factory, pumping out changes in the world in a way that was reliable, scalable, and low-risk. They could look at possible grantees' records to understand what sort of impactful products or services they were capable of creating, and they could strategically invest in expansions of those products and services, but they had no idea how to translate information about relationships into a precise prediction of where and how impact would happen. Their money could not move toward the work of building relationship even when everyone in the room agreed that that's what it should be doing.

It's Hard to Fund Something Unpredictable

In chapter 3 we introduced the curse of transactionality, the idea that we can predict the conditions that will lead to relationship but not where those relationships will lead. Every decision to allocate capital, whether a philanthropic grant or a child's birthday present, is based on a kind of prediction. As individuals, we have little trouble deploying resources based on a relational prediction: we invest in flying to visit an old friend or go all out to host a massive family barbecue. These investments in relational containers are difficult to justify in terms of ROI. We can't predict precisely how the relationships we're investing in will come back to benefit us, but we know on an intuitive and often a conceptual level that our investments are creating the conditions for relationships that will make our lives better. When networks of people deploy resources this way, as often happens in social movements and networks of mutual aid, they are engaging in a sophisticated form of relational prediction. Organizers see not only where relationships are but where they could be: where lonely people could be connected, where conflicts could be smoothed over, where sites of emerging possibility could be nurtured. Then they deploy resources in the form of time, money, food, music, mentorship, and a myriad of other skills to create the conditions where those possible relationships can come to pass.

This practice of relational prediction sits in fundamental mathematical tension with the kind of prediction that many institutions use to invest. Transactional prediction is primarily concerned with the specific state of the world, not the relationships that continually shape it. Like a pool player lining up a shot, transactional prediction seeks to turn a precisely controlled intervention into a precisely predicted outcome. A rural community has to walk to get clean drinking water? Let's build them some pipes. Literacy rates are dropping? Let's invest in software that is proven to make reading fun and then buy kids iPads. Transactional investment hinges on the ability to know what, precisely, your money is buying and why it will create the outcome you want. These investments often come with risks, but these risks are things to be managed and minimized. In a complex and chaotic world, transactional prediction is often only possible when elaborate systems of monitoring and control allow deviations from the expected outcome to be quickly recognized and corrected, like a mechanic fine-tuning an engine. To prove that something is worth investing in, one generally needs to be able to precisely predict the outcome, provide a clear plan for how that outcome will be achieved, and demonstrate an understanding of possible risks and the way that those risks will be managed.

These two modes of prediction are in tension because there is an unavoidable trade-off between predictability and relationality. If you throw an amazing party, people will jostle your pool table. If your top priority is ensuring that everything goes according to plan, there is a limit to how great a party you can host. Successfully investing in relationship undermines the conditions for transactional prediction because relationships create outcomes that are aligned but unpredictable. To be in balanced relationship, we must both change and be changed, and this equitable distribution of power undermines the conditions for precise monitoring and control. The systems of monitoring and control necessary to ensure that things go according to plan will see all but the least disruptive forms of relationship as sources of uncertainty and risk to be eliminated.

This trade-off between relationality and predictability is at the heart of why so many attempts to fund movements and communities fail. Though this chapter will focus largely on failures in philanthropy and political organizing, similar failures abound in health care, education, government, and the corporate world. In all of these places, individuals, including those in positions of power, recognize the resilient and transformative power of relationship. If they are worried about employee retention in the face of a turbulent labor market, if they want to drive cross-disciplinary innovation in their research institution, if they want to improve the conditions for struggling small business in their community or support an art scene that will boost the local economy, they will try to invest in relationship. But when they seek to deploy capital, they'll look for an appealing transactional investment to deploy it to: one with a clearly defined outcome and a plan to minimize risk but little shared understanding of what it means for relationships to happen or how to engage with and support those relationships that already exist. It's spending millions on a conference promoting cross-disciplinary collaboration only to pack people into a lecture hall where they are forbidden to speak. It's supporting the local arts scene creating an art expo in which local artists are selected by outside consultants and dragged on stage while the people already convening and supporting those artists are extracted from and sidelined.

In the summer of 1999, one of Seattle's largest rape crisis centers, Seattle Rape Relief, closed its doors after twenty-seven years in operation.[1] Several former volunteers, aware of the need to support survivors of sexual and domestic violence, founded Communities Against Rape and Abuse (CARA), which saw community organizing as a powerful tool to increase support for survivors. Their work focused on creating resilience and transformative healing by building relationships among community members and seeing where those relationships took them. As described by Alicia Bierria in *The Revolution Will Not Be Funded*, CARA's focus on relationships among survivors and between survivors and staff organically built power within the community.

> *We prioritize leadership development among the people we organize, which results in many of those individuals eventually being hired as interns or staff, or becoming board members. We organize regular community gatherings, parties, and meals to facilitate community building among CARA workers, our families, our constituents, and even the people who live in the neighborhood where our office is located. CARA's office location is not confidential and is instead open to organizational members; they can come in, use computers and other resources, or hang out in the meeting space to work on projects, peruse our library, watch videos, have conversations and debates,*

or just take a nap. We attend weddings, funerals, baby showers, and graduations of our members. We have arguments and conflicts among staff, among members, and between staff and members, and we figure out ways to move through it.[2]

These networks of support and power among survivors of domestic violence were not content simply providing services to other survivors; emerging leaders wanted to focus on the root causes of violence in their community. Members began creating education and advocacy campaigns. When a racist program sought to sterilize women currently or formerly addicted to drugs, the community recognized it as a form of violence and pushed back.[3] After connecting with the broader antiviolence movement, they began to partner with organizations that shared their values, openly critiquing the role of prisons in perpetuating gender violence and organizing "community-based accountability responses to sexual and domestic violence as alternatives to the criminal justice system."[4]

As has been true in movements throughout history, healing together led to relationships that built power, and that power demanded expression. It was common for those who arrived seeking services to become leaders in the community or eventually staff.

For example, one CARA member is a young Chicana who was first interested in CARA as a survivor of abuse, but then became intimately involved in the CARA community by participating in events or simply hanging out at the CARA space and building projects such as women's poetry and spoken word groups. She was eventually hired as a part-time organizer.[5]

CARA's focus on community organizing began to grow a rich relational ecology for survivors of violence, and people took notice. Local government officials, impressed with the community's impact, approached the organizers to offer a funding relationship. But the discussions hit a roadblock. When the government funder sent CARA a Request for Proposal (RFP), they referred to the survivors in CARA's community as "customers" and requested a concrete definition of

the "products" that CARA would offer to serve them.[6] Funders pressured the organization to hire staff that was more professional: outside
experts with masters' degrees in social work rather than fellow survivors from the local community. Funders objected to the growing list
of activities that the community was engaged in, some of which were
politically controversial, and pressured them to focus on defining and
efficiently delivering a consistent core service.

Like many movements and other communities, CARA was an
ecology, a growing garden that was fruiting an increasingly diverse
mix of art, mutual aid, and political power centered on its shared
struggle and values. This ecology was beginning to put down roots
that could not only heal survivors of violence but address the systemic
causes of that violence, both goals that funders, on some level, shared.
If a funder's goal had been to build relationships with the power to
heal and prevent domestic violence, then these signs of a healthy ecology would have been a compelling reason to build trust and move
resources. But funders did not see a garden; they saw an overgrown
factory. The community was clearly producing a valuable service, but
they needed to focus on defining and standardizing that core product and clear all of the extraneous projects away, especially those that
introduced risk of political blowback. Buried within CARA's messy
ecology was a core product or service, something that could reliably
and consistently help survivors of domestic violence heal, and the next
step for the organization was to refine and standardize that product
so that it could be delivered efficiently at scale. To execute that transition, CARA would need to bring in qualified professionals, people
with degrees who understood service delivery and client management
and who could ensure that clients received a clinical experience that
met the industry's standards of care.

This kind of clinical environment would have been much more
predictable, much less risky, and much less relational. Survivors may
have connected in chance encounters in the waiting room; they
would have been explicitly barred from forming supportive personal
relationships with staff, and would have had no voice in the organization's operations beyond the occasional feedback form. This relational

environment is almost certainly less effective than a community of thriving relationships, especially when it comes to addressing the systemic causes of gender violence, but it is easier to predict. The problem is not that trained clinicians and dependable operations have nothing to offer a community like CARA; they almost always do. The problem is not transactional prediction either: if the goal is to disinfect a wound or prepare a meal for a hundred people, then by all means, pursue an efficient path to a predictable outcome. The problem is that these more transactional strategies are institutionally prioritized even when they are less effective. When funding institutions see thriving communities as overgrown factories, when they use the tools of transactional prediction to assess efforts that grow and succeed through relationship, the result is funding that either does not move or comes with constraints that kill the communities it moves to.

This need not be the case. We can and should live in a world where a community that is a thriving source of relationship can go to funders not with a funding proposal promising a precise outcome, but concrete proof that their community is good at building relationships that the world needs. Funding institutions, whether they exist in philanthropy, political organizing, corporate innovation, or health care, should have an opinion about what kinds of relationships create the kind of transformation and resilience that they wish to see in the world, and should be more than happy to deploy resources to people who are capable of making those relationships happen. Institutions with money should be able to switch between using transactional prediction and relational prediction in the scenarios where each are appropriate, but they don't. From Facebook to philanthropic foundations, wealthy institutions whose explicit goal is to support communities and movements draw almost exclusively on the tools of transactional prediction to do so, even when those tools are clearly less effective.

It's worth naming that the concept of effectiveness here is a bit nuanced. There are times when wealthy funders genuinely do not want movements to succeed because that success would undermine the systems that allow them and their wealthy friends to maintain power, but this is not always the case. It would be overly naive to think that funders only want what's best for movements, even when those movements are toppling the systems that keep them in power, and overly cynical to think that all wealthy people's desire to support movements is disingenuous.

Funder Power in the Civil Rights Movement

In "The Price of Civil Rights: Black Lives, White Funding and Movement Capture," Megan Ming Francis recounts the story of the relationship of the National Association of Colored People (NAACP) with its primary philanthropic funder during the first half of the twentieth century, the white-led Garland Fund.[7] In 1922, when the funding relationship began, the NAACP was a member-led organization whose strategic goals reflected the priorities of its membership: economic empowerment and addressing anti-Black violence. Thirty-two years later, the NAACP would achieve a significant legal victory in *Brown v. Board of Education,* a historic victory in an area that was far from the top priority of a membership still facing widespread violence. Francis traces how decisions by the Garland Fund shifted its focus away from its successful and member-driven anti-lynching work to a legal battle around education driven mostly by a professional legal team.

As funders go, the Garland Fund was unusually focused on radical social change. According to Francis:

> *In 1919, Charles Garland refused his million-dollar inheritance, declaring he would not take money from "a system, which starves thousands while hundreds are stuffed." A supporter of the American Left, Garland did not want to take part in an exploitative capitalist system which he "wanted to destroy" but eventually accepted the money after Baldwin convinced him it could be put to use in a national trust "directed to social and economic freedom" of the masses. There were no rigid restrictions placed on the funds, but there were two charges by Garland meant to guide the administrators of the fund in their grant-making duties. The first was "that the money*

should be distributed as fast as it can be put into reliable hands."
Garland had little interest in the maintenance of a long-standing
foundation that would dole out small grants over time; he felt there
were plenty of worthy causes that would greatly benefit from money
in the present. The second was that the funds be used "to the benefit
of mankind—to the benefit of poor as much as rich, of black as much
as white, of foreigners as much as citizens, of so-called criminals as
much as the condemned." As far as Garland was concerned, building
a just social order required the Fund to ally itself with some of the
most marginalized groups in American society.[8]

Garland collected prominent radical activists to form a governing
board, though only one of these activists was Black. This board was
not threatened by the NAACP's anti-lynching work; it was this work
that brought the NAACP to their attention and inspired an initial
round of funding. In the NAACP, the Garland Fund saw everything
it was looking for: a growing national movement working to build
around a more just social order. The NAACP conducted a far-reaching
education campaign designed to challenge white complicity in the
process of lynching, pursued a federal anti-lynching bill, and won a
landmark case in 1923, *Moore* v. *Dempsey,* which established for the
first time that the presence of a violent mob in a courtroom violated
a defendant's right to a fair trial.[9] These victories were all recognized
and celebrated by the Garland Fund as aligned with its core values.

A wrinkle came just a few months later when a member of Garland's board became "frustrated with the snail's pace of radical progress amidst the numerous grants the Fund had administered."[10] Simply
responding to grants from prospective grantees was not going to
bring about the systemic change that the board was seeking; they
would need to take bold, decisive action to bring about change. The
board divided into subcommittees and came up with plans to create
the kind of radical change that their shared values demanded. One
of these plans focused on education. None, in a board with only one
Black member, focused on lynching. Emboldened with its new strategic clarity, the board began to shift its funding to align with its

new grand strategy. The NAACP pushed back, trying to creatively reframe its anti-lynching advocacy as public education about the atrocities of lynching, but the reframe only got them so far. Areas of work such as anti-lynching campaigns that were values-aligned but adjacent to Garland's plan were allowed for a time but defunded when resources became scarce. The goal was radical change, and the only path to that change that Garland's board could see clearly involved a plan that centered education. Struggling to find other sources of funding, the NAACP acquiesced, refocusing their efforts on a professionally staffed, educationally focused effort that was legible to and aligned with their funder, even if it was poorly aligned with their membership.

This process, which Francis refers to as *movement capture,* does not necessarily happen because the values of funders and the movements that they resource are misaligned. It happens because funders have a hard time believing that anything meaningful is happening unless there is a plan with a clear, predictable outcome. The "snail's pace of radical progress" used as a justification for the Garland board to seize power over their grantees is debatable at best. Just months earlier, the NAACP had won a major victory in *Moore* v. *Dempsey,* building on strong momentum that already existed among their base. The NAACP's growing movement offered a clear pathway to exactly the kind of radical change that the Garland board was complaining about the lack of, but what it did not offer was a predictable, tightly controlled series of events that would lead to victory. Because it did not fit neatly into the Garland board's system of predictions, the movement that the NAACP was building was rendered invisible, and the cost of losing alignment with that movement was never considered.

It's not hard to imagine an alternative history where the board meeting at Garland went differently. In this alternative history, the complaint that there was no clear progress on a plan toward radical change was challenged by another board member who pointed out that a movement was growing with the power to make exactly that radical change possible. Rather than trying to set a strategy for that movement, they should trust it and focus their efforts on understanding how they might support its growth. In this history, the growth of values-aligned relationships, not the presence of a defensible plan, guided the board's strategy to invest in radical change. In this reality, the NAACP was actively supported in the anti-lynching work that built power in their base. As a result they made significant advances in countering anti-Black violence and expanded into the other issue of greatest concern to their base: economic empowerment. This alternative reality, with a greatly strengthened civil rights movement in the early 1950s, would almost certainly be preferable to a funder focused on the work of liberation. But they could not see the path to that reality.

Relational Invisibility in American Democracy

In 1945, W. E. B. Du Bois, founding member of the NAACP, declared that "democracy has failed because so many fear it."[11] To Du Bois, "the essence of the democratic process is free discussion,"[12] spaces where people can speak and be heard, change and be changed. To Du Bois, the tremendous potential of American Democracy was held back by a deep fear of hearing and being changed by Black communities.[13] Democracy was not just about voting; it was about creating places for conversation, often uncomfortable conversation, that allowed people to be heard and to come together as much as possible around shared values. Democracy is not merely about getting people to the polls; it is about supporting relational containers where people can change one another and build power. This is especially true in communities where the promise of democracy has a long history of failure.

As I write this book in the summer of 2023, organizers across the political spectrum are preparing for what all expect to be a turbulent and highly unpredictable election year in 2024. My friends in integrity teams, many of which have lost significant head count, are preparing as best they can for back-to-back elections in almost every major democracy on earth. Alongside the US presidential election, there will be similarly large-scale elections in India, Indonesia, Mexico, Great Britain, the European Union, Canada, and Australia, to name just a few.[14] These elections, which face intersecting threats from rising global autocracies and generative AI, which can produce targeted misinformation at an unprecedented scale, cry out for the sites of trusted conversation that Du Bois spoke of. Democratic institutions need relational containers to function, places where people can have conversations with other people that build trust. It looks likely that the 2024 US electoral cycle will shatter the $14.4 billion spending record set in 2020,[15] and it sure would be nice if some of that money wound up supporting organizers who were focused on creating relational containers that strengthen trust and build power.

Deep canvassing, a method of voter contact where volunteers focus on story-sharing, mutual honesty, and creating nonjudgmental space, instead of on delivering canned talking points, has been proven to be mutually transformative. An extensive series of randomized controlled trials have found that the approach can lastingly change hearts and minds among voters while also building trust across political and socioeconomic divides.[16] The process of inviting people from similar kinds of conversations into positions of emerging leadership was core to the successful efforts of Stacey Abrams and a network of grassroots groups to increase voter turnout in Georgia,[17] where 2020 saw a 10 percent increase in youth voter turnout.[18] Political scientists' measurement of the deep canvass persuasion program of the group People's Action in the 2020 presidential election found that their conversations were anywhere from 17 times to 102 times more effective per person than advertising,[19] particularly when the process was grounded in sound relational practice and properly contextualized in the communities being engaged. Democracy is about conversations as well as voting, and conversations that create space for mutual change seem to go a long way toward restoring the trust necessary for voting to happen.

Unfortunately, the vast majority of staff and consultants who run political campaigns are afraid of investing in these sites of shared change. In *Producing Politics,* Daniel Laurison explores how the teams behind political campaigns have become dominated by political operatives who focus on identifying and broadcasting the messages designed to change voters rather than on inviting those voters into relationship.[20] These operatives are estimated to spend $11 billion on advertising in 2024,[21] even though these ads have been scientifically proven to have little to no effect.[22] A constant deluge of communication over email, text messaging, advertising, and junk mail has been proven to make people less likely to vote,[23] even when the explicit goal of that communication is to get them to the polls. The desire to change voters without being changed back, especially poor, Black, and brown voters, sits in the heart of American democracy like a poison.

While writing this book, I attended Netroots Nation, a progressive political organizing conference where these teams were discussing the data infrastructure that would drive the 2024 presidential cycle. In the halls there was a deep-seated frustration about this focus on transactional messaging. Many people had joined politics from movements that thrived on processes of trust-building and shared change, and they wanted to bring that wisdom to the campaigns they believed in. Even though research had proven that they didn't work, the vast majority of attention and resources were oriented toward targeting voters with just the right deluge of one-way messaging to shift their behavior. When volunteers were engaged, it was generally to be a mouthpiece for these pre-scripted messages, whether on phone calls, through text messages to their friends, or through hand-written postcards.

When I asked, organizers were filled with anecdotal stories of times when containers for meaningful conversation had driven change. Often it was the memory of these moments that kept them motivated in their work, even though such mutually transformative organizing generally had to exist in the slim margins of their jobs. The problem was data. Everyone seemed to agree in principle that conversation was the way to support democracy and build long-term power, but there was no way to know which organizers and which conversations were most effective at getting voters to do what campaigns wanted them to do. Ads and text messages were far less effective overall, but they created clean data in the form of click-through and response rates. A campaign staffer could go back to her boss, and her boss could go back to a funder, with data about how many voters they had contacted and an estimate of how likely those voter contacts were to change their voting behavior because messages were well tested and relatively homogeneous. Strategies for winning elections by making voters predictable were getting funded, not strategies for winning elections by making voters powerful in unpredictable ways, even when all evidence pointed to the fact that strategies like deep canvassing were vastly more effective.

In the halls of Netroots Nation, the relational invisibility that I describe in chapter 1 felt especially salient. Something was present in the bodies and lived experiences of the organizers in the room, something that those bodies, the communities they fought for, and the thriving multiracial democracy that they envisioned all desperately needed. Detailed analyses of electoral maps and messaging strategies had an important role to play, but they needed to be balanced by another kind of predictive thinking that was being entirely lost. Organizers were not afraid of building relational power; they craved it and didn't know how to justify it to their funders. As soon as a strategy was considered in which messages stopped being pre-scripted, as soon as a strategy required investing in a campaign's capacity to be changed back, that strategy became labeled as unpredictable, indefensible, unfundable, and even unimaginable. When it came time to allocate funding, something was rendering strategies involving sound relational prediction invisible.

The Roots of the Loneliness Crisis

This book opened with a mystery: If so many powerful institutions have goals that are furthered by building relationship, why are so many of us so lonely? Examining the failures of philanthropy through the lens of the curse of transactionality, an answer is beginning to emerge. When institutions make decisions to invest resources, even when their mission (as with organizations like Meta) is explicitly to build community, they do so by crafting plans with outcomes that are predictable, consistent, and scalable. They build powerful systems of measurement and control to ensure that those plans are executed with minimal risk. The result is a system of dominance and homogeneity that both fails to create the conditions for relationship and ignores, undermines, or actively dismantles the lineages of relational wisdom that already exist. Our world is getting less relational because, in the vast majority of cases, the criteria for fundability are also the conditions for disconnection.

This need not be the case, and has not been the case for much of human history. In *The Dawn of Everything,* David Graeber and David Wengrow provide substantial archaeological evidence that cities governed by coalitions of people in relationship with one another were fairly common throughout human history.[24] Monarchs and other centralized authorities occurred but were only one of a wide range of institutional forms that human societies adopted. Less centralized and more relational forms of government, including the Iroquois Confederation that inspired the democratic federation of the United States, existed in societies across the globe and thrived for most of human history, often by effectively deploying resources to create the conditions for relationship. La Donna Harris's definition of indigeneity, discussed in chapter 4, with its focus on relationship and reciprocity, hints at some of the wisdom about the deployment of resources that still exist in relational lineages today. This wealth of historical knowledge about how to effectively invest in relationship puts the predicament of funders from Garland to the Ford Foundation in a new light. The question is not "Why are funders so bad at embracing relational strategies that more effectively achieve their goals?" but "Why are so many of our well-resourced institutions so disconnected from an understanding of relational strategy that has been present for most of human history?"

In the 1540s, a group of British merchant traders got together in a pub and began scheming ways to fundraise for a new wharf. The merchants were part of a guild, the kind of relational network that dominated much of the British economy at the time, but the funds that their members had access to were insufficient. To bring money in the door, they dreamed up a new institutional form in which investors would help to pay for their wharf and other shared supplies in return for a share of the profits from their voyages. In 1551, the Company of

Adventures to New Lands was established and attracted 240 investors, becoming the world's first joint stock corporation.[25] As commerce blossomed and investors saw expanding returns, this nascent organizational form was refined, becoming less like a decentralized guild and more like one of the rigidly commanded ships that its merchant members owned. In 1600 the first truly modern corporation, the British East India Company, was founded.[26] It was destined to become one of the most powerful and destructive institutions in human history.

Guilds were messy, and so funding guilds was often messy. Guilds tended to operate in the same community as their investors, so supporting a particular tradesman (since guild membership was generally limited to men) brought with it a complex set of relational circumstances that had to be navigated. If one tradesman was funded over another, it could be seen as a personal slight; if the tradesman you funded gave someone a shoddy product or ran over someone's foot with their cart, the consequences could very well come back to the investor. Investment, in other words, was an unavoidably relational as well as a financial decision.

After its test run in the Company of Adventures to New Lands, the British East India Company offered to make the process of investing far easier. Investors' money would be turned into ships that would sail away to the exotic lands of the subcontinent and come back laden with treasures. Investors need not concern themselves with what was happening in the communities where these ships made port; they needed only concern themselves with the return on their investment and the risk, inevitable in any oceangoing voyage but entirely manageable, that came along with that return. The complex relational prediction required to invest in a guild was reduced to the utter simplicity of choosing the highest number. Investment in the British East India Company and other corporations that soon followed soared, and a fleet of ships sailed with orders to maximize investor returns by any means necessary.

In 1601, eighteen years before the first enslaved Africans landed on the shores of what would eventually become the United States, the budding corporation's first ship sailed. Its captain, Sir James Lancaster, was invited to embody this new and powerful disconnection from the complex relational world. On British shores he was to remain a gentleman who participated in polite society, but away from those shores the only things that mattered were the risks to his ship and the amount of treasure in its hold. Forms of relationship that were unimaginably harmful at home were encouraged if they minimized risk and maximized returns. In the ports where Lancaster landed, he was instructed to form whatever relationships most efficiently extracted resources, and this required ignoring what was destroyed through that process of extraction. Whatever feelings these relationships brought up, whatever complex thoughts he had about the relational world he was navigating were distractions to be ignored, and if he failed to ignore them, he would be replaced. If the road to profitability involved plunging the lands he visited into war and chaos, his investors would not be concerned. A year into his journey, Lancaster came across a fellow merchant, a Portuguese vessel hauling pepper and spices, and promptly seized its cargo. In violence and theft, the East India Company's road to profitability had begun.

This kernel of disconnection felt by employees of the East India Company was hardly new. The violence and exploitation that this disconnection encourages had a long prior history. But the founding of the first modern corporation created a novel link between this practice of disconnection and the practice of investment. Investors were invited, in a new and radical way, not to care about the relational implications of their investment, which meant that the people charged with implementing their investments were also invited not to care. To care, to be concerned about relationship at all, was a sign of weakness and therefore a liability to one's career, unless the relationships that one was concerned about were with other British men. Seeing and engaging with the rich relational world was relegated to women or, worse yet, was seen as an indication of the kind of uncivilized thinking that the British sought to uplift through colonization. To be deserving of power and prestige, a wealthy British man had to learn to focus solely on the transactional, on the bottom lines that made corporations and, by extension, the British Empire hum. For almost all of human history, our ability to understand and predict the relational world had been the key to our survival, but suddenly, on a small but powerful island and increasingly on the continent that surrounded it, the survival of wealthy colonialists depended on not seeing the relational world at all.

In 1773 a parliamentary committee began investigating the East India Company's activities and came back horrified. "In the East, the laws of society, the laws of nature have been enormously violated. Oppression in every shape has ground the faces of the poor defenseless natives; and tyranny in her bloodless form has stalked abroad." The company had amassed an army and seized the region of Bengal, the first in a wave of expansions that would eventually overtake the entire subcontinent. Once the seizure was complete, the East India Company was setting about turning Bengali wealth into company assets as efficiently as possible. Artisans and laborers from Bengal were forced into slavery, while a great deal of local trade was outlawed and the markets flooded with British goods.[27] East India Company ships landed in Bengal with enslaved Africans, just as earlier Company ships had carried enslaved people to the Americas.[28] It was a testing ground for the violent and exploitative rule that would soon come to cover much of the subcontinent.

The organization that perpetuated these atrocities had been evolving for a decade to ignore the value inherent in the rich relationships that made up a place like Bengal and focus only on what could be extracted for exchange in a transactional marketplace. This focus on extraction led the East India Company to promote the sociopath Robert Clive, who oversaw the atrocities in Bengal. In the East India Company, power flowed away from people who were sensitive to relational concerns and toward those with the capacity to ignore them. A lesson was being reinforced both in the halls of power and in individual minds and bodies: Ignore relationship, focus on the transactional, and vast wealth can be yours.

As the East India Company's atrocities were finally gaining public attention, an aging intellectual named Adam Smith was busily working on his treatise. Feminist economist Katrine Marçal points out that where and how he wrote the defining work of modern economic theory was revealing. Adam Smith never married, and even at the age of fifty he lived with and was cared for by his mother.[29] After a busy day of writing about how butchers and bakers created the conditions for a prosperous society by solely focusing on maximizing their transactional outcomes, he would sit down to a meal purchased and prepared by his mother as an act of love. The relational invisibility that emerged as a tool of corporate dominance, exploitation, and homogeneity had taken root in the heart of economic theory.

Smith argued that the atomic unit of economic progress was the transaction, an exchange of money for a good or service with clearly predictable benefits. If relationships were involved in this transaction, they were too complex to mention. Never mind that transactions required trust that required relationship, or that goods could only be produced and improved in relational environments, or that all of the humans involved very much needed relationships to live. Focusing only on the transactional brought a piercing clarity to Smith's theories, an intoxicating simplicity that painted the unfathomably complex relational world as a thing that could be understood and conquered. To gain this understanding, one needed only to ignore the complex, embodied relational and focus solely on the predictable and rational.

The power of European colonialism to ruthlessly dominate the world around it was deeply caught up in its ability to render relational reality invisible. This relational invisibility is intertwined with the history of patriarchy, since relational labor was often delegated to women and devalued. This relational invisibility created a false justification for European superiority, since it obscured the wisdom of civilizations operating on relational principles and left a dangerously false image of people living in chaos who needed order imposed on them. It also created a fear of and fascination with relational power, a fear and fascination that was projected onto the bodies of women, people of color, and women of color especially. This invisibility, with its undercurrent of fear and fascination, became woven into the culture of professionalism. To behave professionally—that is, as the captain or crew of a corporate enterprise—was to maintain a rational focus on the solidly predictable. In order to get anything economically meaningful done, one needed to break that thing down into a plan made up of distinct transactional steps, then maintain a rigid hierarchy necessary to ensure that those steps unfolded according to plan. To embrace trust in relationships without a clearly defined and well-managed plan is to invite the chaos and inefficiency of the unprofessional world, a world where nothing truly meaningful ever gets done.

This fear of nothing getting done showed up in the board meeting at the Garland Fund that changed the course of the civil rights movement. In the funder panel after the murder of Michael Brown, it was this fear, articulated thousands of times by their managers and governing boards, that tied the hands of program officers who knew in their gut that deploying capital to a powerful movement against anti-Black violence was the right thing to do. It shows up in modern political campaigns, where nothing precisely predictable happening is equated with nothing happening and therefore with defeat. But there is a world of difference between nothing happening and nothing happening that can be precisely predicted. We know from movement history, countless relational lineages, and concrete mathematical analysis that wisely investing in relational containers will reliably lead to values-aligned but unpredictable outcomes, to transformation and resilience that can be profoundly valuable. We can't control where the evolution that drives relationships will lead, but we can trust in the differentiation function that guides that evolution by trusting in shared values. Movements and other relational lineages have a long history of doing just that. When we deploy resources to create the conditions for relationship, a great deal happens, and if we embrace our shared superpowers of relational prediction, there is a great deal we can know about what those happenings will look like, even if they cannot be predicted with precision.

Why are our institutions so bad at deploying resources to build relationship? Why is relational invisibility widespread and especially embedded wherever institutions have extracted and accumulated vast sums of money? Because to access power and wealth, we must embrace a lineage of disconnection, one that heavily prioritizes the transactional over the relational and which has roots in the deeply interwoven histories of corporate finance and colonial atrocities. We have been told for generations, especially if we are white, especially if we are in or aspire to be in the professional class, and especially if we are men, that gaining transactional control over our world is the only way to be happy, healthy, and safe. Not only does this create widespread conditions for loneliness in our own lives, it leads those in charge of institutional resources to chronically underinvest in relational work.

Relational Containers By and For the Wealthy

The link between relational invisibility and professional identity creates a strange bifurcation in the lives of many people who earn a paycheck. When they are on the clock and responsible for a corporate institution's assets, even if that institution is a nonprofit or government entity, they must engage in the sort of rational predictive thinking that renders relationship invisible. There is some wiggle room here, especially when it comes to "soft" concepts like team cohesion, but serious investments in relationship are forbidden unless those relationships clearly and predictably drive transactions. Things are a bit different off the clock. Here people are free to buy concert tickets with their friends, spend money on their kids, and take their partners out for dinner without a clearly defined return on investment, although such thinking is increasingly creeping into these relationships as well. This life outside work is relational but often relationally impoverished, disconnected from the relational lineages that have either been forgotten or colonized and stripped of valuable resources. People are free to turn the money that they have acquired into relationship and find themselves surrounded by products that promise just that: transactional goods that will make us more desirable, more interesting, or simply more noticed. Yet somehow these transactions fail to deliver the relationships we crave.

Buried in this transactional marketplace is another way to mobilize resources for community, one that some communities have been able to leverage to great effect but that still suffers from severe limitations. My co-mom's mother, Laura Lee, is a former pastor who built community, provided spiritual support, and mobilized resources on the frontlines of the AIDS crisis. She would tell stories from an ancient lineage and relate them to the lives and struggles of the people in the pews, some whose worlds were crumbling and some who had simply shown up for services. She would lead them in shared song, instruct them in the sacred act of welcoming newcomers, and then direct them down the hall to a room where snacks, folding tables, and informal conversation were waiting. Because she was skilled at this relational work, the minds and bodies of the people in the room would light up. Despite centuries of indoctrination, the people in the pews felt the power of relationship moving around them and were motivated to move their hearts, bodies, spirits, and wallets along with it. Whether this felt sense of power and purpose was the Holy Spirit or merely a felt sense of relationship is a question beyond the scope of this text, though John 4:16 would imply that the two are intertwined. When people felt this embodied sense of relationship, they could know, with a deep certainty, that deploying resources was worthwhile so long as their more rational and professional selves were not there to suppress that knowledge. The British East India Company lasted for 274 years before its formal dissolution in 1874, but institutions of faith that mobilize resources through this kind of a relational process have lasted a millennium longer. Their behavior over that millennium has at times been far from exemplary. Simply being accountable to relationship is no assurance of moral institutional behavior, but there is a lesson to be learned about institutional resilience.

This pattern of creating a powerful relational space and then asking for resources within it echoed my experience of movement history. When the struggle to confront anti–Black violence and the Jim Crow laws that enabled it reemerged after the setback with the NAACP, one of its leading figures was a pastor in Montgomery, Alabama, with experience using powerful oratory and relational spaces to mobilize both money and action. Unlike the NAACP, the Montgomery Improvement Association, which led the successful bus boycotts that ushered in a new era for the civil rights movement under the leadership of Martin Luther King Jr., received almost no outside funding. Instead, they mobilized resources like a church through passing the plate and through a network of internal affinity groups. The details of this strategy hold so much insight that I will save them for the opening of chapter 7, in which we finally get down to the business of resourcing relational work, but suffice it to say that the results speak for themselves. Even in the queer movements I grew up in, where most people are extremely wary of institutions of faith, grassroots fundraising would take on an almost spiritual air. The moments where resources were mobilized were filled with song, dance, and tears of joy, with queer elders speaking to the scared kids we all once were and the scared kids who were still out there. Money moved when we could feel the power of the relationships that changed us.

This ability of communities to mobilize money through grassroots fundraising can reinforce inequality when money is not moving across lines of class. Wealthy people pay well for the relational containers that they experience directly, creating relational containers such as country clubs, elite universities, and Burning Man. These institutions can mobilize considerable resources by asking the people who directly experience relationship within them to chip in. Such well-funded communities are often limited in their relational potential because the process of acquiring wealth and power has disconnected them from lineages of relational wisdom that would allow them to deploy that wealth and power effectively. Corporate team-building events struggle to feel relationally powerful because they must swim against the deep lineage of disconnection present in corporate culture.

Burning Man, a giant festival in the Nevada desert that generally costs thousands of dollars to attend, illustrates how this lineage of disconnection can be grappled with in relational containers mostly built by and for those with economic privilege.[30] When I attended Burning Man for the first and only time in 2010, I witnessed a frenetic landscape of people who had been starved of connection reinventing themselves to seek it. If the professional selves of the tech workers and social entrepreneurs who surrounded me required a rejection of relational reality, then Burning Man was a full-throated rejection of those professional selves. People adopted new names and personas, and poorly understood relational lineages were appropriated, mixed together without context, and confidently taught as sage wisdom. Plenty of connections were forming, but those connections were predicated on a disconnection from the "default" world and often did not survive a return to it. This presumption that the lives we came from needed to be temporarily rejected rather than grappled with underpinned every conversation I had on the playa, though I respect that the experiences of many who attend this festival may be different. I witnessed people running from a lineage of disconnection by disconnecting further, creating elaborate sensory experiences to escape into rather than investing, especially across lines of class, in the communities that they lived in. While the community around Burning Man holds substantial wisdom about how to create the conditions for relationship, it also illustrates why the resource-intensive spaces built for the wealthy are not a sustainable or accessible model for addressing the crisis of loneliness.

What About Individual Giving?

I believe that the greatest potential for resilience and transformation occurs when resources can flow to relational work across lines of power and privilege. Distributing the resources that have been extracted and centralized through colonial capitalism back to skilled but under-resourced community organizers who hold lineages of relational wisdom is a recipe for supporting communities and movements with immense transformative potential. Unfortunately this is exactly the kind of resourcing that the modern philanthropic ecosystem struggles most to accomplish.

Institutions like CARA or the Montgomery Improvement Association that seek to create the conditions for relationship in marginalized communities have three options when it comes to funding:

1. They can pursue institutional funding, which fails for reasons that we have discussed at length.

2. They can survive on what they can fundraise from their community, even if it means underpaying or not maintaining a staff and getting by on a bare minimum of resources.

3. They can rely on donations from high-net-worth individuals.

This second strategy, which was utilized by both AVEN and CARA, can result in a considerable amount of relational impact but is insufficient to address systemic challenges like the loneliness or climate crises. If individuals possess the capacity to understand and fund relationship in a way that institutions do not, could high-net-worth donors be the key to funding the relational work that we so desperately need? Not necessarily.

If accessing foundation capital requires appealing to the rational and professional side of wealth, mobilizing high net worth donations involves connecting with the somewhat more relational unprofessional side. Because it generally takes as much time to build the trust necessary to move a $1,000 check as it does to move a $500,000 check, conventional wisdom in the development world is to invest heavily in relationships with a handful of high-net-worth individuals who can also mobilize their high-net-worth friends to give. Often these individuals will be offered board seats or other prestigious positions, even if they have no direct connection to communities the nonprofit works with or the challenges facing them. The trick, when mobilizing this sort of capital, is to translate whatever struggle the community is feeling into something that will help wealthy people feel the way that they might feel in Laura Lee's church.

This feeling of embodied relational certainty, the kind of relational prediction necessary to confidently move resources, can be difficult to construct when the community being funded is not one that funders can directly participate in or be changed by. This translation is pulled off haphazardly and often problematically through a kind of relational theater. Wealthy donors will invite their friends to an annual gala dinner, a luxurious event designed to provide a relational container for the wealthy. At this dinner, people from marginalized communities will be invited up on stage or displayed in videos in order to convince the wealthy attendees that the relationships that make up the community are worth funding.

The stories presented at these dinners often differ starkly from the movement stories described in the previous chapter. If I want to connect with another ace person who has struggled with a culture of compulsory sexuality, I can drop a few hints that will resonate with their lived struggle and then focus on the interesting part, where that struggle is met and transformed. When marginalized people are invited to perform at gala dinners, the stories that they are invited to tell rarely focus on this sort of agency. Because the people in the audience do not share their history of trauma, that history must be relived in exhausting and often retraumatizing detail in order to evoke an emotional reaction. If their narrative includes empowerment at all, it is often a dramatic oversimplification of a transformed life in which the nonprofit and its funders, not the person on stage, are the primary protagonists. Jorgen Lissner coined the term *poverty porn* to describe these narratives delivered often by or about poor Black and brown people to largely affluent white audiences.[31] Sophie Otiende coined the term *survivor porn* to refer to the particularly retraumatizing narratives that survivors of sex trafficking and other forms of sexual violence are asked to perform for funders,[32] while Stella Young coined the term *inspiration porn* to refer to images and stories of disabled people used to elicit funding.[33] These stories, rather than inviting wealthy people into potentially transformative multiracial cross-class movements, serve as a form of transactional entertainment at elite social gatherings. Wealthy people are made to feel; they are offered a temporary escape from the confines of a life disconnected from relationship in exchange for a hefty donation, but at the end of the dinner, no one has been changed in a way that was not predictable.

As with foundation funding, this reliance on high-net-worth donors and gala dinners has a profound impact on the structure of the community institutions it funds. Succeeding at this form of fundraising requires a network of wealthy friends and the ability to put on a show that they will find emotionally compelling, two skills that have nothing to do with effectively inviting marginalized people into community with one another. This funding model has led to a wave in which organizations that seek to connect with and serve poor communities of color are led by well-meaning wealthy white people who report to boards mostly composed of other well-meaning wealthy white people. These organizations experience a constant tension between the need to center the communities that they serve and the need to cultivate and maintain relationships with wealthy donors in order to pay their staff and provide services. Because each major donor requires a substantial investment of time from an executive director, development director, and possibly board member, the number of people invited to donate through anything more relational than an email blast is also extremely small.

This focus on high-touch relationships with a tiny network of donors has led to an ecosystem of community funding that is so broken that a great deal of capital is simply not moving. In order for a wealthy person to move money in accordance with their values, they generally either need to find a senior staff member from a nonprofit who earns their trust or hire a wealth manager to build these relationships for them. Both experiences are labor-intensive and invite a risk of fraud and blatant manipulation that many with money would rather avoid. Moving money takes relational work, and people with money are often the least likely to understand how to go about that work or what the benefits are of doing so.

I am far from alone in pointing out that this system is broken. Inside many major foundations, a rebellion is being fomented as staff challenge outdated models of giving, embracing alternative frameworks such as Trust-Based Philanthropy or the Just Transition framework and citing *The Revolution Will Not Be Funded* and Edgar Villanueva's excellent *Decolonizing Wealth* in their slide decks. These valid critiques and alternatives align closely with the arguments in this book, and in the next chapter I will discuss how a grounded approach to institutional relational prediction can complement them. There is a sense within this revolution that the ways in which we deploy capital can be not only radically more effective but radically easier on everyone involved. Development staff will be able to focus on their work without spending months out of the year on preparing grant applications, reports, and gala dinners. Program staff will be able to trust the wisdom of the movements that they are funding rather than laboriously trying to reconstruct that wisdom themselves and will be able to justify that trust to the senior staff and boards that hold them accountable. Individuals, high-net-worth and otherwise, will have an abundance of invitations to relational experiences in the movements and communities that inspire them where they will be supported in moving whatever resources they have access to in ways that are accountable to the movement's values. Just as the invention of the joint-stock corporation birthed a radically new and radically transformative means of deploying resources, a new methodology is slowly emerging for resourcing relational work.

I do not yet know what this new methodology is, but I can describe some of the questions it is answering in the communities and movements it is emerging from. If we are to address the loneliness crisis and build the movements that our world desperately needs, we must relearn the art of investing institutional resources in relational outcomes. Let's explore what that looks like.

Reflection Questions

- How is relational invisibility present in your world?

- Where do you witness institutions being unable to understand and invest in relationship?

- Is that lack of understanding tied to how these institutions make predictions? If so, how?

- Does the culture of professionalism within these institutions limit relational reasoning? If so, how?

- Is that culture of professionalism required more of some people than others? If so, who?

- Where do you witness communities that *do* understand how to see and invest in relationship?

- What might you learn from these communities?

CHAPTER 7

Investing in Relational Outcomes

I AM GRATEFUL to the staff of the North Star Fund for introducing me to the life and work of Georgia Gilmore.

Georgia was a mother, cook, and civil rights leader from Montgomery, Alabama. A "big woman with a swaggering personality, who showed little fear in the face of white bigotry,"[1] Gilmore once snatched a pistol from a white store clerk and hit him with it after he refused to sell her son bread and laundry detergent.[2] She joined the Montgomery Bus Boycott in 1955 and was fired from her job as a cook after testifying in support of Martin Luther King Jr.

Instead of looking for a new job, she and a group of friends formed the "Club from Nowhere," a group that prepared fried chicken, pies, and other meals for the movement.[3] Georgia began showing up at meetings selling plates of hot food. She opened a kitchen in her basement just a few blocks from Dr. King's house that became a critical gathering point for the movement. Dr. King would take meetings there about issues that would have been unsafe to discuss in a public restaurant, as Gilmore's food and the spaces she provided nurtured the relationships that gave the Montgomery Improvement Association its resilience and transformative power. Much of the money that she raised went back into the movement, helping to cover the gas and repairs for the three hundred cars participating in the movement-organized carpool system that provided transportation to boycotters.[4] Gilmore's kitchen became a community and movement staple, serving both Robert F. Kennedy and Lyndon B. Johnson. In 1958 she was part of a lawsuit to desegregate Montgomery's public parks. She passed away in 1990 while in the midst of cooking food that was then served to her mourners.

Unlike the NAACP, the Montgomery Improvement Association received no funding from large foundations. The money it raised, the food it ate, and the other resources that allowed the boycott to achieve victory came primarily from people like Georgia Gilmore who were embedded in the movement itself. This theme of relying largely on internal funding is a pattern in many successful movements, including the Montgomery Improvement Association, the National Farm Workers Association, and the movement for women's suffrage.[5] This internal funding is often not enough. The money extracted from marginalized communities should be returned, and wealthy individuals and institutions can play an important role in doing so. The existence of wealthy donors within the movement for women's suffrage was vital to its success, and examples abound of movements that would not exist at their current strength without institutional support. But there is something about money that flows through lines of trusted relationship, rather than through systems of transactional prediction, that has historically proved vital to movements' success. If we want to fund relationship, we will need to fund it through relationship. In this, Georgia Gilmore and leaders like her are a source of wisdom.

Funding relational infrastructure requires us to step back from the rigorous standards of transactional prediction that have been enshrined in financial thinking since the founding of the first corporation. We cannot fund relationships by deploying capital to make a specific outcome happen through a well-defined plan. If someone writes an elaborate grant proposal and promises to regularly report on the indicators that their plan is unfolding as predicted, then relationships will inevitably lead to an unpredictable outcome that looks like failure. That is not to say that funders should abandon intention entirely, giving money only in the moments when their bodies light up with a sense of connection and community. This results in funds flowing primarily to communities that serve the wealthy or that can put on convincing theater for them—theater that is poorly correlated with actual relational effectiveness. Intention and rigor have an important role to play in resourcing relational work, but one that looks radically different from the ROI calculations that drive most financial decision-making. To fund relationship, we must be intentional and rigorous about predicting relationally.

Throughout this book, we have laid the groundwork for such a rigorous process of relational prediction. In chapter 1 we established the context of a global loneliness crisis and discussed how addressing this crisis by investing in relationship can help to address a wide range of complex challenges. In chapter 2 we looked at three ways to define a relationship as a process of shared change, and in chapter 3 we explored this definition to see how relationships drive resilience and transformation through a process of evolution. In chapter 4 we discussed the lineages of relational wisdom that offer insight about how to create the conditions for this relational evolution, even if we can't predict exactly where that evolution will lead. In chapter 5 we examined movements as one example of a rich ecology that nurtures and aligns relationships at scale, and in chapter 6 we examined the historical reasons why so many well-intentioned investments in relationship fail. With this foundation, we can begin to explore questions that make up the funding process. Many of the strategies in this chapter have been inspired by organizations such as the North Star Fund, the Trust-Based Philanthropy project, Justice Funders, Liberated Capital, the Third Wave Fund, and the Trans Justice Funding Project. This chapter is intended for those inside institutions with access to financial resources, since freeing those resources to invest in relational work is the primary goal of this book, and I hope it will also be useful to people who are primarily seeking resources or have noninstitutional or nonfinancial resources to offer. The world needs people working to build relationship, and those people need support.

Deciding to Invest in Relational Outcomes

Typically, the value of an investment is summed up by calculating ROI. A funder weighs the cost of the investment against the specific outcome that they hope the investment will achieve, the time it will take for that outcome to happen, and the risk that things won't go according to plan. That outcome is generally money flowing into the funder's bank account, though it could just as easily be any other concrete and measurable change in the world. A philanthropic foundation might calculate ROI in terms of children vaccinated, while a political candidate might calculate it in terms of additional votes mobilized. In most cases, this predictable outcome is desirable because it creates a world that the funder wants to live in. They may want a larger bank account because it gives them a sense of self-worth or because it creates security for their grandchildren. They may want votes because it gives them the power to shape the political landscape according to their values. Often these underlying motivations are unstated in the quest to maximize returns: The "why" does not matter as much as the "what," "when," and "how."

Investing in relationship requires a return to this "why." A funder who wants their grandkids to be safe may have reason to support a powerful youth-led climate movement. A politician who wants to see their values shape the political landscape may have reason to want to see a thriving network of Black voters that lasts beyond the current electoral cycle. This return to values is necessary because investing in relationship is often an effective way to create the kind of world that the funder wants to live in but not an effective tool for aggregating power. Investing in relationship may not be a competitive way to make the funder's bank account bigger, but it will often be competitive with that large bank account as a way to create the kind of change that the funder ultimately wants to see. That is true because relational prediction works in different ways and on different timescales than transactional prediction.

Recall from chapter 3 that relationship is tied, at a fundamental mathematical level, to processes of resilience, transformation, and evolution. A 2022 article by Douglas Rushkoff describes the shadowy world of "billionaire preppers," hedge fund managers, and Silicon Valley moguls building luxury bunkers and hiring mercenary guards for what they perceive to be an increasingly likely societal collapse.[6] In the closed-door meetings that Rushkoff was invited to, the billionaires were obsessed with one question: They needed armed guards to keep looters at bay, but once money was worthless and lawlessness reigned, what would stop their well-compensated men with guns from simply taking over? Rushkoff and others gave a wholly unsatisfying answer: If they wanted resilience in the face of collapse, they would need to invest in trust. Spend time building relationships with the guards they were hiring so that they could form a community together. Better yet, find a community that already knew the land they would be on and build relationships with people there so that there would be resilience among more than just people with guns. Maybe spend a few billion less on secret compounds and put some of that money into the communities on whom they would ultimately depend.

Investing in relationship allows us to invest directly in resilience, not in the systems of control that often serve as a poor proxy for it. It allows us to invest directly in transformation. Researcher Jane Wei-Skillern has demonstrated how, in sector after sector, meaningful systemic change has occurred not because any single nonprofit organization successfully scaled its programs but because organizations with disparate missions and capabilities began supporting one another as part of a broader movement. For example, Wei-Skillern discusses how, in the wake of hurricanes Katrina and Rita, Habitat for Humanity responded not by building up their internal capacity but by investing in relationships with a network of trusted partners, amplifying their usual annual production of homes by a factor of fifteen,[7] and no doubt creating numerous unexpected but positive outcomes that were not clearly documented. These networks did not work when they were curated by funders forcing grantees to collaborate, only when grantees had agency over their own relationships and were resourced to pursue them. Whether one wants to see scientific advances, political change, or educational progress, the missing factor is often relationships between the individuals and organizations in a system, not the strength of those individuals and organizations.

Relational prediction allows us to look out into the world and draw relationships where they do not yet exist. Where those relationships are drawn, we can predict an unpredictable but values-directed process of resilience, transformation, and evolution. If we want a more vibrant art scene, we might invest in relationships among artists and those with resources to enable their work. If we want to accelerate cancer research, we might invest in relationships connecting immunologists and epigeneticists, since scientific breakthroughs often come from small teams exploring novel collaborations between fields.[8] The ability to deploy resources to reliably create the conditions for relationship unlocks a tremendously useful tool for leveraging money to shape our world. It allows us to pursue systemic transformations that are otherwise unimaginable, to build networks, communities, and movements that will be resilient for decades to come, and to conjure creative evolution wherever the possibility for relationship exists. We just need to be willing to surrender control to the relationships that we are investing in.

If that willingness exists, we can get about the business of imagining how those relationships might come into being. What exactly will happen, how exactly it will happen, and when exactly it will happen will be murky, since relationships evolve in unexpected ways on non-linear timelines. Things may build slowly for years, then rapidly leap forward in a moment of opportunity or need. That being said, who, where, and why can be crystal clear.

Who

Relational prediction allows us to look out into the world and imagine relationships that do not yet exist, or imagine relationships that already exist becoming deeper and more resilient. Specificity is welcomed here, so long as it is willing to evolve over time. A funder concerned with reproductive justice may imagine a powerful national youth-led reproductive justice movement that largely does not yet exist, but could. As funders build trust with movement organizers, the conversations can be clear about who needs to be invited into relationship, even if they cannot predict the outcome of doing so. For example, organizers may make a case that supporting organizing at historically Black colleges and universities (HBCUs) is critical, or may opt to focus on cultivating the leadership of young mothers outside of colleges. As the movement grows, the funder can anticipate the "who" to grow and change according to the movement's values.

Where

Relational prediction allows us to know that relationships will reliably happen in certain relational containers. In a particular community in a particular cultural context, certain ways of convening people will reliably create relational outcomes. In one community it could be a potluck with lots of dancing and community-provided child care; in another it could be revitalizing a tradition that brings elders and adolescents together to share stories. The people best situated to create these containers will often be rooted in the communities that they are convening. Often they will draw from lineages of relational wisdom that exist in those communities, especially when those lineages are not overly reliant on transactional thinking. Often these relational containers will be fractal in scale. There may be a big annual event interspersed by smaller quarterly gatherings interspersed by smaller weekly meetings interspersed by informal one-on-one conversations interspersed by daily practices where organizers tend to their individual resilience. To survive and thrive, relationships will develop across this range of containers, jumping from a big annual gathering to a one-on-one to a personal journaling session to presence in a weekly meeting. A funder's role is to give on-the-ground organizers the resources and support necessary to learn what kinds of relational containers work and then to follow organizers on that journey of learning.

Why

When people gather in a relational container, they need something to connect around, some shared struggle or creative passion or sense of possibility. Relational prediction tells us that relational containers need a set of shared values to function effectively. Stated formally, the evolutionary process that drives relational growth cannot proceed without an aligned process of differentiation. These values emerge organically from the relationships that make up a community. A funder should not be the source of these shared values, but they can and should resonate with them. Even though the outcomes of a relational system are unpredictable, shared values can give us a sense of what a given network of relationships will produce. A movement of people convened around a passion for open-source software may wind up producing an incredible new genre of music, but they are far more likely to produce lots of open-source software and extremely unlikely to produce a wave of patent litigation. Because values are central, documenting them and incorporating them into a movement's gatherings is essential. Recall that values are not just words like *respect;* they are complex personal stories about the struggles that lead us to value certain things in the world. Values are experienced through stories: shared between funders and organizers, woven into the stories that the movement broadcasts, visible not just as words on the wall but as art, music, and the norms of introductory conversation. Knowing these values allows us to know that a community or a movement is headed in a direction we want even if we cannot know where it will lead.

Deciding to invest in relationship makes sense when a funder's goals involve resilience, transformation, and evolution. These relational goals may complement transactional ones: For example, a county may invest both in a new school building and in the relationships that will allow that building to serve as a center of learning, but they require different methods of prediction and therefore may involve radically different styles of investment, management, and accountability. A funder can prepare to deploy resources relationally by exploring who they want to invite into relationship, where those relationships might happen, and why people in those places might be motivated to come together.

Building Trust and Deploying Resources

After the release of the Netflix documentary *The Social Dilemma* in 2020, I found myself at the center of a surge of resources. I was the Chief Mobilization Officer at the Center for Humane Technology, a leading organization focused on addressing the harms of social media and the main subject of the documentary. Overnight hundreds of people were showing up to our events and clamoring to be invited into leadership. My networks of inside allies within major tech companies began to greatly expand, and with that access came a surge of new strategic opportunity. The resources being piled upon me were not money, but I suddenly felt like a funder who needed to get grants out the door. This surge of interest was more than I or my organization could handle, and if the people showing up were not invited into meaningful relationship soon, that interest would fade. I was sitting on a glut of resources and I needed to get them deployed to the broader movement that I was a part of.

For over a year I had been building trust with that movement, taking one-on-one phone calls with organizations that shared my core values and those of my organization but brought complementary skills and perspectives. Often in these conversations I was the privileged person on the call: a white man from an organization that received a disproportionate amount of the movement's funding, attention, and industry access. I knew that our movement would be stronger if those things flowed from me to others in the movement whose work was just as important but less resourced, and I said as much. After introducing myself with a brief story about the values driving my work and acknowledging the power and privilege that I held, I would inquire about the work that a potential partner organization was doing. I would get curious about what relationships they held, what relationships they were skilled at forming, and what lack of relationship was holding their work back, then I would see if I could use the resources at my disposal to make some of those enabling relationships happen. Thinking in terms of what relationships the movement needed rather than in terms of what would benefit me and my organization revealed paths to unexpected sources of power.

When I left these conversations impressed, I would try my best to pass on something meaningful. Often it was access to internal employees or contextual information that could help to shape their work. Sometimes I would invite these partner organizations to speak at one of our events in order to garner attention and supporters from our growing base. I could not deploy funding, but on occasion I could provide support in the form of staff time working on deeper collaborations. Passing on resources in this way did not diminish my organization's power—it greatly enhanced it by giving us a trusted place in the coalitions that shaped the movement's strategy. To pass them on, I needed to center the work of trust-building over my organization's narrow strategic goals, and I needed to acknowledge and balance the power and privilege that I held.

Shaady Salehi of the Trust-Based Philanthropy project is part of a new wave of philanthropists arguing that deploying resources should center the work of building trust over that of collecting and reviewing grant applications. The latter not only requires an extraordinary amount of time from both grantors and grantees, it forces relational work into a transactional box that often renders it radically less effective. Instead, Salehi and her colleagues assert that funders should center the process of building trust with the communities that they are funding, starting from a place of trust rather than demanding that trust be earned through compliance and reporting. This does not mean immediately trusting everyone; it means starting with an assumption that trust is possible and centering the work of achieving it. Trust-building processes can be slow at first and are never predictable, but ultimately they allow resources to be deployed much more quickly and effectively than models focused on vetting and control.

This trust has to flow both ways. Organizations led by people who have historically been harmed by philanthropy or by other institutions led by people with power and privilege may be understandably hesitant to extend trust, and the Trust-Based Philanthropy project emphasizes that it is important for funders to respect this hesitation. Acknowledging the power and privilege that allowed resources to be centered on a funder in the first place can help, as can expressing a desire to correct that imbalance of power. For me, this is rooted in a belief that resources almost always do more good at the edges of a movement than they do huddled at the middle. Recognizing and resourcing underrecognized sites of relational opportunity will lead to a vastly greater relational capacity. Being part of a larger, thriving movement is almost always more appealing than maintaining a larger domain of personal control in a smaller one.

To recognize and resource new parts of a movement, I need to be invited. The fact that I want to support a movement, even if I hold a position of trusted leadership, does not mean that I should have access to every relational container that it creates. In the ace community there are numerous groups dedicated to the needs of aces of color or to ace survivors of sexual violence, and if I were to show up uninvited, I would disrupt the important work that those containers are doing. For this reason I often pair an offer of support with an inquiry about invitation. How are people like me invited to show up to this community? If I have a one-on-one conversation with someone, how can I hear and honor the invitation and lack of invitation that that conversation brings? I am not entitled to an invitation everywhere, and sometimes an invitation to offer financial support but not to engage in other forms or relationship is completely justified given the limited relational capacity of the people involved. Building the trust necessary to move resources often requires following such threads of invitation.

Invitation can be powerful to observe even when I am not the one receiving it. To nurture relationship, relational leaders must constantly be inviting people to gather, connect with one another, and step into leadership themselves. When I can see them, I can sometimes learn a great deal about a community by following these threads of invitation and observing what I see along the way.

- Does the movement invite me to connect, or simply to like and subscribe?

- When I show up to its gatherings, do I see a healthy network of emerging leadership on display, or a single charismatic personality that dominates the stage?

- Do I see signs that a cohesion layer is smoothing over conflict and weaving alignment, or do I see splinters of conflict and the fear of conflict rippling through the community's after-spaces as guarded gossip?

These signs can help illuminate which communities to invite into my life and which to deprioritize, though the messiness of organizing is to be expected everywhere. When I can't see signs of invitation, it may only mean that the community's invitations aren't intended for me, but observing the invitations that I can see often brings insight into how the communities I am joining operate.

Following my values, the invitations I received, and the relationships that I want to see in the world leads me to a place of trust with people in the action and cohesion layers of the movements around me. Sometimes I discover robust organizing that I can readily plug into; sometimes I discover gaps and allies who can help work to fill them. Sometimes I discover people who have journeyed before me and made networks of trust that I can easily deploy resources to support. Sometimes I need to nurture those networks directly if I want them to exist. As I gradually build trust, I will gain not just the intelligence necessary for a one-time analysis, but the ongoing stream of information necessary for an evolving deployment of resources.

Trust that is built in this way also invites new possibilities for governance. The institutional default is often to take the information gained through systems of trust and use it to inform decisions made by a small number of people in power, such as program officers and those that they report to. Another option is to distribute decision-making authority among trusted movement leaders who have more contextual information about where resources can have the greatest relational impact. The Trans Justice Funding Project, which deploys small grants to grassroots activists supporting trans communities in the United States and US territories, deploys a community-based funding process in which paid fellows help to direct funding.[9] Third Wave Fund, which provides both rapid-response funding and sustained multiyear grants to movement organizations, relies on an advisory council of people rooted in the movements they are part of to help direct funding.[10] As illustrated in the early days of the Black Lives Matter movement, these community-led granting processes are often able to distribute funds more nimbly and effectively than processes centered on expert analysis. If what's being funded is a big, complicated project like building a hospital, then rigorous transactional analysis is warranted, but there is a cost to centering those with an expertise in such analysis over those who understand the communities where a project takes place. The more relational a project becomes, the less helpful this kind of centralized expertise becomes.

Relational work is about building spaces that work and that stick around long enough for communities to grow, which often requires multiyear sustained funding focused on a process of learning how a given community wants to be in relationship. Because crises happen that are both individual and systemic, relational work often requires rapid-response funding that can move relatively small amounts extremely quickly through networks of trust and mutual aid. Relational work can sometimes involve large ambitious projects, like building a new church, but they just as often involve a broad portfolio of small scrappy ones. Knowledge about which of these small projects to fund, where mutual aid is most deeply needed, and where vital institutions require sustained funding sits within the community where relationships are being built, and the power to allocate resources needs to flow from that knowledge.

Shortly before writing this book, I befriended Haley Bash, founder of the Donor Organizer Hub, which works to eliminate the distinction between the people who fund movements and the people who participate in them. Bash argues that many movements were successful because their rank and file were involved in fundraising. This is not because those deepest in a movement's work should bear the sole financial burden of supporting a movement, but because money that flows from the people who understand a movement from the inside is often much more relationally intelligent than money that flows from elsewhere. Such internal resource allocation can provide a powerful signal to money from the outside. Instead of picking one or two organizations to back through a process of exhaustive analysis, people with money outside of a movement can simply choose to match the money fundraised inside it. If someone like Georgia Gilmore is selling dinner to pay for gas in carpools, then paying for gas is probably a good use of funds. When movements fundraise internally, they create lines of trust that others can follow.

Nurturing relationships is hard, but once those relationships exist, everything is easier. If a movement already has a governance system for nimbly deploying resources, and that governance mechanism is aligned with my values, it's easy to just pour money into it. If a movement has a system of managing mutual aid or crowdfunding new projects where people who understand the community are already exchanging resources, it's easy to match them. What we need to do is build trust with the people who hold this understanding and let resources and agency flow to them.

The challenge here is that the trust we build often does not transfer. If a program officer at a foundation takes the time to deeply understand a movement that they want to fund, the rich relational information they possess may come across to their board of directors as nothing more than anecdotes and personal preference. The situation is similar for anyone inside a nonprofit or corporation seeking to invest in an outside community. Trust is how things get done, but it's difficult to put on a slide deck. And while a small but growing group of philanthropic institutions are reorienting their cultures around trust, most funding institutions still put power over funding decisions in the hands of those with little contextual understanding of the movements being funded. Sometimes such systems simply exist as a way to hold on to power; sometimes they exist because of personal and institutional wounds that have made trust feel unsafe. Often rigid policies and bureaucratic procedures exist to cover up such wounds and have the unintended consequence of making trust difficult to achieve.

One such bureaucratic procedure is an overreliance on data-driven decision-making. Verifiable data has an important role to play in building and maintaining trust. It can help us understand where to show up and how to interpret the stories we encounter in context, but making it the only allowable input to decision-making is a recipe for relational invisibility. To understand the roles that data can and can't play in supporting relational outcomes, we will build on the properties of relational systems discussed in chapter 3. Numbers can help us understand relationships, but we need to understand how the math underlying them works differently.

Measuring and Reporting on Relational Outcomes

Relational measurement, while not a substitute for the rich information gathered when building trust, can be a transformative tool for organizers who need to justify the impact of their work to those outside their communities. This process of justification is where most relational work is rendered invisible, and reimagining it will be critical to charting a shared path out of loneliness.

Relationships evolve in containers. When we want to nurture relationships, we do so by creating environments for them to evolve in. To accomplish a relational goal, we might call a meeting or host a dinner party or set up an online community, inviting people to interact in a container that we have created or at the very least contributed to. Relational measurement is about understanding the efficacy of these containers. If a container works, it will exhibit a high evolutionary rate: People will change one another in meaningful ways, and they will be collectively more resilient and generate creative projects that align with their values. If it doesn't work, these things won't happen. Relational measurement is about measuring this rate of evolution across a variety of relational containers to help both organizers and their funders understand how to invite people into relationship and where to focus their attention.

Before diving into the practicalities of this kind of measurement, it may be helpful to clarify what relational measurement is not:

1. **Relational measurement is not constructing a social graph.** A detailed picture of who is exchanging information with who requires an invasive level of surveillance that is not necessary for most relational work. It is more helpful to determine what places and strategies make relationships happen than to map who those relationships are between or what they are focused on.

2. **Relational measurement is not universal.** Because different communities relate differently, there is no set of relational indicators that apply universally. Measuring relationships within a community will always require a mix of qualitative and quantitative tools customized to how that community likes to communicate with one another and its organizers. This means that metrics from two disparate communities can be difficult to compare meaningfully.

3. **Relational measurement is generally more useful for inquiry than for evaluation.** Because relational measurement is in its infancy and relational systems are unpredictable, it is not advisable to use the metrics outlined in this section to hold organizers accountable. Relational measures can help organizers and their funders highlight where interesting things are happening in a community or convey a story about how a powerful thing has happened, but making them go up should never be an organizer's sole focus. Doing so robs both the organizer and the community that they are organizing of the agency necessary to make their relationships thrive.

Measuring relationships creates a sort of heat map of the relational containers that a community or movement is building. This heat map shows where interesting things in the community are happening, inviting us to zoom in and see the nuanced stories in different parts of the community so that those stories can inform our strategy.

It doesn't show us much about the people in our community unless those people are organizers who actively trust us with their data. It can provide proof to outsiders that we are capable of making interesting things happen and therefore deserving of attention and trust. While it provides insight into a community's story, it cannot be used to make an apples-to-apples comparison between communities. Because different communities show up to build relationship in very different ways, the data they produce, especially quantitative data, cannot be directly compared in a meaningful way. It can inform a story about how effective an organization or organizer is at building community, but KPIs that neatly summarize that story do not exist. It is less helpful for asking the question "Who is doing well?" and more helpful for answering the question "Where in our community should we show up?"

To understand why, it will be helpful to explore practical examples. We can know that evolution is happening in a given relational container by looking for three processes:

Exploration: Are new and relevant things emerging in the relational container? Those things could be topics of conversation, possible connections, or dance moves. If exploration is happening, we can expect to see novelty.

Differentiation: Are the new things being prioritized values-aligned with the people in the room and relationally meaningful? This can sometimes be assessed through emotional expression. Is there applause, laughter, and excitement?

Selection: Do people deploy limited resources to realize the possibilities that they find most meaningful? This resource could be time, money, the capacity to provide care, or anything else that is supportive. When members of a community commit limited resources to one another, it is often a sign of relationships forming.

This framework provides an analytical scaffolding to a process that is normally intuitive. Imagine navigating a room filled with art and conversation that feels fresh and relevant. Imagine that people in that room are openly and clearly expressing their emotions: You witness

excitement where excitement is warranted, but also hope, grief, gratitude, and whatever other emotions are true to the room's shared experience. Imagine that all around you, you see people committing to
one another: supporting one another in new projects, taking care of
one another's kids, and offering to dive in deeply with people they
have just met. Observing these signs of exploration, differentiation,
and selection paints a picture of the community's relational health.

The idea that we can measure the relationality of an environment
by tracking indicators of evolutionary rate is fairly theoretically sound,
but as of the writing of this book, still in its infancy. I will provide
several examples of what this measurement might look like, but these
should be regarded as illustrative theoretical examples rather than
thoroughly tested best practices.

Measuring Gathering

A highly relational container will often spawn follow-up conversations. People who meet in the container will take time out of their lives
to meet outside of it, and measuring this process of selection provides
a helpful indicator for relationship formation. One way to capture this
indicator is to measure participation in an afterspace. Earlier I mentioned hosting a series of events where participants regularly participated in an afterspace for up to four hours. Capturing the number of
people who still remain in an afterspace every fifteen minutes after the
close of an event can provide an indicator of relationality, since people
are choosing to remain in conversation with one another rather than
going elsewhere, and since those conversations are themselves often
relationally meaningful.

This measure is strongly impacted by the opportunity cost of time
of the event's participants. If an event happens in the middle of the
workday when participants have prior commitments to scurry off to,
then the afterspace may be empty even though participants would
prefer to stay in it. An event catering to parents will probably have
fewer people staying in the afterspace than one catering to nonparents
unless free child care is provided. This is one example of why measurements from different communities cannot be directly compared.

For this reason, it can also be helpful to track follow-up conversations that occur between events. If an event is recurring, such as a monthly community gathering, the registration form can be programmed to respond differently to first-time and returning attendees. When an attendee is returning, the registration form can ask them questions like "Have you had any follow-up conversations with members of this community since the last event you attended?" If the respondent answers yes, they can be asked if they would like to share a sentence or two about the conversation and its impact. If events are not recurring, then these questions can be delivered via follow-up surveys delivered with permission over SMS.

Measuring gathering through afterspaces and registration surveys can begin to paint a picture of which event designs are effective at generating follow-up conversations and who among an event's attendees are participating in those conversations. It is possible to test a variety of event types in a variety of communities and measure rates of follow-up conversations to assess where there is relational potential.

Measuring Care

Researchers who study the social isolation crisis have identified a set of measures that seem to predict, better than anything else, who will or won't experience the myriad mental and physical health consequences of loneliness. Prompts like "Who can you count on when you need help?"[11] and "How strongly do you agree with the statement 'I can count on my friends when things go wrong'?"[12] focus on the care that people receive from the community. One of the best ways to know if people are on a path away from loneliness seems to be measuring whether they are caring for one another. This concept of care shows up across movement history. Historically, movements have often emerged not from places where people primarily talk about politics but from places where people care for one another. Black churches in Montgomery, Alabama; the Stonewall Inn in New York City; and the Center for Independent Living in Berkeley, California, were all centers of community care before they were centers of political power, as if one naturally flows from the other. This relationship between care and power reflects the interwoven relationship between resilience and transformation discussed in chapter 2. To be transformative, movements and other creative communities need to support small affinity groups through intense periods of uncertainty and disruption. The seeds of transformation rarely bloom without networks of care to water them.

All of this points to the idea that facilitating and measuring acts of care within a community may have an important role to play in enabling relational outcomes. I say "facilitating and measuring" because often supporting acts of care is the best way to acquire information about them. Care data can be captured through surveys with questions such as "Have you felt meaningfully supported by a member of this community in the past three months?" but richer data and stories are accessible if organizers plan an active role in encouraging acts of care. Many relational lineages have rituals for publicly expressing gratitude to people who have performed acts of care, and incorporating these gratitude rituals across a community can provide a point for qualitative and quantitative data capture. Recognizing and supporting people in a community who disproportionately provide care can also yield meaningful insights. Organizers will often conduct one-on-one check-ins with affinity group leaders to stay up to date and offer support, and conducting such check-ins with emerging care providers can provide rich qualitative information on where care is happening, where it is needed, and how the care providers themselves can be supported to avoid burnout. Formal or semiformal mentorship networks, in which new community members are paired with more seasoned members, can be another lens into this support work. Checking in with mentors and mentees about their experience provides a more focused source of care data and can be helpful to identify emerging caregivers among the mentor network.

Occasionally, care can be facilitated through technology, such as through the ask-and-offer systems deployed by companies like Switchboard. When communities use them, such technologies can provide their own fruitful sources of care data. Such systems should be approached with intention, however, as they require community members to know what to ask for and what to offer and to feel comfortable doing so. Care usually does not start with an ask; it starts with a story of struggle. Observable acts of care are indicators that these stories are inviting people to change one another in ways that matter.

Measuring Fundraising

One powerful act of care is moving money. This occurs through networks of mutual aid (though when these networks are relational, they are rarely limited to money); it occurs in churches when plates are passed to support families in need and in the grassroots *sou-sou* networks common in West Africa and the Caribbean.[13] Where trust exists, it is easier for money to flow, especially money that is supporting relational rather than transactional outcomes, so observable money flowing in this way can be an indicator of trust.

Haley Bash of the Donor Organizer Hub argues that this is one reason why incorporating grassroots fundraising into a movement or community can be so powerful. Because money is associated with the professional, transactional, and extractive world, many people have hesitations about discussing it in the context of community. Training people in the art of grassroots fundraising helps to overcome this block, giving community members the skills to fundraise not just for nonprofit organizations and political campaigns, but for grassroots projects and mutual aid. For nascent creative or political projects and in moments of crisis, the first money moved is often moved through personal networks of trust, and equipping these networks to move money can greatly improve a community's resilience and creative potential.

As with other acts of care, organizers can collect data on these financial transactions by providing infrastructure to support them. Trusted community networks can become targets for scams and exploitation, and trusted organizations with relational data on their membership are well positioned to detect and counter such fraud. One tool for facilitating such peer-to-peer financial transactions is Open Collective, which makes it easy for small affinity groups to set up a bank account and even receive fiscal sponsorship provided their finances are openly visible to the public. Although this combination of transparency and technology is not a fit for every movement, Open Collective makes it fairly straight-forward for a network of affinity groups to set up their own fundrais-ing and financial management infrastructure with minimal effort and then provide financial data in a consistent format. Another platform, Cobudget, allows organizers to set up a place for community-specific crowdfunding. For example, the Swiss Climate Fund invited members of the Swiss climate movement to use Cobudget to solicit projects from members of the local climate community and then let the funding deci-sions made by those activists inform their own resource allocation.[14] This sort of funding infrastructure provides an opportunity for mem-bers of a community to discover one another's fundable initiatives and for the convening organization to put these initiatives through a layer of vetting. It also provides a convenient mechanism for outside funders to match and amplify funding flowing at a grassroots level.

That being said, relying solely on financial data invites a wide range of opportunities for misalignment, bias, and downright graft. Organizers who are incentivized primarily to get community mem-bers to fund one another's projects will be disincentivized to do much of the work necessary to make those communities function. Relying solely on total dollars raised or even total number of donors may create a heavy bias toward communities that are comfortable with using and have access to financial resources. Simply matching dollars without any other criteria can create a bias toward relational work by and for the wealthy. For these reasons and more, reliance on financial data must be supplemented by other methodologies for relational measurement discussed in this chapter. A community that shows strong indicators of gathering, collective care, *and* peer-to-peer financial exchange is far more interesting than one that merely demonstrates the latter.

Measuring Creative Action

One of the most powerful ways to measure evolution within a com-munity is to examine what's evolving. As discussed in chapter 5, a social movement will reliably generate affinity groups that generate new strategic options for achieving the movement's goals. Through the same mechanism, a fan community will generate fan fiction and cosplay impressive enough to overtake the franchises that inspire them, and a rural community will generate local gatherings and small businesses. Tracking these initiatives and the affinity groups that birth them can provide an additional layer of insight into a community's relational strength and direction.

Of the measures described in this chapter, creative action is the most complex and therefore the least amenable to quantitative as opposed to qualitative measurement. A coffee date after an event represents the early stage of a developing relationship, which means that as relational measures go, it is likely to be reasonably uniform. A wild idea spawned in that coffee conversation could look like anything, making it difficult to predict what kind of measures are most relevant.

Creative action almost always emerges where the other indicators discussed in this chapter already exist. First a community gathers independently, then they start caring for one another, then they take creative action together. If your relational goal is to engender creative action, then gathering and care can serve as leading indicators. If the goal is to engender care, then you should be prepared to engage with creative actions that emerge out of it.

One approach to measuring creative action relies once again on the pattern of measurement through facilitation. Organizers can proactively identify members of their community interested in pursuing projects and support them or offer low-friction ways for community members to apply for support. When organizers update their colleagues about these check-ins and emerging projects, the summaries can easily be added to a shared database. The result is a feed of updates about emerging projects in the community that can be sorted for alignment, reviewed for strategic opportunity, and when appropriate and with permission, reported to outside groups such as funders.

As these creative actions emerge, they can and should expand the strategic option set of the organizers. A messy but quick way to do this is to rate incoming projects on a 1 to 5 scale:

1. **Values misaligned:** This project reflects values that contradict those that drive our community or movement. For example,

a progressive political campaign sees a proposal that includes transphobic language.

2. **Strategically misaligned:** This project is aligned with our values but potentially undermines one of our core strategic objectives. For example, a campaign with a commitment to nonviolence sees a proposal for an action that comes from a values-aligned place but contains an unnecessarily high risk of escalating to violence.

3. **Values aligned:** This project reflects values that we agree with but is unlikely to contribute meaningfully to our core strategy. For example, the volunteers on a political campaign decide to plan a Christmas party after the election.

4. **Strategically adjacent:** This project is not part of our core strategy but could be. It's values-aligned and has potential; it's just not our organization or community's current focus. For example, young volunteers on an electoral campaign decide to start a Twitch stream where they will encourage other young people to vote.

5. **Strategically aligned:** This project directly aligns with our core strategy and is aligned with our values. For example, a political campaign that invites volunteers to phone-bank finds a volunteer who wants to phone-bank.

When engaging their volunteer communities, most organizations ignore everything but 1s and 5s. If someone can contribute to a predictable outcome or increase the risk that that outcome will not come to pass, then they are worthy of attention; otherwise they are a distraction to be ignored. Relational measurement focuses on proposals in the 2 to 4 range. If a community has many values-aligned proposals that are strategically misaligned, then generative conflict may be needed to align around strategy. If a community is filled with 3s, then there may be an insufficiently compelling story that gives the community the context it needs to understand which actions are meaningful.

A rich influx of 4s is a sign that a community is in a mature state of relational health. To extend the metaphor above, a political campaign that focuses only on 5s will wind up with a large population of phone bankers and door knockers engaging in proven but fairly homogenous forms of voter contact. A campaign with a rich set of 4s will find itself overflowing with new art and music, new channels for connecting with churches and other care networks in hard-to-reach communities, and an ever-widening portfolio of volunteer expertise that it can draw on to inform both strategy and policy.

Creating time for organizing staff to review and support these strategically adjacent proposals is both incredibly powerful and tragically rare. By uplifting such proposals to the reporting process, organizers can ensure that funders, both internally and externally, understand their value and are willing to offer them support. These values-aligned and strategically adjacent actions are where investments in relationship bear fruit, but they can take time to mature.

A cliché in professional settings is to create goals that are SMART: specific, measurable, achievable, relevant, and time-bound. When engaging in relational work, this heuristic quickly breaks down. We cannot predict specific outcomes. While those outcomes are measurable, the measurements only point to a richer story rather than telling it. Because relational work unlocks new forms of power, it often thrives on visions that seem ludicrously unachievable at first, on actions whose relevance is only revealed with time, and on a relationship with time that is both unpredictable and highly nonlinear.

Instead, relational measurement is best when it is pursued with LOVE. Relational measures are strongest when they are:

1. **Localized:** Relational data comes from the communication channels and cultural practices that people in the community find comfortable rather than those that the researchers find convenient.

2. **Observational:** It draws on qualitative and quantitative data to draw a picture of what is happening within the community

without conducting experiments designed to make the community more predictable.

3. **Values-oriented:** The methods used to collect, store, and analyze data are aligned with the community's values and accountable to its governance mechanisms.

4. **Earned:** The data collected flows along lines of trust rather than through subterfuge or surveillance.

Relational measurement is a rich topic, and as of the writing of this book, I have barely scratched the surface. Some reading this book may be inspired to experiment with the measures of gathering, care, resourcing, and creative action outlined here. For others, it may be appropriate to step back to a deeper layer of abstraction and inquire how the evolution of relationships plays out in the system they are seeking to measure so that that process may be observed. Others, such as those with access to communications metadata or other dynamically updating tensors, may be able to directly measure changes in entropy that are indicative of the information exchange that sits at the heart of all relationships. Such measurement has potential applications far beyond reporting on relational outcomes to funders, but in the face of a global loneliness crisis, this may well be its most urgent application.

Generating Buy-in Around Relational Outcomes

If the loneliness crisis has a heart, it lies in the way that we generate buy-in about capital investments. Someone who feels directly changed by a community can happily deploy resources to support its relational outcomes. Someone who has built trust within a movement can skillfully deploy resources to support it. But if those people need to justify their decisions to people who do not deeply trust them and who sit outside the community they are funding, then they are left with only anecdotes and theater to justify their decision. Relational outcomes feel soft and ephemeral not because they are but because they seem that way to people who are trying to create predictable outcomes from far away.

Now, armed with both a rational and a relational understanding of the relational world, we can journey to that heart and invite it to change. We can convince people from far away that predictable outcomes are not the best way to live their values and achieve their deeper goals, that by releasing rigid predictability and passing on power, they can invite far more of the transformation that they wish to see in the world. We can teach them to understand a new kind of data that does not flow into graphs that go up and to the left but that points out where stories exist that demonstrate the complex reality of a community. Most importantly, we can organize. To create a world of abundant connection and powerful movements, the culture of investment must radically transform, and transformation does not happen without relationship.

Getting Buy-in Through Rational Argument

It is my hope that the curse of transactionality outlined in chapter 3 can be a helpful starting point when engaging with organizations that have a strong bias toward decision-making that prioritizes data collection and predictability above all else. Because increasingly relational systems become increasingly complex and therefore decreasingly predictable, there is a fundamental incompatibility between a management style focused on predictability and outcomes that require relationship. These organizations are welcome to stay in their comfort zone of Weberian bureaucracy, but to do so, they must acknowledge a significant strategic cost that has previously gone unacknowledged: They will be able to foster human connection only in its most constrained forms. Their work will be significantly less transformational and significantly less resilient to unforeseen disruption than would otherwise be possible. They will have access to far less creativity, more constrained tools of conflict resolution, and less compelling public narratives. Their need to render the relational reality around them invisible will deny them access to strategic intelligence that can only be delivered through lines of trust and to compelling opportunities for investment that can only be cultivated and discovered through networks of relationship. Their fealty to corporate professionalism will also have a personal cost. They will be less connected to their bodies, their land, their families, and their communities. They will grapple with the deep pain of loneliness, and over time that pain will cause their minds and bodies to fail.

The alternative is understandably terrifying. For many in positions of power, releasing control and listening to their relational selves when allocating resources has, for generations, been a path that leads to failure, then poverty, then classist and sometimes racist violence, then death. For others, swearing fealty to rational professionalism has been the only path out of this cycle of poverty and trauma, and they are understandably hesitant to challenge that loyalty. At the heart of this fear is the idea that joining you will undermine trust from those around them and bring about harsh punishment. You must not only convince them to buy into your relational outcomes but convince them that they will be able to bring those around them along for the journey.

To assuage this fear, they can be offered familiar sources of comfort with a new flavor. There is data, just not the sort of data that they are used to. There is proof, just not proof that can be neatly predicted ahead of time. There is learning, but the kind of learning that centers on data-backed stories rather than on randomized controlled trials and p-values, because relational learnings cannot be statistically removed from context. There is rigorous decision-making, but that decision-making focuses on aligning complex stories with shared values rather than on maximizing KPIs. Most of these institutional processes will be uncomfortable because they are new, and many will be awkward because they are still highly experimental and are adapted from communities that bureaucratic institutions are not used to trusting. Work is required to figure out how to do things differently, and that work takes comfort with a different kind of failure. Not the calculable risks that a plan will fail, but the risk that the relationships that hold a project or an institution together will fail to survive uncertainty. Like all risks, this can be mitigated, mostly by investing in the relationships involved, but like all risks it must also be accepted and held. The plan looks a little different than they may be used to, but there is a plan.

First, a decision needs to be made about where to create relationships in the world. The goal of investing in those relationships may be to support collaborative communication across isolated silos. It may be to enable transformation in a community that is ready to change but doesn't know how, to create resilience in the face of expected disruption, to foster creative innovation, or to unlock a new source of political power. Regardless of which relational outcome resonates as a goal, all of them will happen. There is no way to build resilience among residents in an elder-care facility without also strengthening their political power, for example. So the full range of these outcomes should be taken into account. Once it's clear where you want to see relationships built, it's time to design containers for them to build in. Ideally these containers are rooted in relational lineages with which the community is familiar. Ideally they are being led by someone who is already familiar with and integrated into the community or communities being resourced.

The plans for these containers can be quite detailed, though they are an embarkation point for a learning process and not a commitment to our consistent offering. The containers may invite participants to reflect on and connect around their own personal struggles after seeing such stories modeled by an organizer. They may include specific rituals for welcoming new people and helping them form connections in a new space. They may include embodied activities such as singing, dance, or other forms of movement. They may include after-spaces with food in places that are well suited to small clusters of casual conversation. There may be a range of container sizes, from large annual events to smaller monthly gatherings, one-on-one check-ins, and support for personal practices of rest and reflection. This network of containers should make it easy to imagine how relationships might evolve and how participants in these containers might be exposed to new ideas, differentiate the ones that are meaningful to them, and focus on the ones that are most meaningful.

These containers will generate a steady stream of stories and data, some of which will be summarized and made available to funders as part of a shared process of learning and accountability. Funders will not and should not have access to every piece of data flowing through the community. To maintain trust, the community must be aware of and have agency over how its data and stories will be presented to funders, and funders will respect this agency. What they can expect to see, if the containers are successful, is a growing heat map. Containers with attendance numbers, recurring attendance numbers, and between-event gathering metrics give an early picture of where relationships are forming. These early numbers will sprout into seedlings of care, metrics, and stories that paint a picture of how and where a community is beginning to support one another as it matures. Some of this support will take the form of resourcing, and some will take the form of grassroots initiatives that are adjacent and complementary to the convening organization's core strategy. As reports of these early efforts come in and are rewarded for aligning with the community's core values, more will begin to blossom. Soon, a mix of data and stories will flow in about a maturing community, complete with a growing grassroots cohesion layer that takes on some of the work of managing conflict and setting strategic direction previously executed by staff.

This means that the convening organization may have less responsibility for and control over the community it is convening over time. That's a good thing. The growing community should eventually be able to mobilize its own resources and survive without an ongoing expenditure of staff time if necessary, especially if serving the community it is convening is not the organization's sole mission. This means that the convening organization cannot control the community in the way that it controls its own employees. It can convene them around a set of shared values and hold them accountable to those values, but it cannot ask the community to prioritize its own strategic interests above all else. For this reason, it can be helpful for a convening organization and its community to be separate in the public eye. A community should not be able to speak with the weight of its convening organization's brand, nor should an organization's strict brand controls extend to the voices of the people it convenes. An organization may choose to disaffiliate with people who do not share its values, and in extreme cases, may encourage others to do the same, but it generally cannot stop those people from organizing or speaking publicly. This means that the values that an organization convenes around and invites people into are central—they are the core mechanism that keeps the convening organization and community aligned. Accountability around these values cuts both ways. Organizations should expect to be challenged by communities to live up to their shared values in a transformative process that is challenging but ultimately beneficial. To invite community, we must be ready and willing to be changed by it.

Investing in relationship will be a learning process. Funders can expect reports on learnings about what convening strategies build relationships, who is most strategic to build those relationships with, what new opportunities are emerging from those relationships, and what kinds of resources will bring those relationships to fruition. Funders will be called on to be more than checkbooks. Like everyone in the movement, there may be moments when their expertise, their personal social networks, their public voices, or their personal capacity for mentorship and care may become relevant. Funders won't be struggling to justify this expense to their peers; they'll be sharing a growing portfolio of opportunities to drive the change that those peers want to see in the world.

While there may exist ethical ways to use relational investment to turn a profit, such investment is beyond the scope of this book. A software platform may invest in relationship among developers building on top of it, or a real estate investment firm may invest in relationships that strengthen community and make their properties more appealing. I believe that there are severe limits to what such transactional investments in relational outcomes can accomplish. To understand and access the benefits of investing in relationship, funders must find ways to experience and be changed by the relationships that they are helping to create. Funders will live in a world where relationships exist that did not before, where communities are more resilient, creative, and capable of driving transformation. They can benefit, both directly and indirectly, from the creative evolution that takes place in these communities and the resilience that they provide. While funders are not entitled to be a movement's priority, they can benefit from its existence. When their grandchildren face hardship, that movement can be there to provide support in a way that a bank account cannot. Whatever their own journey out of loneliness looks like, the movement can offer pathways that did not exist before. Understanding that journey, how it has shaped their values, and how it remains an ongoing struggle can be vital to positioning relationship as worthy of investment.

Getting Buy-in Through Relational Organizing

The arguments outlined above, while compelling to some, will be far too unorthodox for many funders to accept. It will not be difficult for them to conduct rational counterarguments and to evoke urgent crises that do not afford time for uncertain relational experimentation, even when relational strategies are the most effective ways to build transformative power and creative resilience in the face of such crises. Fortunately, we need not accept the false premise that funding decisions are the result of rational discussions between isolated individuals and those in power.

To change the way that funding works, we need to organize. If you are reading this book, there is a good chance that you sit in some institution of power that both deploys resources strategically and must justify that deployment to others. Whether you are a UX (user experience) researcher on a product team, a program officer in a foundation, or a field organizer on a political campaign, you are probably frustrated with the ways in which relational work is both extremely impactful and difficult to justify, and you are probably not alone. Others around you almost certainly share your frustrations, even if they have yet to find a container to share their stories. You can create that container.

During my time in the tech reform movement, I supported a wide range of tech workers organizing for change from within large social media companies. Their organizing took place at a time when the tech industry was grappling with a widespread spiritual crisis. A growing number of workers from Meta were heading to increasingly extreme spiritual retreats, and some left Meta to head to divinity school. Tech workers found themselves in a community simultaneously scrambling in their day jobs to support dominance and homogeneity and scrambling outside of them to escape disconnection. In such an environment, a drop of rootedness and purpose found in social movements proved a powerful thing.

The first job of the movement was to arm these workers with language: stories in public consciousness that they could bring up with their coworkers over lunch, professionally acceptable objections that they could raise in a product meeting, and references that could be picked up by those who shared their concerns and were consuming similar media about it. These objections and quiet conversations wouldn't go anywhere at first; the cultural momentum of the institutions they inhabited was far too great, but they would slowly begin to reveal allies. Someone might come to them after the meeting, thank them for speaking up, and then accept an invitation to coffee. They would grow a network of internal allies capable of dreaming up and proposing increasingly well-formulated proposals for change, and those proposals would get rejected until they didn't.

The convenient thing about working in the midst of a crisis is that ideas that have been systematically rejected can become urgently necessary very quickly. Employees working on health misinformation struggled along on little more than passion until a global pandemic made their work vital overnight. After the 2020 election, integrity teams who were monitoring #StopTheSteal groups were told to refocus attention elsewhere, until disaster struck on January 6. Internal coalitions that are organized to address systemic failures are like seeds before a forest fire, ready to sprout when the consequences of those failures come home.

As these networks grew, they would surround and infiltrate the decision-making bodies that held them back. Sometimes a group of workers would find a senior ally who was a peer of the decision-maker who held them back and could exert pressure. Sometimes they would find allies among more junior staff, who had more willingness to take risks to align their careers with their values. Often they would connect with movements that stretched beyond the boundaries of their employers, forging relationships with peers in different organizations who shared their values and connecting with outside advocates with voices that their community needed to hear, such as survivors of harm. They built these relationships by finding or building containers. Sometimes they would co-opt the corner of a company retreat or an industry conference for their gathering, and eventually they began hosting planning calls, happy hours, and conferences of their own.

As more people began to speak up in meetings and connect outside of them, the culture around them began to shift. Punctuated by crises, the easily dismissable arguments that they voiced became harder to ignore. People who were afraid of being rejected by their peers for embracing such radical views started to wonder if they might instead be rejected for failing to seriously consider them. All of this happened in relational time, which is to say incredibly slowly, and then frustratingly backward, and then all at once.

Worker organizing in the tech industry is still nascent, but it provides a hint at the spectrum of options available to people seeking to change how institutional funding is deployed from the inside. These options include whistleblowers who create crises of public opinion, management-approved employee resource groups who leverage those crises to organize internal change, and employees who drop out of established institutions to form values-oriented projects that can take up the space that these institutions vacate when they fail. Pulling coworkers aside after a meeting might create professional risk, but the risk can be worth it. When movements win in the workplace, when they succeed in transforming how work is done and how resources are allocated, the trust that organizers have built tends to open new doors. Some are doors to individual professional opportunity, but there are also doors to new forms of collective power. If we are to change how resources are allocated, address the loneliness crisis, and build movements that meet our world's greatest challenges, this sort of worker organizing is our best hope.

In the process of writing this book, I have been shocked at how widespread the frustration is at the way that funding is allocated. From senior leaders in philanthropy who hold to rigid professionalism so that they can change the system from the inside to the waves of talent entering political organizing only to be burned out by its harsh focus on transactional outcomes, there is a deep pain both felt and hidden at every part of the system. Wherever institutions with a corporate structure seek to build community or grow movements, I have found a rage smoldering somewhere beneath the surface. Sometimes it overflows in rebellion, burning out the most promising talent in a movement before it can find the resilience it needs to drive change. Sometimes it gets buried deep, visible only as forgotten dreams that are sensitive to the touch. I have seen this anger, when given space and held with care, cause rooms to erupt with laughter. I have seen it forge friendships, create backchannels around institutional roadblocks, and help people understand that they love the same thing, even if that thing does not yet have a name. If those of us who feel this rage can invite one another to hold it together, we will find joy, we will find power, and we will find rest.

I hope that, if such organizing comes to pass, it will not target all transactional thinking as backward and exploitative. In a world where relationships thrive, many things need to be predictable. The computer that I write these words on supports me in relationship. So does my famous matzo ball soup recipe, and both are designed to have reliable and predictable outcomes. The lineage that gives us ROI calculations, project plans, and orderly spreadsheets holds wisdom as well as harm. It is a part of the ecosystem that is overgrown, not an enemy to be eliminated. We must cut it back, especially in places where the tasks it undertakes demand relational outcomes. We must resource the relational lineages around it that have been under-resourced and extracted from so that they can grow to a place of balance and integration. Engineering an electricity grid is a transactional task, though citing its infrastructure is a relational one. Maintaining school buildings is a transactional task, though the resources necessary to do so can be sourced relationally.

Sometimes anger can be an invitation to relationship. An invitation first to strength and resilience with those who share our anger, then to the power necessary to invite the causes of that anger into a process of mutual transformation. I hope for a world of abundant invitation to relationship, and in that world I hope that the lineage of dominance, homogeneity, and disconnection that has made us so lonely will be radically transformed but not eliminated. I hope that it will be supported in grappling with the harm that it has caused itself and others, and I hope that it will be able to find its way to relationships of healing and transformation. I cannot chart a path to a world where movements greatly surpass corporations in power and wealth, where invitations to meaningful connection are more abundant than invitations to purchase products, and the work of building relationship is resourced for all of the value it produces. I do not know exactly what role corporate investment such as stock markets and traditional philanthropy might play in such a world or how it might be transformed by a sophisticated understanding of relational prediction and resource allocation. But, messily, I can articulate a vision.

Reflection Questions

- How might you help money flow toward relational work?

- In what ways are you close to relational work that needs resourcing?

- How might you help with the work of inviting money to build trust with it?

- How might you educate funders about the importance of funding relational work?

- How might data and stories about gathering, care, and action support your efforts to move resources?

- In what ways are you close to resources that could move toward relational work?

- How might you build trust to deploy these resources and invite others to do the same?

- If you are part of an institution with resources to deploy, what conversations might help you find allies in deploying them relationally?

CHAPTER 8

What Happens If We Invest in Relationship:

A Speculative Future

THERE IS EVERY REASON to believe that our civilization's down-ward spiral toward loneliness will continue. The root cause of our loneliness is deeply entrenched in our most powerful institutions, in the way that our economy operates and the way that we are taught to make meaning in the world. This culture of loneliness is closely interwoven with a history of racism, patriarchy, and environmental devastation that has profoundly shaped our world, and imagining that any of these things might simply disappear is unhelpfully naive. But the culture of loneliness can be transformed. Every day, billions of dollars around the world are being wasted because the people allocating them cannot see the power of relationship. This book has explored how people in and around those institutions might begin to redirect those dollars and how we might both discover and relearn the power of relationship and invite individual and institutional capital to unlock that power. These decisions about money are far from the only decisions that matter, but they are an intriguing pressure point. What happens if people who hold lineages of relational wisdom start getting resourced for the value that they create in the world? What happens if institutions held back by a culture of transactional prediction learn to think relationally and are financially rewarded for doing so?

Even as I write this book, I struggle to answer these questions. A world without relational invisibility and the resulting loneliness crisis would be so radically transformed that it can be difficult to imagine. The speculative future I present here is not a prediction, nor is it a logical argument about what will come to pass. It is a messy and intentionally naive attempt to find hope. Like identity, it is a tool to be picked up and modified, to spur imagination and discussion about a more relational future. This imagined future leans toward the hopeful because on balance, hope is what is needed. But I welcome just as strongly imagination that notices and seeks to mitigate causes of harm. All too often the culture of dominance and homogeneity limits our imaginations, and to move away from that world, we must play with setting them free. It can be difficult to imagine in an environment of scarcity, so let's start our journey envisioning an abundance of money surrounded by relationships that decide to do something new.

Where Might the Money Come From?

In 2022, wealthy individuals in the United States avoided taxes by contributing $72.67 billion to donor-advised funds (DAFs). This amount has increased 46.6 percent since 2020.[1] Of the almost $73 billion that flowed into these funds, only about $45 billion flowed out of them to any kind of charitable work. The remaining $27 billion, which is roughly equivalent to the net income of Meta, was simply too labor-intensive to deploy in a way that wealthy DAF holders could justify to themselves or their friends. As a result, the money is piling up. At the end of 2022 about $235 billion unallocated dollars sat in DAFs,[2] the equivalent of just under 1 percent of US GDP. All that money just sitting there uncertain what to do with itself is far from alone.

There's also the $1.057 trillion in assets held by philanthropic foundations,[3] which are only legally required to distribute 5 percent of their assets per year and often struggle to do so. There's the $1.7 trillion budget that the US Department of Health and Human Services has to promote Americans' health and well-being,[4] some fraction of which could no doubt benefit from investing in relational outcomes. There is the $29 billion directly given by corporations through direct grants and employee matching,[5] and the budgets of social enterprises that seek to prioritize values and mission over profit.[6] Though it is small monetarily, let's also not overlook the $14.4 billion in electoral spending that would almost certainly be more effectively spent on bringing people into conversation than on political spam.[7] Not all of this money can or should be invested relationally, but even a modest fraction would constitute a major emerging sector of the US economy.

Let us imagine a giant dam that prevents this money from flowing toward relational outcomes that are aligned with its values and stated goals. Now imagine that the dam has a small crack. This breach would almost certainly happen through relationship, through a mix of supported personal transformation, organized advocacy among staff, and public pressure from grantees and other communities in need of support. Let's imagine that this dam is already riddled with hairline breaches, places where resources drip through despite a system intent on holding them back, and that these thin cracks start to grow and reach toward one another. The dam is not about to dramatically burst, but the money moving through it will clear a path for more money to move in the future. Let's imagine that once people and institutions start to invest in relationship, they like the results and are changed such that they invest more. Let's imagine that people want to flow toward relationship like water wants to flow downhill and that no barrier that keeps them from doing so can be permanent.

Where would this money flow? No doubt Silicon Valley entrepreneurs will raise millions on the promise that they will be able to capture it in a vast global net and direct it back to the coffers of the superwealthy, but they will be doomed to failure because the most important tool for building relationship is incompatible with this colonial approach. To create relationship, we must create the conditions for relationship, and those conditions can only be created by human minds working in collaboration. These minds must deeply understand local context in a way that a centralized corporate headquarters cannot. They will be more powerful if they are rooted in relational lineage, in their bodies and in the more-than-human world that surrounds them. Money looking to resource relationship will need to move away from places where it has been centralized and toward organizers with the skills and knowledge to deploy it effectively.

More often than not, this will involve distributing resources back to communities that they have been extracted from. Black, brown, rural, and Indigenous communities that have maintained connections to relational lineage as a means of survival will be uniquely suited to turn money into relational impact. Money may flow to a mutual aid network among disabled folks, an annual block party arranged by a Black matriarch who has been helping to hold the neighborhood together for decades, or a network of supportive spaces for trans youth rooted in the knowledge of trans elders. These small rooted spaces will be far better suited to make relationship happen than anything centrally controlled or massively scaled. As the dam cracks, money will flow out to individuals and small- to medium-scale projects, as a counterforce to rising income inequality. It will flow to places where powerful relational lineages are in need of repair. This money is distinct from reparations paid for the impacts of slavery and institutional racism or to Indigenous survivors of genocide, broken treaties, and cultural erasure, but it will be a collective investment in repairing those disruptions in lineage. If we are to navigate our way back to a place of abundant connection, we will need to revive, repair, and evolve that which has been damaged by centuries of focus on dominance and homogeneity. When money starts seeking the best possible way to create relationship, a good deal of it inevitably flows to this work of repair.

Let's imagine that this money flows through a network of trust, rooted in accountability to shared values, that is wholly unlike any financial infrastructure that we know today. It resembles and is inspired by the mycelial network that runs beneath the floor of a forest, a complex and intelligent web that directs resources from sites of abundance to sites of potential through threads that are small and constantly evolving. This network resembles a movement that is infused with and evolved to better manage flows of capital, although that description is an oversimplification because a movement is never just one thing.

How Might the Money Flow?

Imagine a church basement in North St. Louis, perhaps one of the same church basements where organizers gathered to plan actions in nearby Ferguson, Missouri, in 2014. Today the church basement is hosting fellowship after Sunday services. Located in a predominantly Black neighborhood with a rich history of worship, the space is alive with homemade food and lively conversation. Money is being raised for a successful affordable housing program alongside raucous laughter and more than a little gossip. An eight-year-old boy named Malcolm is eager to run and play with other kids after spending the day sitting in the pews, but his mother Naomi is holding him back. Malcolm has just been diagnosed with asthma, and Naomi's caution elicits support from a grandpa and an auntie who are sitting nearby. Many of the kids in their lives are struggling with asthma or other health issues, and getting support from the health care system is a struggle. Inspired by the conversation, Naomi starts a conversation within the church and a WhatsApp group for families supporting kids with asthma.

Naomi and a few parents and grandparents give the group life, and before long they're offering advice on how to navigate racism in the medical system and inviting one another to cookouts. It's no secret that environmental racism is impacting North St. Louis, where pollution from highways and power plants is more concentrated than in any other part of the city. At one cookout, a debate starts up about how bad this pollution is, which leads Naomi to discover that North St. Louis also has fewer air-quality monitoring stations than anywhere else in the city. Backed by others in the group, she begins looking into what it would take to get one set up at the church.

Naomi starts looking around for advice and gets connected with organizers who are eager to plug her into a broader movement. Down the Mississippi, a "cancer alley" stretches from Baton Rouge to New Orleans, where petroleum refinement has led to widespread pollution primarily impacting Black communities. In response, a robust network of relationships have grown up to support families impacted by cancer, monitor pollution, and advocate for environmental justice. Organizers there love what Naomi is doing and offer her advice on university collaborations, ways to secure monitoring equipment, and possible sources of funding. There is money flowing to the kind of work that Naomi is doing: work that touches environmental justice and is rooted in communities of care. The way to learn about it would be to have a conversation with Rita.

Rita is an artist in Albuquerque, a veteran of the protests at Standing Rock and a widely respected elder in the environmental justice movement. Every year, Rita and five of her closest friends take a backpacking trip to catch up and discuss the state of the movement that brought them together. A DC lobbyist, an urban farmer from Detroit, a land-use attorney from Tulsa, and the executive director of an environmental education program in the Bronx all meet up with Rita to reconnect with the land and one another. During one of these trips, they floated the idea of starting a Movement Fund. Informed by the trusted relationships that they had build across the environmental movement, the five friends would create a constantly updating story about where resources could flow to the movement's underappreciated edges to have the most impact. This story would be validated by relational data collected from these edges and by the trust that each of them had built and would provide a point of invitation for money interested in flowing into the movement. With the data that they provided, it would be easy for people with money unfamiliar with the movement to understand Rita and her friends' understanding of what relationships the movement most needed and deploy their funds to support the work necessary to make those relationships possible.

Rita and her friends are one of many such funds. Over the past several years, Rita has become interested in the role of communities of care centered in sites of environmental injustice. The environmental movement needs to build a broad, diverse base of political power to meet the challenges ahead, and it needs to spend proportionally more time and attention supporting communities directly impacted by climate change. To Rita, investing in communities of care and advocacy focused on environmental injustice is a way to build this capacity, a site of relational possibility that the broader movement needs but fails to appreciate. After some convincing, the other members of the Movement Fund agree with her. They manage the fund as a side project, aggregating relational data that they have earned access to in a shared workspace and discussing it in a meme-filled Signal thread. Together they conduct a level of analysis that rivals foundations with dedicated full-time teams. Because they have easier access to information through networks of trust and well-honed instincts from their organizing experience, they can come to insightful consensus in a fraction of the time. As a result, the fund does not need to be their primary source of income. It provides small stipends, allocated according to a values-based money exercise that they engaged in together, respecting the work that they put in while pushing the vast majority of resources to the places that they recommend.

Although Naomi's work is nascent, Rita is excited to connect and build trust. As this trust is built, Rita gets a deeper understanding of how Naomi is gathering her community in ways that lead to care and action and helps her find lightweight ways to use relational measurement to make the impact of her work communicable to others. She lays out a path for Naomi to start getting microgrants for food at community gatherings and lays out a plan over the next few months to getting a stream of funding that would allow Naomi to leave her low-paying job and focus on organizing. Naomi needs to keep doing what she's doing: building relationships, building trust within the movement around her, and staying accountable to the values that she and her community share. Doing this will generate data and stories that people like Rita and her friends can use to mobilize resources.

As Rita and Naomi's relationship grows, Rita is contacted by Adam, a marketing executive from a wealthy suburb just outside Chicago. Concerned by the wildfire smoke that is having an increasing impact on his community and his kids, Adam and his husband hosted a dinner party for their friends focused on the practical steps that they could take around climate action. After the party, Adam was motivated to look for invitations to get involved that resonated with his values, and he found the invitation from Rita's Movement Fund. As someone used to analyses of audiences and impact, he found the Fund's mix of stories and data impressive. They had a clear thesis about how and where to build power and proof that that power was being built, even if it was all structured in a way that felt new to him. In their first conversation, Rita modeled the kind of trust-building work that is necessary between funders and movements. If Adam wanted to show up, there were ways for him to show up, both with his skills in marketing and as a donor organizer among his friends. Asking friends for money sounded intimidating at first, but Rita clarified that the work was focused on agency. His job was to find a path toward supporting the movement, including with his money, and to support his friends in finding paths that worked for them. Motivated, Adam began having follow-up conversations with some of his guests, starting with two who held DAFs that had gone largely unallocated. The resources flowing into the movement fund and to hundreds of small projects like Rita's became more abundant.

Accountability sits at every level of this process. Naomi is accountable to the community around her to produce the relational results that drive funding, though once she has these results, she will have several funders to choose from. Rita is accountable to the values that drive her relationships, to the people like Naomi that she serves, to her five friends, and to others in the movement that volunteer to hold them accountable. The data in the Fund's shared workspace is sensitive, but it is reviewed by others in the movement who occupy positions of trust to ensure that it is values-aligned, and any concerns are resolved through generative conflict. Organizing and messiness are expected, and reputable movement funds are expected to have records of this kind of conflict in their public profiles. Adam is accountable to both the values of his community and to people like Rita who provide him with access to the information he needs to make good decisions and invite his friends to do the same. Adam's invitation into the movement relies on his ability to stay aligned with its values.

How Might Our World Transform?

Now imagine that this process of money flowing through networks of relationship toward networks of relationship is unfolding with greater and greater frequency. Billions start flowing through relationships based on trust toward projects brimming with relational potential. Foundations, seeing how impactful these new mechanisms are, begin to internally reform to focus less on the labor-intensive process of funding predictable projects and more on the trust-based process of funding movements. Small values-driven businesses pop up to serve movements and find a rich relational potential that helps them outcompete businesses focused purely on profit. In increasingly creative ways, money is flowing anywhere that has transformative relational potential. The culture at schools shifts as they are resourced as critical sites of community rather than as engines for producing test scores. Money concerned with public safety flows toward creating supportive relationships for those who are being released from incarceration and toward relational alternatives to incarceration as a movement of growing power dismantles the policies that keep the system of mass incarceration in place.

In science, the barriers that keep fields siloed, postgrads miserable, and academic departments gridlocked with petty politics begin to melt away. The greatest minds of a generation have easy access to colleagues outside their field, recognition outside a rat race to publish in prestigious journals, and movements that can both inform and directly apply their work. Everywhere the pace of discovery accelerates, driven by shared values that prevent many harmful discoveries from being resourced with collaboration, funding, and attention. A team creating next-generation protein printers for synthetic biology is well aware that they will lose the support of the movement around them if they fail to think long and hard about how to prevent their technology from being used to create bioweapons. Their research, along with a growing understanding of the deep links between relationships and human health, rapidly makes health care affordable and accessible in a way that was previously unthinkable. Health care is increasingly a thing that the medical community supports families and communities in doing, rather than a thing it performs itself, as our individual experiences of medicine gradually become less like fixing a car and more like preparing a family meal. These medical advances play out most profoundly in a radically transformed experience of aging.

Everywhere that the crisis of social isolation has taken root, a sense of invitation begins to creep in. It is slow at first, but as more and more organizers and community leaders gain the financial stability necessary to do what they love, it grows. Elders are one of the first groups to experience the shift. An exponentially growing set of relational experiments reveal two patterns: we desperately need the relational wisdom that is being lost, and there is an undeniable magic to an intergenerational moment of celebration. Communities of elders begin to experience invitations to help create the relationships that the world needs, offers that are interwoven with care. Not all of these offers need to be accepted. Those who want to enjoy time alone still have it in abundance, but thoughtful invitations to intergenerational community are abundant, and those who accept them are often happier and invite their friends. They help first-time parents, they cook for community gatherings, they serve as mentors to a generation of leaders that is coming into being, and much more.

The communities that elders are joining and often co-leading also draw in young people seeking their own paths out of loneliness. Here, invitations flow through a rapidly transforming social media landscape, one in which creators have found that it is far more fulfilling and sustainable to invite people into community than it is to use their influence to sell products. The relational agency generated by these communities redefines the algorithmic landscape for the attention economy: Instead of the most engaging content floating to the top, platforms emerge that focus on connecting people with the invitations that they find most personally relevant and fulfilling. Integrity workers networked across tech companies and governments use the data coming off these communities to spot and down-rank invitations that lead to harm. They do not oppose any political standpoint or view of reality but they do prevent the growth of communities that actively harm their members or others. Some conspiracy theories still exist, but they struggle to take hold of the public imagination without evidence. Some hate groups still exist, but their membership dwindles without a population of lonely and resentful people being fed their content. When discovering a new community online, it is easy to see not only how popular that community is, but the basic indicators of its relational health. The internet is filled with containers you can trust to generate whatever kind of relationships you want, and there is transparency and accountability when those relationships generate harm. Where there was loneliness there is now a blossoming of relational agency.

Everywhere, money and human talent flow toward the work of creating relationship. High school students follow invitations into movements and other communities and regularly wind up in positions of leadership, shattering ageism and positioning them for lives of meaning and purpose. College students increasingly find that the trust built in community and movement work is far more valuable than good grades at a top school when it comes to establishing a career. Student organizing is increasingly interwoven with intergenerational organizing as campuses and other youth-focused communities become recognized as hubs of relational creativity and political power for others to follow. College, while worthwhile for many, is no longer a barrier to a lucrative and influential career.

Deeper experience with relational lineage and conflict mediation means that more young people are comfortable living in sophisticated forms of community. College roommates start cooperatives and pool their resources to purchase property far earlier than their parents' generation was able to. They are less likely to move away from their communities when they have kids and more likely to have committed intergenerational communities of care that prevent them from being isolated in parenthood with their romantic partners. Having kids is far less burdensome economically, professionally, and emotionally. Instead of pressuring young people to get married and have kids, it becomes fashionable to ask them what relationships with kids they are looking for at this time in their lives. Aunties and uncles of choice abound, maintaining regular supportive relationships with kids in their communities even when they don't feel like biologically producing kids of their own. Primary parents' relationships have room to breathe and community support when they inevitably enter conflict, so they are less overwhelmed and better able to show up as the parents they want to be. Everywhere infants, toddlers, and elementary school kids are thriving. Though the birthrate is just below the replacement rate, far more adults have far more children in their lives and are happier for it.

Land use shifts. Isolated suburbia loses its appeal while both urban and rural communities flourish. A network of supportive relationships means that it is easier for communities in areas rendered uninhabitable by climate change to relocate without losing everything. Farmers are supported in shifting their crops as the average age of a farmer in the United States drops from 57 to 36, with new blood eager to tackle the challenges of labor exploitation and climate fragility at the heart of the US food supply. Where antiquated water rights created a gridlocked and untenable system, mediation strategies begin to move things forward. More renewable energy and transmission are being built, and there is better and better science to build them with. Just as more people have deeper relationships with children, more people have deeper relationships with land. It is not uncommon for even diehard New Yorkers to be co-stewards of a land project and to deeply understand a particular ecosystem as it moves through the seasons. More land is governed collectively; more land moves back to Indigenous lineages with a history of stewardship. In helpful ways, this relationship with land changes us.

Jobs, too, are different. Being part of a community with resources flowing through it creates a wide range of options for financial survival, some of which involve working toward transactional outcomes and many of which do not. Some survive and thrive mostly through participation in mutual aid networks, creating relational value for those around them with minimal participation in the traditional economy and no sense of shame about it. Some survive and thrive by focusing entirely in and on community, tapping into income streams that value the work of creating relational containers and regularly finding additional opportunities through the trust that they build there. Black communities and other sites of underrecognized relational labor see an influx of wealth as they are appropriately recognized and rewarded for the value that they create. Black lineages that have been disrupted by centuries of exploitation and violence are resourced for repair. Even those who maintain lucrative traditional jobs often find it helpful to keep a foot or two in the relational economy since it gives them access to a wealth of professional opportunities and meaningful personal experiences that money can't buy. It turns out that a luxury villa in Tuscany is often not as fun as a trusting relationship with a loving family down the hill who has a nice guest room and a thick book of family recipes. As relational agency goes up, a flush bank account becomes steadily less appealing as a measure of wealth. A senior position in a corporate hierarchy is no longer synonymous with success. People in corporate jobs that feel unfulfilling or misaligned with their values are far more likely to leave, confident that movements can catch them.

Bleeding talent and facing an increasingly organized group of values-driven employees, customers, investors, and suppliers, the power of corporate executives rapidly constricts. Amazon's investors want to know why they only have a single stock to bet on both web services and a TV studio when the two could just as easily be governed in federation. Increasingly organized vendors want to know why the marketplace Amazon has built can't be a community-governed protocol, and they wield growing technical and political power to make that question a reality. There is pressure from all sides to turn one of the world's largest corporations into something more closely resembling a movement: a network of more locally governed projects woven together by a shared story and values rather than a shared brand and balance sheet. Such a system is more relational, and therefore more agile and innovative, making it more appealing to investors.

Investors, after all, don't care as much about profitability as they do about being better than others at predicting it. All of the relational data flowing off movements is extremely useful for predicting where transformation, resilience, and therefore money will flow, which means that investors who have access to it are more successful. The only investors who get that access are those who are values-aligned enough to earn movements' trust. Gradually, control of the global financial markets starts to shift from Wall Street to people rooted in the communities where the economy lives. This new generation of investor-organizers, many of whom moonlight managing Movement Funds, see no reason to keep giant corporations like Amazon under centralized autocratic rule. The movements they come from can more easily integrate with and make use of the pieces of Amazon, providing them with values-aligned economic opportunities and their employees with myriad benefits in return. The corporate form persists in a much less dominant state, as something broken up and integrated with the communities and movements around it, rather than as a dominant economic titan.

In Washington, DC, and other centers of democracy around the globe, the power games of corporate lobbyists are replaced by an ecology of democratic movements. These movements mobilize votes to keep politicians in office and work directly with their staff to shape policy, making congressional offices something akin to a powerful affinity group that sits between several movements with intersecting values. A high school student who cannot yet vote may nonetheless wind up serving with congressional staffers to shape a policy proposal around federal education funding. By leveraging talent and insight from the movements around them, elected leaders can get far more done while facing far fewer impenetrable political roadblocks. Political parties lose power, and so does partisanship, as people increasingly identify with movements that are adept at working across party lines to achieve their goals. Movements empower and accelerate the work of democratic governments, strengthening national and international bodies that serve as points of agreement for people with vastly differing backgrounds and values. A populace increasingly familiar with collective governance in their homes, families, and workplaces begins to evolve the mechanics of democracy. There is more capacity to agree across lines of difference and more capacity to address the inequities that hold our democracies back.

While the governments and economies of democracies thrive, the world's autocracies grow increasingly fragile. They must suppress movements in order to maintain centralized control, and that suppression grows ever more costly as the tools of organizing grow more sophisticated. Limited to hierarchical structures, their economic engines are less innovative and less productive. Forced to suppress rather than work with movements, their governments are far less nimble and resilient. Their people increasingly see what is possible and demand change. Across the globe, authoritarian power structures either crumble or scramble to transition to more democratic forms. Police violence, state surveillance, and risk of nuclear escalation are down; peaceful demonstrations and investigative journalism are up.

Across the globe the wealth gap that has been rising steadily for the past half century begins to drop. So do carbon emissions. People live well on less land that we manage more mindfully. Relationship is not forced upon us but is there for us to safely explore, and as we explore it, it makes us happier, healthier, and more capable. We busy ourselves pruning the lineage of dominance and homogeneity that has taken hold of so many of our imaginations so that we can reconnect with and evolve the many lineages of relational wisdom that are our birthright. Some of us may have less transactional power, and some of us have less freedom to cause harm without relational consequence, but we will have a sense of relational agency that is as welcome as it is unimaginable today.

From this place of connectedness, resilience, and adaptability we will face the hardest century in our species' long history. Billions of us will be displaced. The food and water we have built our civilizations around will shift radically as our forests burn, our ecosystems grow increasingly fragile, and our oceans die and rise. I know that we will survive, but we will not survive through a strategy of isolation and conflict. Our best hope is to relearn the hard, messy work of coming together, to embrace it with our imagination, and move it back to its rightful place in our economy. This will require change—change that is no doubt far messier and more complex than the simplistic and rosy picture I have painted here. But one way or another, that change is coming. We cannot know exactly how; we cannot know exactly which strategies will result in our survival, but we know that now is a critical time to invest in the work of transformation and resilience. Some of that investment will come from the individual transformation of people in power, but the majority will come because the people around those people choose to organize. The first steps toward this organizing are not hard: a few conversations with friends, the creation of a space for people to come together, an open curiosity about the movements that you might join and contribute to. Choosing to invest in relationship will be our greatest challenge, our greatest joy, and our greatest victory.

Reflection Questions

- What might your world look like with more relationship in it?

- What might your day-to-day life look like in a world with abundant access to relationship?

- What might happen in this world that aligns with your values?

- What might happen that is misaligned with your values, for example if people who do not share your values also gain relational power?

- How might resources move to make that world possible?

- Who might they move to?

Conclusion

THESE DAYS A LOT of my time is spent parenting. I take my kid to a reservoir near our house, and she discovers a secret path to a grassy hill topped by a single tree. She asks to be lifted up into its branches, but instead I casually lean against it. My arms become handholds and my shoulders become footholds until she is up in the tree and I am watching her, still relaxed, ready to catch her or be her ladder down. Parenting is about a lot of things, but for me a great deal of it is about the places I take her to and the ways we are present there.

When she was four we went camping and the night grew unexpectedly cold. We spent the night huddled together under a pile of sleeping bags and blankets and emerged from our tent to find the campsite covered in frost. I quickly lit our small stove to make hot chocolate for her to drink in our warm car. The hot chocolate felt like an expression of love, and so did the cold. My love as a parent is not conditional in the way that a contract is conditional, but it is expressed through the steady creation of conditions. Through those conditions I do my best to invite deeper relationship into the world that we share.

I channel my own father, inviting me to wait in stillness on the edge of the Grand Canyon. There is a sense of ease that comes from letting the shaping flow through me. After deciding to form a family, Avary, Zeke, and I sat down to talk about what from our families of origin we wanted to re-create and what from those families we wanted to reimagine. The lineages were there, not just from those who shared our genes but from all of the communities and movements that had shaped us. We weren't in this alone. We didn't need to invent something new from scratch; we needed to weave with intention.

The conditions that we create together for relationship come from that weaving.

I've come to think of this process of weaving and evolving as a sort of relational practice, one that shows up not just in my life as a parent but in my life as a son, an organizer, a partner, and a friend. This relational practice requires presence and it requires foresight. It requires acts of care and it requires the courage to instigate conflict. It is deeply practical, and for me it is also deeply spiritual. I practice gratitude for the relationships that have shaped me. I try my best to see how the world is made of relationship and to let it guide me to the places where I might invite more relationship into being. The journey away from loneliness has become a path toward something. I do not know where the path is headed, but I have many teachers to guide me.

Sometimes on this journey I get the sense that something immensely important is being held back. Sometimes the loneliness that used to leave me hopeless instead crackles with a feeling of potential. Sometimes the loneliness that is so radically reshaping the world around me feels deeply and tragically unnecessary. I have many movements that I show up for, and I am learning to show up for the movement to end this loneliness. I do this by helping to create the conditions for relationship in the world around me: by cooking food and extending invitations, by arranging furniture and by getting outside, by planning the complex logistics of gathering, and by practicing my quality of presence.

I do this with a respect for my own limited relational capacity. I can't connect with everyone, but I can listen for invitations that feel right in my body and create a few invitations of my own. This can be overwhelming because the movement to end loneliness deeply intersects with every other movement that I believe in. Even movements that do not explicitly talk about loneliness are generally deeply engaged in the work of inviting people out of it, so I find that work and support it as best I can. I pass on money, and help others to pass on theirs, because proximity to money is part of my position in the world. I help with the work of organizing when such help is invited because it gives me a chance to invite relationship into the world and to learn.

Showing up for movements is about transformation and struggle and deep moments of caring connection, but more than any of those things, it is about showing up.

If you are reading this book, then my hope is that it will help you reflect on how you show up. Every day, you create the conditions for connection with the people around you and with yourself. You tend to the relationships that make up your mind and body and pass their multifaceted resilience and lack thereof on to others. You decide how to show up to the communities you are a part of and the land that you are on. You decide which lineages to embody, which lineages to challenge, and which to evolve. You decide what values to let guide your life and in what communities you will hold those values, and in doing so, you decide which movements to show up to.

I hope that this book will help you to make these decisions in ways that invite more relationships into being. Where you already do relational work, I hope that that work will be recognized and resourced for the value it creates. Where you notice that relationships are missing in the world, I hope that you will be able to build trust with and resource those who are positioned to bring those relationships into being. We live in a world that is spiraling toward loneliness only because the immense power of relationship is being held back. I hope that together we can find a way to a world where that relationship can flourish and where its immense potential for transformation and resilience can be unleashed.

Glossary

action layer: The affinity groups that perform the work of the movement and the people who participate in them.

broadcast layer: The public narrative that a movement tells about itself and the people who have heard this story but have yet to show up to connect with others.

cohesion layer: The work of shaping a movement's narrative and mediating conflict, and the trusted leaders who perform that work.

curse of transactionality: A property of relational systems that states that we can know the conditions that lead to relationship but not where that relationship will lead. If we try to make a system have a precisely predictable outcome, then we will inevitably make it less relational in the process.

differentiation: The process of receiving and integrating information about many possible states.

evolution: The gradual development of an entity or system to a greater state of relationality through a process of exploration, differentiation, and selection.

evolutionary rate: The speed at which evolution happens in an environment, which is closely tied to that environment's relationality.

exploration: The process of testing many possible states.

gathering layer: The relational containers that a movement builds and the people who show up in these containers but have yet to step into deeper responsibility.

information: Anything that changes anything else, mathematically measured as a reduction in entropy.

loneliness: The subjective feeling of not having the relationships one wants and not knowing how to find them.

movement: A relational network of people focused on transforming their world to better align with a set of shared values.

relational: Viewed through the lens of relationship, with a focus on aligned outcomes that cannot be precisely predicted.

relational agency: One's capacity to find relationships that improve their life, usually by finding and creating containers where those kinds of relationships can grow.

relational container: An environment in which relationships form, often an environment that has been shaped to have a high relationality.

relational entity: A dense network of stable relationships that can form relationships of its own. An example is the human body.

relational invisibility: The tendency of individuals and institutions not to recognize relational work or the potential that investing in that work can bring.

relational lineage: An understanding of how to create the conditions for relationship that has been developed through a long history of trial and error.

relational measurement: The process of collecting stories and data that illustrate the effectiveness of a relational container or a set of relational containers in order to facilitate trust.

relational prediction: A set of techniques for understanding what can be understood about how relationships will unfold in the future, usually by observing and analyzing the environments in which they will evolve.

relational system: A network of relationships changing one another in an environment.

relational work: The skilled effort required to create the conditions for relationship.

relationality: The capacity of a particular time and place to generate relationship. This is often correlated with a localized reduction in entropy.

relationship: A dynamic process in which two or more relational entities change one another through an exchange of information.

selection: The process of focusing resources on a small set of states and releasing others based on information received.

social isolation: The state of having few meaningful relationships in one's life.

speculative future: An articulation of a possible future designed to spark conversation by eliciting feelings of fear and hope.

transactional: Viewed through the lens of ownership and control, with a focus on outcomes that can be precisely predicted.

value: A sense of purpose that directs one's actions, usually communicated through a personal story that creates a felt resonance in the body of the listener.

Notes

Chapter 1: Why We Need Relationship

1 Clare Gardiner, Gideon Geldenhuys, and Merryn Gott, "Interventions to Reduce Social Isolation and Loneliness among Older People: An Integrative Review," *Health & Social Care in the Community* 26, no. 2 (March 2018): 147–57, https://doi.org/10.1111/HSC.12367.

2 Robin I. M. Dunbar, "Neocortex Size as a Constraint on Group Size in Primates," *Journal of Human Evolution* 22, no. 6 (June 1992): 469–93, https://doi.org/10.1016/0047-2484(92)90081-J.

3 Marcus E. Raichle and Debra A. Gusnard, "Appraising the Brain's Energy Budget," *Proceedings of the National Academy of Sciences of the USA* 99, no. 16 (August 2002): 10237–39, https://doi.org/10.1073/PNAS.172399499.

4 Federica Laricchia, "Global Smartphone Penetration 2016–2022," *Statistica,* May 24, 2023, www.statista.com/statistics/203734/global-smartphone -penetration-per-capita-since-2005.

5 US Department of Health and Human Services, "New Surgeon General Advisory Raises Alarm about the Devastating Impact of the Epidemic of Loneliness and Isolation in the United States," news release, May 3, 2023, www.hhs.gov/about/news/2023/05/03/new-surgeon-general-advisory -raises-alarm-about-devastating-impact-epidemic-loneliness-isolation -united-states.html.

6 Daniel A. Cox, "The State of American Friendship: Change, Challenges, and Loss," *The Survey Center on American Life* (blog), June 8, 2021, www .americansurveycenter.org/research/the-state-of-american-friendship -change-challenges-and-loss.

7 Viji Diane Kannan and Peter J. Veazie, "US Trends in Social Isolation, Social Engagement, and Companionship—Nationally and by Age, Sex, Race/Ethnicity, Family Income, and Work Hours, 2003–2020," *SSM— Population Health* 21 (March 2023): 101331, https://doi.org/10.1016/J. SSMPH.2022.101331.

8 Sabrina Martins Barroso, Heloísa Gonçalves Ferreira, and Felipe Costa Araujo, "Brazilian Loneliness Scale: Evidence of Validity Based on

Relations to Depression, Anxiety and Stress," *Psico-USF* 26, no. 3 (December 2021): 559–70, https://doi.org/10.1590/1413-82712021260313.

9 Mayor of London, "London's Loneliness Epidemic," news release, October 31, 2019, www.london.gov.uk/press-releases/assembly/londons -loneliness-epidemic.

10 National Institutes of Health, "The Benefits of Slumber," NIH News in Health, April 2013, https://newsinhealth.nih.gov/2013/04/benefits -slumber.

11 Teruo Hayashi, "Conversion of Psychological Stress into Cellular Stress Response: Roles of the Sigma-1 Receptor in the Process," *Psychiatry and Clinical Neurosciences* 69, no. 4 (April 2015): 179–91, https://doi.org /10.1111/PCN.12262.

12 Suzanne C. Segerstrom and Gregory E. Miller, "Psychological Stress and the Human Immune System: A Meta-Analytic Study of 30 Years of Inquiry," *Psychological Bulletin* 130, no. 4 (July 2004): 601, https://doi.org /10.1037/0033-2909.130.4.601.

13 Martin Picard and Bruce S. McEwen, "Psychological Stress and Mitochondria: A Systematic Review," *Psychosomatic Medicine* 80, no. 2 (February 2018): 141, https://doi.org/10.1097/PSY.0000000000000545.

14 American Psychological Association, "Stress Effects on the Body," APA.org, March 8, 2023, www.apa.org/topics/stress/body.

15 Julianne Holt-Lunstad, Timothy B. Smith, and J. Bradley Layton, "Social Relationships and Mortality Risk: A Meta-Analytic Review," *PLoS Medicine* 7, no. 7 (July 2010): e1000316, https://doi.org/10.1371/journal.pmed .1000316.

16 Nicole K. Valtorta, Mona Kanaan, Simon Gilbody, Sara Ronzi, and Barbara Hanratty, "Loneliness and Social Isolation as Risk Factors for Coronary Heart Disease and Stroke: Systematic Review and Meta-Analysis of Longitudinal Observational Studies," *Heart* 102, no. 13 (July 2016): 1009–16, https://doi.org/10.1136/heartjnl-2015-308790.

17 Stephanie Brinkhues, Nicole H. T. M. Dukers-Muijrers, Christian J. P. A. Hoebe, Carla J. H. van der Kallen, Annemarie Koster, Ronald M. A. Henry, Coen D. A. Stehouwer, et al., "Social Network Characteristics Are Associated with Type 2 Diabetes Complications: The Maastricht Study," *Diabetes Care* 41, no. 8 (August 2018): 1654–62, https://doi.org/10.2337 /dc17-2144.

18 Carlo Lazzari and Marco Rabottini, "COVID-19, Loneliness, Social Isolation and Risk of Dementia in Older People: A Systematic Review and Meta-Analysis of the Relevant Literature," *International Journal of Psychiatry in Clinical Practice* 26, no. 2 (June 2022): 196–207, https://doi.org /10.1080/13651501.2021.1959616.

19 Farhana Mann, Jingyi Wang, Eiluned Pearce, Ruimin Ma, Merle Schlief, Brynmor Lloyd-Evans, Sarah Ikhtabi, and Sonia Johnson, "Loneliness and the Onset of New Mental Health Problems in the General Population," *Social Psychiatry and Psychiatric Epidemiology* 57, no. 11 (November 2022): 2161, https://doi.org/10.1007/S00127-022-02261-7.

20 Steven M. Southwick, Lauren Sippel, John Krystal, Dennis Charney, Linda Mayes, and Robb Pietrzak, "Why Are Some Individuals More Resilient than Others: The Role of Social Support," *World Psychiatry* 15, no. 1 (February 2016): 77–79, https://doi.org/10.1002/wps.20282.

21 Sheldon Cohen, "Psychosocial Vulnerabilities to Upper Respiratory Infectious Illness: Implications for Susceptibility to Coronavirus Disease 2019 (COVID-19)," *Perspectives on Psychological Science* 16, no. 1 (January 2021): 161, https://doi.org/10.1177/1745691620942516.

22 World Health Organization, "Substantial Investment Needed to Avert Mental Health Crisis," news release, May 14, 2020, www.who.int/news/item/14-05-2020-substantial-investment-needed-to-avert-mental-health-crisis.

23 M. Hawker and R. Romero-Ortuno, "Social Determinants of Discharge Outcomes in Older People Admitted to a Geriatric Medicine Ward," *The Journal of Frailty & Aging* 5, no. 2 (2016): 118–20, https://doi.org/10.14283/JFA.2016.89.

24 Raheel Mushtaq, Sheikh Shoib, Tabindah Shah, and Sahil Mushtaq, "Relationship Between Loneliness, Psychiatric Disorders and Physical Health: A Review on the Psychological Aspects of Loneliness," *Journal of Clinical and Diagnostic Research* 8, no. 9 (2014): WE01, https://doi.org/10.7860/JCDR/2014/10077.4828.

25 Matthew Solan, "The Secret to Happiness? Here's Some Advice from the Longest-Running Study on Happiness," *Harvard Health Blog* (blog), October 5, 2017, www.health.harvard.edu/blog/the-secret-to-happiness-heres-some-advice-from-the-longest-running-study-on-happiness-2017100512543.

26 Louise C. Hawkley, Mary Elizabeth Hughes, Linda J. Waite, Christopher M. Masi, Ronald A. Thisted, and John T. Cacioppo, "From Social Structural Factors to Perceptions of Relationship Quality and Loneliness: The Chicago Health, Aging, and Social Relations Study," *Journals of Gerontology. Series B, Psychological Sciences and Social Sciences* 63, no. 6 (2008), https://doi.org/10.1093/GERONB/63.6.S375.

27 Liana DesHarnais Bruce, Joshua S. Wu, Stuart L. Lustig, Daniel W. Russell, and Douglas A. Nemecek, "Loneliness in the United States: A 2018 National Panel Survey of Demographic, Structural, Cognitive, and Behavioral Characteristics," *American Journal of Health Promotion* 33, no. 8 (November 2019): 1123–33, https://doi.org/10.1177/0890117119856551.

28 Electronics—United States," September 2023, Statista, "Consumer www
    .statista.com/outlook/cmo/consumer-electronics/united-states.

29 Christopher Spera, Robin Ghertner, Anthony Nerino, and Adrienne
    DiTommaso, "Out of Work? Volunteers Have Higher Odds of Getting
    Back to Work," *Nonprofit and Voluntary Sector Quarterly* 44, no. 5 (September 2015): 886–907, https://doi.org/10.1177/0899764015605928.

30 Raj Chetty, Matthew O. Jackson, Theresa Kuchler, Johannes Stroebel,
    Nathaniel Hendren, Robert B. Fluegge, Sara Gong, et al., "Social Capital I:
    Measurement and Associations with Economic Mobility," *Nature* 608, no.
    7921 (August 2022): 108–21, https://doi.org/10.1038/s41586-022-04996-4.

31 Hannah Arendt, *The Origins of Totalitarianism* (New York: Harcourt,
    1976), 323.

32 Arendt, *Origins of Totalitarianism,* 317.

33 Global State of Democracy Initiative, *The Global State of Democracy 2022:
    Forging Social Contracts in a Time of Discontent* (Stockholm: International
    Institute for Democracy and Electoral Assistance, 2022), https://doi.org
    /10.31752/idea.2022.56.

34 Global State of Democracy Initiative, *Global State of Democracy 2022.*

35 Global State of Democracy Initiative, *Global State of Democracy 2022.*

36 Natasha R. Wood, "Adventures in Solitude: The Link Between Social
    Isolation and Violent Extremism" (master's thesis, University of Pittsburgh, 2020), https://d-scholarship.pitt.edu/38639/7/Natasha%20Wood
    %20Final%20ETD.pdf.

37 Ian Lovett and Adam Nagourney, "Video Rant, Then Deadly Rampage in
    California Town," *New York Times*, May 25, 2014, www.nytimes.com
    /2014/05/25/us/california-drive-by-shooting.html.

38 Bruce Hoffman, Jacob Ware, and Ezra Shapiro, "Assessing the Threat
    of Incel Violence," *Studies in Conflict & Terrorism* 43, no. 7 (July 2020):
    565–87, https://doi.org/10.1080/1057610X.2020.1751459.

39 Gillian Reagan, "The Evolution of Facebook's Mission Statement," *The
    Observer*, July 13, 2009, https://observer.com/2009/07/the-evolution-of
    -facebooks-mission-statement.

40 Reagan, "Evolution of Facebook's Mission Statement."

41 Michael Garfield, "Mason Porter on Community Detection and Data
    Topology," *Complexity,* podcast, Santa Fe Institute, April 5, 2023, https://
    complexity.simplecast.com/episodes/105.

42 Mark Granovetter, "The Strength of Weak Ties: A Network Theory
    Revisited," *Sociological Theory* 1 (1983): 201, https://doi.org/10.2307
    /202051.

43 Wikipedia, s.v. "Relationship," last modified October 13, 2023, https://
    en.wikipedia.org/wiki/Relationship.

44 Wikipedia, s.v. "Interpersonal relationship," last modified October 19, 2023, https://en.wikipedia.org/wiki/Interpersonal_relationship.

45 Wikipedia, s.v. "Interpersonal relationship."

46 Julia Carrie Wong, "Facebook Overhauls News Feed in Favor of 'Meaningful Social Interactions,'" *The Guardian,* January 12, 2018, www .theguardian.com/technology/2018/jan/11/facebook-news-feed-algorithm -overhaul-mark-zuckerberg.

47 Georgia Wells, Jeff Horwitz, and Deepa Seetharaman, "Facebook Knows Instagram Is Toxic for Teen Girls, Company Documents Show," *Wall Street Journal,* September 14, 2021, www.wsj.com/articles/facebook -knows-instagram-is-toxic-for-teen-girls-company-documents-show 11631620739.

48 Keach Hagey and Jeff Horwitz, "Facebook Tried to Make Its Platform a Healthier Place. It Got Angrier Instead," *Wall Street Journal,* September 15, 2021, www.wsj.com/articles/facebook-algorithm-change-zuckerberg -11631654215.

49 M. J. Crockett, "Moral Outrage in the Digital Age," *Nature Human Behaviour* 1, no. 11 (September 2017): 769–71, https://doi.org/10.1038 /s41562-017-0213-3.

Chapter 2: Three Definitions of Relationship

1 Lauri Nummenmaa, Enrico Glerean, Riitta Hari, and Jari K. Hietanen, "Bodily Maps of Emotions," *Proceedings of the National Academy of Sciences of the USA* 111, no. 2 (January 2014): 646–51, https://doi.org/10.1073 /PNAS.1321664111.

2 Lisa Blaker, "The Islamic State's Use of Online Social Media," *Military Cyber Affairs* 1, no. 1 (December 2015): 4, https://doi.org/10.5038 /2378-0789.1.1.1004.

3 Jackson Katz, *Macho Paradox: Why Some Men Hurt Women and How All Men Can Help* (Naperville, IL: Sourcebooks, 2006).

4 adrienne maree brown, *Emergent Strategy: Shaping Change, Changing Worlds* (Chico, CA: AK Press, 2017); adrienne maree brown, *Pleasure Activism: The Politics of Feeling Good* (Chico, CA: AK Press, 2019).

5 Octavia E. Butler, Parable of the Sower (New York: Four Walls Eight Windows, 1993).

6 Re:Power, "Voices From the Frontlines: What Organizers Need in 2022," RePower.org, August 5, 2022, https://repower.org/2022-organizer-survey.

7 Justin Scheck, Newley Purnell, and Jeff Horwitz, "Facebook Employees Flag Drug Cartels and Human Traffickers. The Company's Response Is Weak, Documents Show," *Wall Street Journal,* September 16, 2021,

www.wsj.com/articles/facebook-drug-cartels-human-traffickers-response
-is-weak-documents-11631812953.

8   Julia Carrie Wong, "How Facebook Let Fake Engagement Distort Global
Politics: A Whistleblower's Account," *The Guardian,* April 12, 2021, www
.theguardian.com/technology/2021/apr/12/facebook-fake-engagement
-whistleblower-sophie-zhang.

9   Wong, "How Facebook Let Fake Engagement Distort Global Politics."

10   Ezra Klein, "A Legendary World Builder on Multiverses, Revolution and
the 'Souls' of Cities," interview with N. K. Jemisin, *The Ezra Klein Show,*
podcast, audio, October 18, 2022, www.nytimes.com/2022/10/18/opinion
/ezra-klein-podcast-nk-jemisin.html.

11   Carlo Rovelli, *Reality Is Not What It Seems: The Journey to Quantum Gravity* (New York: Penguin, 2017).

12   John Smythies, "Intercellular Signaling in Cancer—the SMT and TOFT
Hypotheses, Exosomes, Telocytes and Metastases: Is the Messenger in
the Message?," *Journal of Cancer* 6, no. 7 (2015): 604–9, https://doi.org
/10.7150/JCA.12372. The article includes the revealing quote, "Most
common cancers are not primarily caused by genetic or chromosomal
lesions, but by a sustained failure to communicate between interacting
cell lineages living in the complex society of the organism."

13   James Gleick, *The Information: A History, a Theory, a Flood* (New York:
Knopf Doubleday, 2011).

14   C. E. Shannon, "A Mathematical Theory of Communication," *Bell System
Technical Journal* 27 (July/October 1948), 379–423, 623–56, https://doi.org
/10.1002/j.1538-7305.1948.tb01338.x, https://people.math.harvard.edu
/~ctm/home/text/others/shannon/entropy/entropy.pdf.

15   "TWL Dictionary Scrabble Letter Frequency Statistics," Unscramblerer
.com, accessed June 9, 2023, www.unscramblerer.com/scrabble-twl
-dictionary-statistics.

16   Wikipedia, s.v. "Human genome," last modified October 26, 2023, https://
en.wikipedia.org/wiki/Human_genome#Information_content; "Star
Wars: A New Hope," Microsoft Store, accessed November 1, 2023,
www.microsoft.com/en-us/p/star-wars-a-new-hope/8d6kgwzxzdz3.

17   Peter Godfrey-Smith and Kim Sterelny, "Biological Information," in *The
Stanford Encyclopedia of Philosophy,* ed. Edward N. Zalta (Stanford, CA:
Stanford University, 2016), https://plato.stanford.edu/archives/sum2016
/entries/information-biological.

18   Duke University Department of Physics, "Introduction to the Information Velocity," accessed November 1, 2023, https://physics.duke.edu
/introduction-information-velocity.

Chapter 3: Understanding Relational Systems

1 Eric Klinenberg, *Heat Wave: A Social Autopsy of Disaster in Chicago* (Chicago: University of Chicago Press, 2002).

2 Thomas Hale, "We've Found One Factor That Predicts Which Countries Best Survive Covid," *The Guardian,* March 24, 2022, www.theguardian .com/commentisfree/2022/mar/24/countries-covid-trust-damage -pandemic.

3 Laura Pappano, "The Year of the MOOC," *New York Times*, November 2, 2012, www.nytimes.com/2012/11/04/education/edlife/massive-open -online-courses-are-multiplying-at-a-rapid-pace.html.

4 Daniel Onah and Jane Sinclair, "Dropout Rates of Massive Open Online Courses: Behavioural Patterns," *Proceedings of the 6th International Conference on Education and New Learning Technologies (EDULEARN14)*, Barcelona, July 2014, https://doi.org/10.13140/RG.2.1.2402.0009.

5 Rene F. Kizilcec and Emily Schneider, "Motivation as a Lens to Understand Online Learners: Toward Data-Driven Design with the OLEI Scale," *ACM Transactions on Computer-Human Interaction* 22, no. 2 (March 2015): 1–24, https://doi.org/10.1145/2699735.

6 James Gleick, *Genius: The Life and Science of Richard Feynman* (New York: Knopf Doubleday, 1993).

7 Ilkka Hanski and Michael E. Gilpin, *Metapopulation Biology: Ecology, Genetics, and Evolution* (San Diego: Academic Press, 1997).

8 Andreas Pavlogiannis, Josef Tkadlec, Krishnendu Chatterjee, and Martin A. Nowak, "Construction of Arbitrarily Strong Amplifiers of Natural Selection Using Evolutionary Graph Theory," *Communications Biology* 1, no. 1 (December 2018): 71, https://doi.org/10.1038/s42003-018-0078-7.

9 Cameron K. Ghalambor, Kim L. Hoke, Emily W. Ruell, Eva K. Fischer, David N. Reznick, and Kimberly A. Hughes, "Non-adaptive Plasticity Potentiates Rapid Adaptive Evolution of Gene Expression in Nature," *Nature* 525:7569 (2015) 372–75, https://doi.org/10.1038/nature15256.

10 P. L. Forey, "Biological Radiations and Speciation," *Encyclopedia of Geology,* 2005, 266–79, https://doi.org/10.1016/B0-12-369396-9/00014-9.

11 Herman Goldstein, *The Computer from Pascal to von Neumann* (Princeton, NJ: Princeton University Press, 1972).

12 James Gleick, *Chaos: Making a New Science* (New York: Viking, 1987).

13 Edward N. Lorenz, "Predictability: Does the Flap of a Butterfly's Wings in Brazil Set Off a Tornado in Texas?" (presentation, American Association for the Advancement of Science, Washington, DC, December 29, 1972), https://static.gymportalen.dk/sites/lru.dk/files/lru/132_kap6_lorenz _artikel_the_butterfly_effect.pdf.

Chapter 4: Lineages of Relational Wisdom

1 I include the footnote as it was presented in *How We Show Up:* See Shawn Fremstad, Sarah Jane Glynn, and Angelo Williams, "The Case Against Marriage Fundamentalism: Embracing Family Justice for All," Family Story, April 4, 2019, https://familystoryproject.org/case-against-marriage-fundamentalism.

2 Mia Birdsong, *How We Show Up: Reclaiming Family, Friendship, and Community* (New York: Hachette, 2020), 84–85.

3 Cari Shane, "The First Self-Proclaimed Drag Queen Was a Formerly Enslaved Man," *Smithsonian Magazine,* June 9, 2023, www.smithsonianmag.com/history/the-first-self-proclaimed-drag-queen-was-a-formerly-enslaved-man-180982311.

4 David Brooks, "The Nuclear Family Was a Mistake," *The Atlantic,* February 10, 2020, www.theatlantic.com/magazine/archive/2020/03/the-nuclear-family-was-a-mistake/605536.

5 Brooks, "Nuclear Family."

6 La Donna Harris and Jacqueline Wasilewski, "Indigeneity, an Alternative Worldview: Four R's (Relationship, Responsibility, Reciprocity, Redistribution) vs. Two P's (Power and Profit). Sharing the Journey toward Conscious Evolution," *Systems Research and Behavioral Science* 21, no. 5 (September 2004): 489–503, https://doi.org/10.1002/SRES.631.

7 Harris and Wasilewski, "Indigeneity."

8 Robin Wall Kimmerer, *Braiding Sweetgrass: Indigenous Wisdom, Scientific Knowledge and the Teachings of Plants* (Minneapolis: Milkweed Editions, 2015), 28.

9 Mary Annette Pember, "Death by Civilization," *The Atlantic,* March 8, 2019, www.theatlantic.com/education/archive/2019/03/traumatic-legacy-indian-boarding-schools/584293.

Chapter 5: How Movements Nurture Relationship

1 Gustave Le Bon, *The Crowd: A Study of the Popular Mind* (1926; repr., Mineola, NY: Dover, 2002).

2 John D. McCarthy and Mayer N. Zald, "Resource Mobilization and Social Movements: A Partial Theory," *American Journal of Sociology* 82, no. 6 (May 1977): 1212–41, https://doi.org/10.1086/226464.

3 David A. Snow, Rens Vliegenthart, and Pauline Ketelaars, "The Framing Perspective on Social Movements," in *The Wiley Blackwell Companion to Social Movements*, eds. David A. Snow, Sarah A. Soule, Hanspeter Kriesi, and Holly J. McCammon (John Wiley & Sons, 2018), 392–410. https://doi.org/10.1002/9781119168577.ch22.

4 Grace Lee Boggs and Scott Kurashige, *The Next American Revolution: Sustainable Activism for the Twenty-First Century* (Berkeley, CA: University of California Press, 2012).

5 David A. Aaker, *Building Strong Brands* (New York: Free Press, 1996).

6 National Democratic Institute, "Public Narrative Participant Guide," June 2012, adapted from Marshall Ganz, "Leading Change: Leadership, Organization and Social Movements," in *Handbook of Leadership Theory and Practice,* eds. Nitin Nohria and Rakesh Khurana (Cambridge, MA: HBS Press, 2010), ch. 19, www.ndi.org/sites/default/files/Public %20Narrative%20Participant%20Guide.pdf.

7 Marshall Ganz, *Why David Sometimes Wins: Leadership, Organization, and Strategy in the California Farm Worker Movement* (New York: Oxford University Press, 2009).

8 Jack Drescher, "Out of *DSM:* Depathologizing Homosexuality," *Behavioral Sciences* 5, no. 4 (December 2015): 565–75, https://doi.org/10.3390 /BS5040565.

9 Hahrie Han, Elizabeth McKenna, and Michelle Oyakawa, *Prisms of the People: Power & Organizing in Twenty-First-Century America* (University of Chicago Press, 2021), 17.

10 Julie Quiroz and Kristen Zimmerman, "OUR Walmart: Caring Communities, Courageous Action. Love with Power: Practicing Transformation for Social Justice," Story Series No. 3, Movement Strategy Center, March 2016, https://movementstrategy.org/resources/our-walmart-caring -communities-courageous-action-love-with-power-3.

11 Quiroz and Zimmerman, "OUR Walmart."

12 Quiroz and Zimmerman, "OUR Walmart."

13 Zeynep Tufekci, *Twitter and Tear Gas: The Power and Fragility of Networked Protest* (New Haven, CT: Yale University Press, 2017), 105.

14 Luther P. Gerlach, "The Structure of Social Movements: Environmental Activism and Its Opponents," in *Networks and Netwars: The Future of Terror, Crime, and Militancy,* eds. John Arquilla and David Ronfeldt (Santa Monica, CA: Rand Corp., 2001), 289–310.

15 Darcy K. Leach, "Culture and the Structure of Tyrannylessness," *Sociological Quarterly* 54, no. 2 (2013): 181–91, https://doi.org/10.1111/tsq.12014.

16 Alicia Garza, *The Purpose of Power: How We Come Together When We Fall Apart* (One World/Random House, 2020), 130.

17 Garza, Purpose of Power, 185–86.

18 Max Weber, *Economy and Society: An Outline of Interpretative Sociology* (1921; repr., New York: Bedminster Press, 1968).

19 Larry Buchanan, Quoctrung Bui, and Jugal K. Patel, "Black Lives Matter May Be the Largest Movement in U.S. History," *New York Times,* July 3, 2020,

www.nytimes.com/interactive/2020/07/03/us/george-floyd-protests-crowd
-size.html.

20 Erica Chenoweth and Maria J. Stephan, *Why Civil Resistance Works: The Strategic Logic of Nonviolent Conflict* (New York: Columbia University Press, 2011).

Chapter 6: Why We Fail to Invest in Relationship

1 Alisa Bierria, "Pursuing a Radical Antiviolence Agenda Inside/Outside a Non-profit Structure," in *The Revolution Will Not Be Funded: Beyond the Non-Profit Industrial Complex,* ed. INCITE! Women of Color Against Violence (Durham, NC: Duke University Press, 2017), 151.

2 Bierria, "Pursuing a Radical Antiviolence Agenda," 160.

3 Bierria, "Pursuing a Radical Antiviolence Agenda," 153.

4 Bierria, "Pursuing a Radical Antiviolence Agenda," 155.

5 Bierria, "Pursuing a Radical Antiviolence Agenda," 160.

6 Bierria, "Pursuing a Radical Antiviolence Agenda," 157.

7 Megan Ming Francis, "The Price of Civil Rights: Black Lives, White Funding, and Movement Capture," *Law Society Review* 53:1 (2019), 275–309, https://doi.org/10.1111/lasr.12384.

8 Francis, "Price of Civil Rights."

9 Francis, "Price of Civil Rights."

10 Francis, "Price of Civil Rights."

11 W. E. B. Du Bois, *Color and Democracy: Colonies and Peace* (New York: Harcourt, Brace, 1945).

12 W. E. B. Du Bois, "Socialism and the American Negro," speech to the Wisconsin Socialist Club, April 9, 1960, Madison, WI, transcript, https:// credo.library.umass.edu/view/full/mums312-b206-i053.

13 Chad Williams, "W. E. B. Du Bois and the Fight for American Democracy," *Washington Post,* August 27, 2018, www.washingtonpost.com/news /made-by-history/wp/2018/08/27/w-e-b-du-bois-and-the-fight-for -american-democracy.

14 Wikipedia, s.v. "List of Elections in 2024," last modified November 4, 2023, https://en.wikipedia.org/wiki/List_of_elections_in_2024.

15 Karl Evers-Hillstrom, "Most Expensive Ever: 2020 Election Cost $14.4 Billion," OpenSecrets News, February 11, 2021, www.opensecrets.org /news/2021/02/2020-cycle-cost-14p4-billion-doubling-16.

16 Joshua Kalla and David Broockman, "Voter Outreach Campaigns Can Reduce Affective Polarization among Implementing Political Activists," *American Political Science Review,* 116:4 (November 2022), 1516–22, https://doi.org/10.1017/S0003055422000132.

17 Brittany Gibson, "How Georgia Got Organized," *The American Prospect*, January 2, 2021, https://prospect.org/politics/how-georgia-got-organized -stacey-abrams-democrats-elections.

18 Poppy Noor, "Surge in Youth Voter Turnout May Have Helped Propel Biden to Victory," *The Guardian*, November 9, 2020, www.theguardian .com/us-news/2020/nov/09/youth-turnout-us-election-biden-victory -young-voters.

19 People's Action, "How to Defeat Trump and Heal America: Deep Canvassing," 2021, accessed November 8, 2023, https://peoplesaction.org/wp -content/uploads/PA-ReportDeepCanvassingResults09.14-FINAL.pdf.

20 Daniel Laurison, *Producing Politics: Inside the Exclusive Campaign World Where the Privileged Few Shape Politics for All of Us* (Boston: Beacon Press, 2022).

21 Steve Passwaiter, "Political Ad Spending Projected to Top $11 Billion in 2024," AdAge, July 12, 2023, https://adage.com/article/opinion/2024 -elections-political-ad-spending-projected-top-11-billion-2024/2504126.

22 Alexander Coppock, Seth J. Hill, and Lynn Vavreck, "The Small Effects of Political Advertising Are Small Regardless of Context, Message, Sender, or Receiver: Evidence from 59 Real-Time Randomized Experiments," *Science Advances* 6, no. 36 (September 2, 2020): eabc4046, https://doi.org/10.1126 /sciadv.abc4046.

23 Levi Bankston and Barry C. Burden, "Voter Mobilization Efforts Can Depress Turnout," *Journal of Elections, Public Opinion and Parties* 33, no. 1 (January 2, 2023): 94–104, https://doi.org/10.1080/17457289.2021.1949328.

24 David Graeber and David Wengrow, The Dawn of Everything: A New History of Humanity (New York: Farrar, Straus and Giroux, 2021).

25 J. Hamel, *Early English Voyages to Northern Russia: Comprising the Voyages of John Tradescant the Elder, Sir Hugh Willoughby, Richard Chancellor, Nelson, and Others*, trans. John Studdy Leigh (London: Richard Bentley, 1857; reprinted London: Forgotten Books, 2018).

26 Ted Nace, *Gangs of America: The Rise of Corporate Power and the Disabling of Democracy* (San Francisco: Berrett-Koehler, 2003).

27 William Dalrymple, "The East India Company: The Original Corporate Raiders," *The Guardian*, March 4, 2015, www.theguardian.com/world /2015/mar/04/east-india-company-original-corporate-raiders.

28 Bonnie Pinkston, "Documenting the British East India Company and Their Involvement in the East Indian Slave Trade," *SLIS Connecting* 7 (July 1, 2018): 53–59, https://doi.org/10.18785/slis.0701.10.

29 Katrine Marçal, *Who Cooked Adam Smith's Dinner?: A Story about Women and Economics* (Berkeley, CA: Pegasus, 2016).

30 DailyMail.com, "Burning Man Census Reveals the Average Burner Has a Household Income of Up to $100,000, Is 35, Male, White and Will Spend Nearly $2,500." *Daily Mail,* July 30, 2019, www.dailymail.co.uk/news /article-7302645/Burning-Man-census-reveals-average-burner-35-male -white-worth-65K.html.

31 Jorgen Lissner, "Merchants of Misery," *New Internationalist,* June 1, 1981, https://newint.org/features/1981/06/01/merchants-of-misery.

32 Amy Costello and Frederica Boswell, "The Ethics of Nonprofit Storytelling: Survivor Porn and Parading Trauma," *Nonprofit Quarterly,* April 5, 2019, https://nonprofitquarterly.org/the-ethics-of-nonprofit-storytelling -survivor-porn-and-parading-trauma.

33 Stella Young, "We're Not Here for Your Inspiration," ABC News, July 2, 2012, www.abc.net.au/news/2012-07-03/young-inspiration-porn/4107006.

Chapter 7: Investing in Relational Outcomes

1 John T. Edge, *The Potlikker Papers: A Food History of the Modern South* (New York: Penguin, 2017).

2 Klancy Miller, "Overlooked No More: Georgia Gilmore, Who Fed and Funded the Montgomery Bus Boycott," *New York Times,* July 31, 2019, www.nytimes.com/2019/07/31/obituaries/georgia-gilmore-overlooked .html.

3 Miller, "Overlooked No More."

4 Miller, "Overlooked No More."

5 Joan Marie Johnson, *Funding Feminism: Monied Women, Philanthropy, and the Women's Movement, 1870–1967* (Chapel Hill, NC: University of North Carolina Press, 2017).

6 Douglas Rushkoff, "The Super-Rich 'Preppers' Planning to Save Themselves from the Apocalypse," *The Guardian,* September 4, 2022, www.theguardian.com/news/2022/sep/04/super-rich-prepper-bunkers -apocalypse-survival-richest-rushkoff.

7 Jane Wei-Skillern and Sonia Marciano, "The Networked Nonprofit," *Stanford Social Innovation Review,* Spring 2008, https://doi.org/10.48558 /gcy2-rn71.

8 Lingfei Wu, Dashun Wang, and James A. Evans, "Large Teams Develop and Small Teams Disrupt Science and Technology," *Nature* 566 (February 2019): 378–82, https://doi.org/10.1038/s41586-019-0941-9.

9 Trans Justice Funding Project, "FAQs," n.d., accessed November 12, 2023, www.transjusticefundingproject.org/about-faq.

10 Third Wave Fund, "Third Wave Fund Resources and Supports Youth-Led, Intersectional Gender Justice Activism," n.d., accessed November 12, 2023, www.thirdwavefund.org/about.

11 Irwin G. Sarason, Barbara R. Sarason, Edward N. Shearin, and Gregory R. Pierce, "A Brief Measure of Social Support: Practical and Theoretical Implications," *Journal of Social and Personal Relationships* 4, no. 4 (November 1987): 497–510, https://doi.org/10.1177/0265407587044007.

12 Gregory D. Zimet, Nancy W. Dahlem, Sara G. Zimet, and Gordon K. Farley, "The Multidimensional Scale of Perceived Social Support," *Journal of Personality Assessment* 52, no. 1 (March 1, 1988): 30–41, https://doi.org /10.1207/s15327752jpa5201_2.

13 Lihle Z. Mtshali, "Everything You Ever Wanted to Know About Those Sou-Sou Savings Clubs African and Caribbean Women Love," *Essence,* December 6, 2020, www.essence.com/news/money-career/what-is-a -sou-sou-savings-club-facts.

14 Cobudget, "You're in Good Company," n.d., accessed July 25, 2023, https://cobudget.com.

Chapter 8: What Happens If We Invest in Relationship

1 High Ground Advisors, "The 2022 DAF Report Is Here," December 6, 2022, www.highgroundadvisors.org/blog/the-2022-daf-report-is-here, summarizing National Philanthropic Trust, *Donor-Advised Fund Report,* 2022, www.nptrust.org/reports/daf-report.

2 High Ground Advisors, "2022 DAF Report."

3 Candid Philanthropy News Digest, "U.S. Foundation Assets Fell $246 Billion in Value in 2022, Study Finds," January 27, 2023, https:// philanthropynewsdigest.org/news/u.s.-foundation-assets-fell-246-billion -in-value-in-2022-study-finds.

4 US Department of Health and Human Services, "HHS FY 2024 Budget in Brief," March 3, 2023, www.hhs.gov/about/budget/fy2024.

5 Steve Biever, "Giving USA 2023 Report Insights," BWF, June 20, 2023, www.bwf.com/giving-usa-2023-report-insights.

6 Ben Thornley, "The Facts on U.S. Social Enterprise," HuffPost, November 8, 2012, www.huffpost.com/entry/social-enterprise_b_2090144.

7 Karl Evers-Hillstrom, "Most Expensive Ever: 2020 Election Cost $14.4 Billion," OpenSecrets News, February 11, 2021, www.opensecrets.org /news/2021/02/2020-cycle-cost-14p4-billion-doubling-16.

Bibliography

Aaker, David A. *Building Strong Brands.* New York: Free Press, 1996.

American Psychiatric Association. *Diagnostic and Statistical Manual of Mental Disorders,* Fifth Edition *(DSM-5).* Washington, DC: American Psychiatric Publishing, 2022.

American Psychological Association. "Stress Effects on the Body." APA.org. March 8, 2023. www.apa.org/topics/stress/body.

Arendt, Hannah. *The Origins of Totalitarianism.* New York: Harcourt, 1976.

Bankston, Levi, and Barry C. Burden. "Voter Mobilization Efforts Can Depress Turnout." *Journal of Elections, Public Opinion and Parties* 33, no. 1 (January 2, 2023): 94–104. https://doi.org/10.1080/17457289.2021.1949328.

Bierria, Alisa. "Pursuing a Radical Antiviolence Agenda Inside/Outside a Non-profit Structure." In *The Revolution Will Not Be Funded: Beyond the Non-Profit Industrial Complex,* edited by INCITE! Women of Color Against Violence, 151–64. Durham, NC: Duke University Press, 2017.

Biever, Steve. "Giving USA 2023 Report Insights." BWF, June 20, 2023. www.bwf.com/giving-usa-2023-report-insights.

Birdsong, Mia. *How We Show Up : Reclaiming Family, Friendship, and Community.* New York: Hachette, 2020.

Blaker, Lisa. "The Islamic State's Use of Online Social Media." *Military Cyber Affairs* 1, no. 1 (December 2015): 4. https://doi.org/10.5038/2378-0789.1.1.1004.

Boggs, Grace Lee, and Scott Kurashige. *The Next American Revolution: Sustainable Activism for the Twenty-First Century.* Berkeley, CA: University of California Press, 2012.

Brinkhues, Stephanie, Nicole H. T. M. Dukers-Muijrers, Christian J. P. A. Hoebe, Carla J. H. van der Kallen, Annemarie Koster, Ronald M. A. Henry, Coen D. A. Stehouwer, Paul H. M. Savelkoul, Nicolaas C. Schaper, and Miranda T. Schram. "Social Network Characteristics Are Associated with Type 2 Diabetes Complications: The Maastricht Study." *Diabetes Care* 41, no. 8 (August 2018): 1654–62. https://doi.org/10.2337/dc17-2144.

Brooks, David. "The Nuclear Family Was a Mistake." *The Atlantic,* February 10, 2020. www.theatlantic.com/magazine/archive/2020/03/the-nuclear -family-was-a-mistake/605536.

brown, adrienne maree. *Emergent Strategy: Shaping Change, Changing Worlds.* Chico, CA: AK Press, 2017.

brown, adrienne maree. *Pleasure Activism: The Politics of Feeling Good.* Chico, CA: AK Press, 2019.

Brown, Sherronda J. *Refusing Compulsory Sexuality: A Black Asexual Lens on Our Sex-Obsessed Culture.* Berkeley, CA: North Atlantic Books, 2022.

Bruce, Liana DesHarnais, Joshua S. Wu, Stuart L. Lustig, Daniel W. Russell, and Douglas A. Nemecek. "Loneliness in the United States: A 2018 National Panel Survey of Demographic, Structural, Cognitive, and Behavioral Characteristics." *American Journal of Health Promotion* 33, no. 8 (November 2019): 1123–33. https://doi.org/10.1177/0890117119856551.

Buchanan, Larry, Quoctrung Bui, and Jugal K. Patel. "Black Lives Matter May Be the Largest Movement in U.S. History." *New York Times,* July 3, 2020. www.nytimes.com/interactive/2020/07/03/us/george-floyd -protests-crowd-size.html.

Butler, Octavia E. *Parable of the Sower.* New York: Four Walls Eight Windows, 1993.

Candid Philanthropy News Digest. "U.S. Foundation Assets Fell $246 Billion in Value in 2022, Study Finds." January 27, 2023. https://philanthropy newsdigest.org/news/u.s.-foundation-assets-fell-246-billion-in-value-in -2022-study-finds.

Chen, Angela. *Ace: What Asexuality Reveals About Desire, Society, and the Meaning of Sex.* Boston: Beacon, 2020.

Chenoweth, Erica, and Maria J. Stephan. *Why Civil Resistance Works: The Strategic Logic of Nonviolent Conflict.* New York: Columbia University Press, 2011.

Chetty, Raj, Matthew O. Jackson, Theresa Kuchler, Johannes Stroebel, Nathaniel Hendren, Robert B. Fluegge, Sara Gong, Federico Gonzalez, Armelle Grondin, and Matthew Jacob. "Social Capital I: Measurement and Associations with Economic Mobility." *Nature* 608, no. 7921 (August 2022): 108–21. https://doi.org/10.1038/s41586-022-04996-4.

Cohen, Sheldon. "Psychosocial Vulnerabilities to Upper Respiratory Infectious Illness: Implications for Susceptibility to Coronavirus Disease 2019 (COVID-19)." *Perspectives on Psychological Science* 16, no. 1 (January 2021): 161. https://doi.org/10.1177/1745691620942516.

Coppock, Alexander, Seth J. Hill, and Lynn Vavreck. "The Small Effects of Political Advertising Are Small Regardless of Context, Message, Sender, or Receiver: Evidence from 59 Real-Time Randomized Experiments." *Science Advances* 6, no. 36 (September 2, 2020): eabc4046. https://doi.org/10.1126 /sciadv.abc4046.

Costello, Amy, and Frederica Boswell. "The Ethics of Nonprofit Storytelling: Survivor Porn and Parading Trauma." *Nonprofit Quarterly,* April 5, 2019. https://nonprofitquarterly.org/the-ethics-of-nonprofit-storytelling -survivor-porn-and-parading-trauma.

Cox, Daniel A. "The State of American Friendship: Change, Challenges, and Loss." *The Survey Center on American Life* (blog). June 8, 2021. www .americansurveycenter.org/research/the-state-of-american-friendship -change-challenges-and-loss.

Crockett, M. J. "Moral Outrage in the Digital Age." *Nature Human Behaviour* 1, no. 11 (September 2017): 769–71. https://doi.org/10.1038/s41562 -017-0213-3.

DailyMail.com. "Burning Man Census Reveals the Average Burner Has a Household Income of Up to $100,000, Is 35, Male, White and Will Spend Nearly $2,500." *Daily Mail,* July 30, 2019. www.dailymail.co.uk/news /article-7302645/Burning-Man-census-reveals-average-burner-35-male -white-worth-65K.html.

Dalrymple, William. "The East India Company: The Original Corporate Raiders." *The Guardian,* March 4, 2015. www.theguardian.com/world/2015 /mar/04/east-india-company-original-corporate-raiders.

Drescher, Jack. "Out of *DSM:* Depathologizing Homosexuality." *Behavioral Sciences* 5, no. 4 (December 2015): 565–75. https://doi.org/10.3390/BS5040565.

Du Bois, W. E. B. *Color and Democracy: Colonies and Peace.* New York: Harcourt, Brace, 1945.

Du Bois, W. E. B. "Socialism and the American Negro." Speech to the Wisconsin Socialist Club, April 9, 1960. Madison, WI. Transcript. https:// credo.library.umass.edu/view/full/mums312-b206-i053.

Duke University Department of Physics. "Introduction to the Information Velocity." Accessed November 1, 2023. https://physics.duke.edu /introduction-information-velocity.

Dunbar, Robin I. M. "Neocortex Size as a Constraint on Group Size in Primates." *Journal of Human Evolution* 22, no. 6 (June 1992): 469–93. https:// doi.org/10.1016/0047-2484(92)90081-J.

Edge, John T. *The Potlikker Papers: A Food History of the Modern South.* New York: Penguin, 2017.

Evers-Hillstrom, Karl. "Most Expensive Ever: 2020 Election Cost $14.4 Billion." OpenSecrets News, February 11, 2021. www.opensecrets.org/news /2021/02/2020-cycle-cost-14p4-billion-doubling-16.

Forey, P. L. "Biological Radiations and Speciation." *Encyclopedia of Geology,* 2005, 266–79. https://doi.org/10.1016/B0-12-369396-9/00014-9.

Francis, Megan Ming. "The Price of Civil Rights: Black Lives, White Funding, and Movement Capture." *Law Society Review* 53:1 (2019), 275–309. https://doi.org/10.1111/lasr.12384.

Fremstad, Shawn, Sarah Jane Glynn, and Angelo Williams. "The Case Against Marriage Fundamentalism: Embracing Family Justice for All." Family Story, April 4, 2019. https://familystoryproject.org/case-against-marriage -fundamentalism.

Ganz, Marshall. *Why David Sometimes Wins: Leadership, Organization, and Strategy in the California Farm Worker Movement.* New York: Oxford University Press, 2009.

Gardiner, Clare, Gideon Geldenhuys, and Merryn Gott. "Interventions to Reduce Social Isolation and Loneliness among Older People: An Integrative Review." *Health & Social Care in the Community* 26, no. 2 (March 2018): 147–57. https://doi.org/10.1111/HSC.12367.

Garfield, Michael. "Mason Porter on Community Detection and Data Topology." *Complexity.* Podcast. Santa Fe Institute. April 5, 2023. https:// complexity.simplecast.com/episodes/105.

Garza, Alicia. *The Purpose of Power: How We Come Together When We Fall Apart.* One World/Random House, 2020.

Gerlach, Luther P. "The Structure of Social Movements: Environmental Activism and Its Opponents." In *Networks and Netwars: The Future of Terror, Crime, and Militancy,* edited by John Arquilla and David Ronfeldt, 289–310. Santa Monica, CA: Rand Corp., 2001.

Ghalambor, Cameron K., Kim L. Hoke, Emily W. Ruell, Eva K. Fischer, David N. Reznick, and Kimberly A. Hughes. "Non-adaptive Plasticity Potentiates Rapid Adaptive Evolution of Gene Expression in Nature." *Nature* 525:7569 (2015) 372–75. https://doi.org/10.1038/nature15256.

Gibson, Brittany. "How Georgia Got Organized." *The American Prospect,* January 2, 2021. https://prospect.org/politics/how-georgia-got-organized -stacey-abrams-democrats-elections.

Gleick, James. *Chaos: Making a New Science.* New York: Viking, 1987.

Gleick, James. *Genius: The Life and Science of Richard Feynman.* New York: Knopf Doubleday, 1993.

Gleick, James. *The Information: A History, a Theory, a Flood.* New York: Knopf Doubleday, 2011.

Global State of Democracy Initiative. *The Global State of Democracy 2022: Forging Social Contracts in a Time of Discontent.* Stockholm: International Institute for Democracy and Electoral Assistance, 2022. https://doi.org /10.31752/idea.2022.56.

Goldstein, Herman. *The Computer from Pascal to von Neumann.* Princeton, NJ: Princeton University Press, 1972.

Graeber, David, and David Wengrow. *The Dawn of Everything: A New History of Humanity.* New York: Farrar, Straus and Giroux, 2021.

Granovetter, Mark. "The Strength of Weak Ties: A Network Theory Revisited." *Sociological Theory* 1 (1983): 201. https://doi.org/10.2307/202051.

Hagey, Keach, and Jeff Horwitz. "Facebook Tried to Make Its Platform a Healthier Place. It Got Angrier Instead." *Wall Street Journal,* September 15, 2021. www.wsj.com/articles/facebook-algorithm-change-zuckerberg -11631654215.

Hale, Thomas. "We've Found One Factor That Predicts Which Countries Best Survive Covid." *The Guardian,* March 24, 2022. www.theguardian.com /commentisfree/2022/mar/24/countries-covid-trust-damage-pandemic.

Hamel, J. *Early English Voyages to Northern Russia: Comprising the Voyages of John Tradescant the Elder, Sir Hugh Willoughby, Richard Chancellor, Nelson, and Others.* Translated by John Studdy Leigh. London: Forgotten Books, 2018. First published 1857 by Richard Bentley (London).

Han, Hahrie, Elizabeth McKenna, and Michelle Oyakawa. *Prisms of the People: Power & Organizing In Twenty-First Century America.* University of Chicago Press, 2021.

Hanski, Ilkka, and Michael E. Gilpin. *Metapopulation Biology: Ecology, Genetics, and Evolution.* San Diego: Academic Press, 1997.

Harris, La Donna, and Jacqueline Wasilewski. "Indigeneity, an Alternative Worldview: Four R's (Relationship, Responsibility, Reciprocity, Redistribution) vs. Two P's (Power and Profit). Sharing the Journey toward Conscious Evolution." *Systems Research and Behavioral Science* 21, no. 5 (September 2004): 489–503. https://doi.org/10.1002/SRES.631.

Hawker, M., and R. Romero-Ortuno. "Social Determinants of Discharge Outcomes in Older People Admitted to a Geriatric Medicine Ward." *The Journal of Frailty & Aging* 5, no. 2 (2016): 118–20. https://doi.org /10.14283/JFA.2016.89.

Hawkley, Louise C., Mary Elizabeth Hughes, Linda J. Waite, Christopher M. Masi, Ronald A. Thisted, and John T. Cacioppo. "From Social Structural Factors to Perceptions of Relationship Quality and Loneliness: The Chicago Health, Aging, and Social Relations Study." *Journals of Gerontology. Series B, Psychological Sciences and Social Sciences* 63, no. 6 (2008). https:// doi.org/10.1093/GERONB/63.6.S375.

Hayashi, Teruo. "Conversion of Psychological Stress into Cellular Stress Response: Roles of the Sigma-1 Receptor in the Process." *Psychiatry and Clinical Neurosciences* 69, no. 4 (April 2015): 179–91. https://doi.org /10.1111/PCN.12262.

High Ground Advisors. "The 2022 DAF Report Is Here." December 6, 2022. www.highgroundadvisors.org/blog/the-2022-daf-report-is-here.

Hoffman, Bruce, Jacob Ware, and Ezra Shapiro. "Assessing the Threat of Incel Violence." *Studies in Conflict & Terrorism* 43, no. 7 (July 2020): 565–87. https://doi.org/10.1080/1057610X.2020.1751459.

Holt-Lunstad, Julianne, Timothy B. Smith, and J. Bradley Layton. "Social Relationships and Mortality Risk: A Meta-Analytic Review." *PLoS*

Medicine 7, no. 7 (July 2010): e1000316. https://doi.org/10.1371/journal.
pmed.1000316.

INCITE! Women of Color Against Violence, ed. *The Revolution Will Not
Be Funded: Beyond the Non-Profit Industrial Complex.* Durham, NC: Duke
University Press, 2017.

Jackson Katz, *Macho Paradox: Why Some Men Hurt Women and How All Men
Can Help* (Naperville, IL: Sourcebooks, 2006).

Johnson, Joan Marie. *Funding Feminism: Monied Women, Philanthropy, and the
Women's Movement, 1870–1967.* Chapel Hill, NC: University of North
Carolina Press, 2017.

Kalla, Joshua, and David Broockman. "Voter Outreach Campaigns Can
Reduce Affective Polarization among Implementing Political Activists." *American Political Science Review,* 116:4 (November 2022), 1516–22.
https://doi.org/10.1017/S0003055422000132.

Kannan, Viji Diane, and Peter J. Veazie. "US Trends in Social Isolation,
Social Engagement, and Companionship—Nationally and by Age, Sex,
Race/Ethnicity, Family Income, and Work Hours, 2003–2020." *SSM—
Population Health* 21 (March 2023): 101331. https://doi.org/10.1016/J.
SSMPH.2022.101331.

Kimmerer, Robin Wall. *Braiding Sweetgrass: Indigenous Wisdom, Scientific
Knowledge and the Teachings of Plants.* Minneapolis: Milkweed Editions,
2015.

Kizilcec, Rene F., and Emily Schneider. "Motivation as a Lens to Understand
Online Learners: Toward Data-Driven Design with the OLEI Scale."
ACM Transactions on Computer-Human Interaction 22, no. 2 (March 2015):
1–24. https://doi.org/10.1145/2699735.

Klein, Ezra. "A Legendary World Builder on Multiverses, Revolution and
the 'Souls' of Cities." Interview with N. K. Jemisin. *The Ezra Klein Show.*
Podcast, audio. October 18, 2022. www.nytimes.com/2022/10/18/opinion
/ezra-klein-podcast-nk-jemisin.html.

Klinenberg, Eric. *Heat Wave: A Social Autopsy of Disaster in Chicago.* Chicago:
University of Chicago Press, 2002.

Laricchia, Federica. "Global Smartphone Penetration 2016–2022." *Statistica,*
May 24, 2023. www.statista.com/statistics/203734/global-smartphone
-penetration-per-capita-since-2005.

Laurison, Daniel. *Producing Politics: Inside the Exclusive Campaign World Where
the Privileged Few Shape Politics for All of Us.* Boston: Beacon Press, 2022.

Lazzari, Carlo, and Marco Rabottini. "COVID-19, Loneliness, Social Isolation and Risk of Dementia in Older People: A Systematic Review and
Meta-Analysis of the Relevant Literature." *International Journal of Psychiatry in Clinical Practice* 26, no. 2 (June 2022): 196–207. https://doi.org/10.10
80/13651501.2021.1959616.

Le Bon, Gustave. *The Crowd: A Study of the Popular Mind.* London: T. Fisher Unwin, 1926. Reprinted Mineola, NY: Dover, 2002.

Leach, Darcy K. "Culture and the Structure of Tyrannylessness." *Sociological Quarterly* 54, no. 2 (2013): 181–91. https://doi.org/10.1111/tsq.12014.

Lissner, Jorgen. "Merchants of Misery." *New Internationalist,* June 1, 1981. https://newint.org/features/1981/06/01/merchants-of-misery.

Lorenz, Edward N. "Predictability: Does the Flap of a Butterfly's Wings in Brazil Set Off a Tornado in Texas?" Presentation at the American Association for the Advancement of Science, Washington, DC, December 29, 1972. https://static.gymportalen.dk/sites/lru.dk/files/lru/132_kap6_lorenz_artikel_the_butterfly_effect.pdf.

Lovett, Ian, and Adam Nagourney. "Video Rant, Then Deadly Rampage in California Town." *New York Times,* May 25, 2014. www.nytimes.com/2014/05/25/us/california-drive-by-shooting.html.

Mann, Farhana, Jingyi Wang, Eiluned Pearce, Ruimin Ma, Merle Schlief, Brynmor Lloyd-Evans, Sarah Ikhtabi, and Sonia Johnson. "Loneliness and the Onset of New Mental Health Problems in the General Population." *Social Psychiatry and Psychiatric Epidemiology* 57, no. 11 (November 2022): 2161. https://doi.org/10.1007/S00127-022-02261-7.

Marçal, Katrine. *Who Cooked Adam Smith's Dinner?: A Story about Women and Economics.* Berkeley, CA: Pegasus, 2016.

Martins Barroso, Sabrina, Heloísa Gonçalves Ferreira, and Felipe Costa Araujo. "Brazilian Loneliness Scale: Evidence of Validity Based on Relations to Depression, Anxiety and Stress." *Psico-USF* 26, no. 3 (December 2021): 559–70. https://doi.org/10.1590/1413-82712021260313.

Mayor of London. "London's Loneliness Epidemic." News release. October 31, 2019. www.london.gov.uk/press-releases/assembly/londons-loneliness-epidemic.

McCarthy, John D., and Mayer N. Zald. "Resource Mobilization and Social Movements: A Partial Theory." *American Journal of Sociology* 82, no. 6 (May 1977): 1212–41. https://doi.org/10.1086/226464.

Miller, Klancy. "Overlooked No More: Georgia Gilmore, Who Fed and Funded the Montgomery Bus Boycott." *New York Times,* July 31, 2019. www.nytimes.com/2019/07/31/obituaries/georgia-gilmore-overlooked.html.

Mtshali, Lihle Z., "Everything You Ever Wanted to Know About Those Sou-Sou Savings Clubs African and Caribbean Women Love." *Essence,* December 6, 2020. www.essence.com/news/money-career/what-is-a-sou-sou-savings-club-facts.

Mushtaq, Raheel, Sheikh Shoib, Tabindah Shah, and Sahil Mushtaq. "Relationship Between Loneliness, Psychiatric Disorders and Physical Health: A Review on the Psychological Aspects of Loneliness." *Journal of Clinical and*

Diagnostic Research 8, no. 9 (2014): WE01. https://doi.org/10.7860/JCDR
/2014/10077.4828.

Nace, Ted. *Gangs of America: The Rise of Corporate Power and the Disabling of
Democracy.* San Francisco: Berrett-Koehler, 2003.

National Democratic Institute. "Public Narrative Participant Guide."
June 2012. Adapted from Marshall Ganz, "Leading Change: Leadership,
Organization and Social Movements." In *Handbook of Leadership Theory
and Practice,* edited by Nitin Nohria and Rakesh Khurana, chapter 19.
Cambridge, MA: HBS Press, 2010. www.ndi.org/sites/default/files/Public
%20Narrative%20Participant%20Guide.pdf.

National Institutes of Health. "The Benefits of Slumber." NIH News in Health.
April 2013. https://newsinhealth.nih.gov/2013/04/benefits-slumber.

National Philanthropic Trust. *Donor-Advised Fund Report,* 2022. www.nptrust
.org/reports/daf-report.

Noor, Poppy. "Surge in Youth Voter Turnout May Have Helped Propel
Biden to Victory." *The Guardian,* November 9, 2020. www.theguardian
.com/us-news/2020/nov/09/youth-turnout-us-election-biden-victory
-young-voters.

Nummenmaa, Lauri, Enrico Glerean, Riitta Hari, and Jari K. Hietanen.
"Bodily Maps of Emotions." *Proceedings of the National Academy of Sciences
of the USA* 111, no. 2 (January 2014): 646–51. https://doi.org/10.1073
/PNAS.1321664111.

Onah, Daniel, and Jane Sinclair. "Dropout Rates of Massive Open Online
Courses: Behavioural Patterns." *Proceedings of the 6th International Conference on Education and New Learning Technologies (EDULEARN14).* Barcelona, July 2014. https://doi.org/10.13140/RG.2.1.2402.0009.

Orlowski-Yang, Jeff, dir. *The Social Dilemma.* 2020; Los Angeles: Exposure
Labs. Netflix video.

Pappano, Laura. "The Year of the MOOC." *New York Times,* November 2,
2012. www.nytimes.com/2012/11/04/education/edlife/massive-open
-online-courses-are-multiplying-at-a-rapid-pace.html.

Passwaiter, Steve. "Political Ad Spending Projected to Top $11 Billion in
2024." AdAge, July 12, 2023. https://adage.com/article/opinion/2024
-elections-political-ad-spending-projected-top-11-billion-2024/2504126.

Pavlogiannis, Andreas, Josef Tkadlec, Krishnendu Chatterjee, and Martin A.
Nowak. "Construction of Arbitrarily Strong Amplifiers of Natural Selec-
tion Using Evolutionary Graph Theory." *Communications Biology* 1, no. 1
(December 2018): 71. https://doi.org/10.1038/s42003-018-0078-7.

Pember, Mary Annette. "Death by Civilization." *The Atlantic,* March 8, 2019.
www.theatlantic.com/education/archive/2019/03/traumatic-legacy-indian
-boarding-schools/584293.

People's Action. "How to Defeat Trump and Heal America: Deep Canvassing." 2021. Accessed November 8, 2023. https://peoplesaction.org/wp -content/uploads/PA-ReportDeepCanvassingResults09.14-FINAL.pdf.

Peter Godfrey-Smith and Kim Sterelny, "Biological Information," in *The Stanford Encyclopedia of Philosophy,* ed. Edward N. Zalta (Stanford, CA: Stanford University, 2016), https://plato.stanford.edu/archives/sum2016 /entries/information-biological.

Picard, Martin, and Bruce S. McEwen. "Psychological Stress and Mitochondria: A Systematic Review." *Psychosomatic Medicine* 80, no. 2 (February 2018): 141. https://doi.org/10.1097/PSY.0000000000000545.

Pinkston, Bonnie. "Documenting the British East India Company and Their Involvement in the East Indian Slave Trade." *SLIS Connecting* 7 (July 1, 2018): 53–59. https://doi.org/10.18785/slis.0701.10.

Quiroz, Julie, and Kristen Zimmerman. "OUR Walmart: Caring Communities, Courageous Action. Love with Power: Practicing Transformation for Social Justice." Story Series No. 3. Movement Strategy Center, March 2016. https://movementstrategy.org/resources/our-walmart-caring -communities-courageous-action-love-with-power-3.

Raichle, Marcus E., and Debra A. Gusnard. "Appraising the Brain's Energy Budget." *Proceedings of the National Academy of Sciences of the USA* 99, no. 16 (August 2002): 10237–39. https://doi.org/10.1073/PNAS.172399499.

Re:Power. "Voices From the Frontlines: What Organizers Need in 2022." RePower.org. August 5, 2022. https://repower.org/2022-organizer-survey.

Reagan, Gillian. "The Evolution of Facebook's Mission Statement." *The Observer,* July 13, 2009. https://observer.com/2009/07/the-evolution-of -facebooks-mission-statement.

Rovelli, Carlo. *Reality Is Not What It Seems: The Journey to Quantum Gravity.* New York: Penguin, 2017.

Rushkoff, Douglas. "The Super-Rich 'Preppers' Planning to Save Themselves from the Apocalypse." *The Guardian,* September 4, 2022. www.theguardian .com/news/2022/sep/04/super-rich-prepper-bunkers-apocalypse-survival -richest-rushkoff.

Sarason, Irwin G., Barbara R. Sarason, Edward N. Shearin, and Gregory R. Pierce. "A Brief Measure of Social Support: Practical and Theoretical Implications." *Journal of Social and Personal Relationships* 4, no. 4 (November 1987): 497–510. https://doi.org/10.1177/0265407587044007.

Scheck, Justin, Newley Purnell, and Jeff Horwitz. "Facebook Employees Flag Drug Cartels and Human Traffickers. The Company's Response Is Weak, Documents Show." *Wall Street Journal,* September 16, 2021. www.wsj .com/articles/facebook-drug-cartels-human-traffickers-response-is-weak -documents-11631812953.

Segerstrom, Suzanne C., and Gregory E. Miller. "Psychological Stress and the Human Immune System: A Meta-Analytic Study of 30 Years of Inquiry." *Psychological Bulletin* 130, no. 4 (July 2004): 601. https://doi.org/10.103 7/0033-2909.130.4.601.

Shane, Cari. "The First Self-Proclaimed Drag Queen Was a Formerly Enslaved Man." *Smithsonian Magazine,* June 9, 2023. www.smithsonianmag.com /history/the-first-self-proclaimed-drag-queen-was-a-formerly-enslaved -man-180982311.

Shannon, C. E. "A Mathematical Theory of Communication." *Bell System Technical Journal* 27 (July/October 1948), 379–423, 623–56. https://doi .org/10.1002/j.1538-7305.1948.tb01338.x, https://people.math.harvard .edu/~ctm/home/text/others/shannon/entropy/entropy.pdf.

Smythies, John. "Intercellular Signaling in Cancer—the SMT and TOFT Hypotheses, Exosomes, Telocytes and Metastases: Is the Messenger in the Message?" *Journal of Cancer* 6, no. 7 (2015): 604–9. https://doi.org/10 .7150/JCA.12372.

Snow, David A., Rens Vliegenthart, and Pauline Ketelaars, "The Framing Perspective on Social Movements." In *The Wiley Blackwell Companion to Social Movements*, edited by David A. Snow, Sarah A. Soule, Hanspeter Kriesi, and Holly J. McCammon, 392–410. John Wiley & Sons, 2018. https://doi.org/10.1002/9781119168577.ch22.

Solan, Matthew. "The Secret to Happiness? Here's Some Advice from the Longest-Running Study on Happiness." *Harvard Health Blog* (blog), October 5, 2017. www.health.harvard.edu/blog/the-secret-to-happiness -heres-some-advice-from-the-longest-running-study-on-happiness -2017100512543.

Southwick, Steven M., Lauren Sippel, John Krystal, Dennis Charney, Linda Mayes, and Robb Pietrzak. "Why Are Some Individuals More Resilient than Others: The Role of Social Support." *World Psychiatry* 15, no. 1 (February 2016): 77–79. https://doi.org/10.1002/wps.20282.

Spera, Christopher, Robin Ghertner, Anthony Nerino, and Adrienne DiTommaso. "Out of Work? Volunteers Have Higher Odds of Getting Back to Work." *Nonprofit and Voluntary Sector Quarterly* 44, no. 5 (September 2015): 886–907. https://doi.org/10.1177/0899764015605928.

Statista. "Consumer Electronics—United States." September 2023. www.statista .com/outlook/cmo/consumer-electronics/united-states.

Third Wave Fund. "Third Wave Fund Resources and Supports Youth-Led, Intersectional Gender Justice Activism." N.d., accessed November 12, 2023. www.thirdwavefund.org/about.

Thornley, Ben. "The Facts on U.S. Social Enterprise." HuffPost, November 8, 2012. www.huffpost.com/entry/social-enterprise_b_2090144.

Trans Justice Funding Project. "FAQs." N.d., accessed November 12, 2023. www.transjusticefundingproject.org/about-faq.

Tufekci, Zeynep. *Twitter and Tear Gas: The Power and Fragility of Networked Protest.* New Haven, CT: Yale University Press, 2017.

US Department of Health and Human Services. "HHS FY 2024 Budget in Brief." March 3, 2023. www.hhs.gov/about/budget/fy2024.

US Department of Health and Human Services. "New Surgeon General Advisory Raises Alarm about the Devastating Impact of the Epidemic of Loneliness and Isolation in the United States." News release. May 3, 2023. www.hhs.gov/about/news/2023/05/03/new-surgeon-general-advisory -raises-alarm-about-devastating-impact-epidemic-loneliness-isolation -united-states.html.

Valtorta, Nicole K., Mona Kanaan, Simon Gilbody, Sara Ronzi, and Barbara Hanratty. "Loneliness and Social Isolation as Risk Factors for Coronary Heart Disease and Stroke: Systematic Review and Meta-Analysis of Longitudinal Observational Studies." *Heart* 102, no. 13 (July 2016): 1009–16. https://doi.org/10.1136/heartjnl-2015-308790.

Villanueva, Edgar. *Decolonizing Wealth: Indigenous Wisdom to Heal Divides and Restore Balance.* Oakland, CA: Berrett-Koehler, 2018.

Weber, Max. *Economy and Society: An Outline of Interpretative Sociology,* 1921. Reprinted. New York: Bedminster Press, 1968.

Wei-Skillern, Jane, and Sonia Marciano. "The Networked Nonprofit." *Stanford Social Innovation Review,* Spring 2008. https://doi.org/10.48558/gcy2-rn71.

Wells, Georgia, Jeff Horwitz, and Deepa Seetharaman. "Facebook Knows Instagram Is Toxic for Teen Girls, Company Documents Show." *Wall Street Journal,* September 14, 2021. www.wsj.com/articles/facebook-knows -instagram-is-toxic-for-teen-girls-company-documents-show-11631620739.

Williams, Chad. "W. E. B. Du Bois and the Fight for American Democracy." *Washington Post,* August 27, 2018. www.washingtonpost.com/news/made -by-history/wp/2018/08/27/w-e-b-du-bois-and-the-fight-for-american -democracy.

Wong, Julia Carrie. "Facebook Overhauls News Feed in Favor of 'Meaningful Social Interactions.'" *The Guardian,* January 12, 2018. www.theguardian .com/technology/2018/jan/11/facebook-news-feed-algorithm-overhaul -mark-zuckerberg.

Wong, Julia Carrie. "How Facebook Let Fake Engagement Distort Global Politics: A Whistleblower's Account." *The Guardian,* April 12, 2021. www .theguardian.com/technology/2021/apr/12/facebook-fake-engagement -whistleblower-sophie-zhang.

Wood, Natasha R. "Adventures in Solitude: The Link Between Social Isolation and Violent Extremism." Master's thesis, University of Pittsburgh,

2020. https://d-scholarship.pitt.edu/38639/7/Natasha%20Wood %20Final%20ETD.pdf.

World Health Organization. "Substantial Investment Needed to Avert Mental Health Crisis." News release. May 14, 2020. www.who.int/news/item/14 -05-2020-substantial-investment-needed-to-avert-mental-health-crisis.

Wu, Lingfei, Dashun Wang, and James A. Evans. "Large Teams Develop and Small Teams Disrupt Science and Technology." *Nature* 566 (February 2019): 378–82. https://doi.org/10.1038/s41586-019-0941-9.

Young, Stella. "We're Not Here for Your Inspiration." ABC News, July 2, 2012. www.abc.net.au/news/2012-07-03/young-inspiration-porn /4107006.

Zimet, Gregory D., Nancy W. Dahlem, Sara G. Zimet, and Gordon K. Farley. "The Multidimensional Scale of Perceived Social Support." *Journal of Personality Assessment* 52, no. 1 (March 1, 1988): 30–41. https://doi.org /10.1207/s15327752jpa5201_2.

Index

Acknowledgments

This book is the result of a decade-long journey during which I received extensive support and endless patience from my community. My co-parents, Avary Kent and Zeke Hausfather, have made countless personal sacrifices to support me in the time-intensive and financially risky project of researching and writing this text. They have been a backbone of emotional support along with our child, Tavi Kent. My partner, Hyunhee Shin, has been an incredible guide through the many uncertainties and insecurities involved in writing this text alongside my friends Bex Mui, Haley Bash, Christine Lai, Molly Alloy, Brandon Bosch, Lennon Flowers, Liz Lee, Lydia Laurenson, Meetali Jain, Deepti Doshi, Lauren Beach, Dharmishta Rood, Poonam Kapoor, Ollie Gillette, Yvan Shafer, Jules Vivid, and Sandy Folker.

I am appreciative for the many content experts who informed the thinking in this book, some of whom have already been mentioned, including Marianne Manilov, who has been a source of significant wisdom about organizing and who turned me on to the power of care, and Shaady Salehi, who graciously helped me understand the practices of trust-based philanthropy. Others include Ambika Kamath, who helped me discover the concept of evolutionary rate; Steve Deline, who helped me understand the power of deep canvassing; Jillian Racoosin of the Foundation for Social Connection, for her inspirational work moving resources to combat loneliness; Veronica Garcia of WRAP, for introducing me to the Just Transition framework and supporting me on my personal journey around resource mobilization; Cat Huang, who has been a thought partner in understanding the academic study of organizing; Eben Lazarus, who has been a guide to make sense of relational understanding and invisibility in economics; Fabian Pfortmüller, who has helped me to understand the intersection of relationality and philanthropy; Serena Bian of US Surgeon General Vivek Murthy's office, for helping me understand the scope of the loneliness crisis; Sahar Massachi and Jeff Allen, for the work of organizing integrity workers, which brought a much needed perspective to my life and this book; Andrew Hanauer and Laura Lee Kent, for helping me understand the wisdom of communities of faith; Shamil Idriss and Lisa Schirch, for giving me the term *cohesion* and the rich history of peace-building behind it; and Julie Hayes for providing feedback on my approach to relational systems modeling. I'm excited to thank the reviewers of this book who have not already been mentioned. This text was made substantially stronger because of your input: Ravon Ruffin, Suparna Chhibber, Camille Carlton, Andrew Dunn, James Rohrbach, Darren Kwong, and Lara Galinsky.

I would like to thank the community on AVEN, especially the administrators and moderators whose tireless work has kept the community running for all these years. I am grateful to the team at the Center for Humane Technology for giving me an incredible platform to explore ideas of relationship and community: Randy Fernando, Rebecca Lendl, Brooke Clinton, Maria Bridge, Camille Carlton, Tristan Harris, Sari Harrison, and Aza Raskin, alongside the numerous other friends and allies who worked with me to help the tech reform movement to progress.

I owe a huge debt of gratitude to the team at North Atlantic Books for making this project a reality: Shayna Keyles, Susan Bumps, Margeaux Weston, Janelle Ludowise, Emily Shapiro, Joe Finlaw, and Kelly Bolding. Thank you for bringing to the art of publishing all of the values that I have struggled to articulate in this book. Thank you also to Tessa Shanks for supporting me from my earliest questions about identity through the process of navigating the publishing industry.

Finally, I would like to thank my family of origin. My parents, Mary Ann Lazarus and Daniel Jay, who have held unwavering faith in me even when my life makes no sense. My brother, Michael Jay, for all the ways that you have believed in me and shown up in my life, and to my sister, Laura Jay, for also always showing up for me even though you seem to be better than me at pretty much everything. Finally I would like to thank my grandparents: Bob Jay, whose love of connection with land, water, and stillness was passed on to me through my father; Cynthia Jay, who remains an inspiration and to whom I owe much of my love of family, kids, and community; Betty Lazarus, who taught me through her children to build my life around a sense of purpose; and David Lazarus, whose love of both physics and family shaped my earliest understanding of beauty in the world.

About the Author

Born and raised in St. Louis, Missouri, David Jay is a community organizer with a background in physics. From founding the Asexual Visibility and Education Network to working in the heart of the tech reform movement, David has centered the work of building relationship as a tool of healing and driving social change. His research and writing centers on the reasons why these important relational tools so often go underappreciated and underfunded and on how that reality might change. David is regularly invited to speak at conferences and universities on topics that include asexuality, movement organizing, tech reform, and queer family structure. He lives with his two co-parents and two children in Oakland, California.

About
North Atlantic Books

North Atlantic Books (NAB) is an independent, nonprofit publisher committed to a bold exploration of the relationships between mind, body, spirit, and nature. Founded in 1974, NAB aims to nurture a holistic view of the arts, sciences, humanities, and healing. To make a donation or to learn more about our books, authors, events, and newsletter, please visit www.northatlanticbooks.com.